Heartbeat and Beyond

Heartbeat and Beyond

Memoirs of 50 Years of Yorkshire Television

Edited by

John Fairley and Graham Ironside

PEN & SWORD
HISTORY

First published in Great Britain in 2017 by
Pen & Sword History
an imprint of
Pen & Sword Books Ltd
47 Church Street
Barnsley
South Yorkshire
S70 2AS

ISBN 978 1 47384 826 9

A CIP catalogue record for this book is available from the British Library

Typeset in Ehrhardt by
Mac Style Ltd, Bridlington, East Yorkshire
Printed and bound in China by Imago.

Pen & Sword Books Limited incorporates the imprints of Atlas,
Archaeology, Aviation, Discovery, Family History, Fiction, History, Maritime,
Military, Military Classics, Politics, Select, Transport, True Crime, Air World,
Frontline Publishing, Leo Cooper, Remember When, Seaforth Publishing,
The Praetorian Press, Wharncliffe Local History, Wharncliffe Transport,
Wharncliffe True Crime and White Owl

For a complete list of Pen & Sword titles please contact
PEN & SWORD BOOKS LIMITED
47 Church Street, Barnsley, South Yorkshire, S70 2AS, England
E-mail: enquiries@pen-and-sword.co.uk
Website: www.pen-and-sword.co.uk

Contents

Preface

This is the story of a group of young people who landed up in a derelict trouser factory in a rundown part of Leeds in Yorkshire and, between them, produced programming to conquer the television world.

They attracted – or, indeed, created – stars of international fame: Catherine Zeta Jones, James Mason, Alan Whicker, David Jason, David Frost.

They produced programmes which changed our society.

And the Dales and Wolds of Yorkshire earned new renown as 'Heartbeat Country' or just the 'real Emmerdale'.

In the process, the young producers and crews found themselves in all sorts of dramatic and absurd situations. This book has vivid personal accounts of crises and comedy, both in front of and behind the camera.

The Yorkshire Television crews seemed always to contain someone who delighted in capturing with their own camera the private moments that amused them – and many of the most intriguing pictures in this book come from the sound recordists, make-up artists or production secretaries who worked on the shows.

Together, these things paint a fascinating picture of the making, from nothing, of one of the great television studios of its time.

Chapter 1

John Fairley

JF in India. (Terry Ricketts)

Donald Baverstock. (Yorkshire Post Newspapers)

The phone rang on my desk in BBC Radio's *Today* programme office in Portland Place in London. A Welsh voice said, 'You look out of your window, boyo, and you'll see who's talking to you.'

Thus began a journey that took me to the most creative, ambitious and successful of television companies.

The Welshman was Donald Baverstock, who had commandeered a small set of chambers on the other side of Portland Place to conjure up an entire new TV station for Yorkshire which was due to go on air that summer of 1968.

By the time I arrived in Leeds, there were only three weeks to go. The studios were unfinished; the offices were in an ex-trouser factory. But Baverstock was determined to launch the station with a new nightly Yorkshire news programme to be called *Calendar*.

I had never seen a TV studio, or ever worked in television. But instantly I was despatched to do a film about a man who kept a bluebottle farm, hatching maggots on hunks of rotting meat for sale to fishermen.

It got on air that first night, 29 July 1968. But a lot didn't. *Calendar* fell about technically and editorially, and within a week I found myself shanghaied by my *Calendar* colleagues into the editorship of the programme.

Elsewhere in this book are some glorious glimpses of how we took the wreckage of these early shows and made *Calendar* into the most successful regional news programme in terms of ratings there has ever been.

All shoulders were applied to the wheel. It was quite usual for me, producing the programme, to nip out of the gallery, read the news and then get back to production – though Richard Whiteley famously summed

up my news-reading abilities by saying, 'He always looked as though he knew more about the news than he was prepared to tell you.'

Scarcely a year later, Donald Baverstock summoned me to his office and announced, 'Bloody Alan Whicker needs a producer. Can you get out there this weekend?'

It transpired that this meant descending on the island of Mustique to kick off a three-month tour of the West Indies. What was not to like?

I arrived, with researcher Nigel Turner, on Mustique a day before Whicker. We found out what we could, before being summoned to the great man's suite.

'What are we going to do?' he enquired.

To my dismay, he then sat at his typewriter and simply wrote down all the questions I had prepared for him. No discussion.

I thought, 'Gosh, is this how it's going to be for the next three months?'

The next morning, we set up to film the opening interview with Colin Tennant. The theme was to be the beautiful attractions of his tropical island. Right on cue, as the camera rolled, the heavens opened. Tennant obviously expected me to stop the interview. But Whicker gripped him firmly by the elbow and, as the water poured down on their heads, made him tell us all about his idyllic island. It was to make a most wonderfully ironic opening to our film. And on day one I saw the relentless professionalism and sense of story which made *Whicker's World* the most popular and legendary TV series of its time.

I was to have some wonderful years with Whicker for Yorkshire Television, across the Far East from Bali to Thailand and Malaysia, and then, more sedately, as his executive

Whicker's fascination with the rich and famous took him to the island of Mustique in the Caribbean, owned by Colin Tennant, Lord Glenconner, and here driving the Whicker team to their next location. Cameraman Frank Pocklington, assisted by Alan Pyrah, checks the light readings.

Lord Glenconner, who bought the island for £45,000 in 1958 as a present for his wife, was seldom out of the gossip columns of the popular newspapers and he loved the limelight, mainly through his friendship with Princess Margaret, a regular visitor. (Terry Ricketts)

producer at home. David Green then became his producer, and there is an account of some of those years later in this book.

By this time I was running our Yorkshire Television documentary department. Going to live in Yorkshire, I had fallen completely for the charms not only of the Dales but also of the North Yorkshire Moors. Starting with smaller film features for *Calendar*, with director Barry Cockcroft, we had begun to unearth the lode of riveting life stories which were to be epitomized by Hannah Hauxwell and her lone Dales farm in the film *Too Long a Winter*. The Moors were also to be the setting for the splendid drama series *Heartbeat*, which Keith Richardson describes in this book.

The ITV network at that time was a jungle. It was a matter of *sauve qui peut*. One day Baverstock came back and said, 'I've told them we can do science programmes. They want the first one in six weeks time.'

Thus began not only the distinguished documentary series *The Scientists*, but also the hugely popular *Don't Ask Me* with Magnus Pyke and Miriam Stoppard, both new to television. Simon Welfare, David Taylor and Miriam describe those frantic days later in the book.

We had also persuaded Robert Kee to join us. Robert was perhaps the most forensic, intellectual and yet popular journalist I ever worked with. We made what remains one of the most defining documentary series of the Cold War era, *Faces of Communism*, travelling across much of the then Soviet zone of Eastern Europe. It was in East Berlin, beyond the Wall, that Robert sat down casually on a

The steam train powers across North Yorkshire in a scene from *Heartbeat*, a ratings winner from Yorkshire TV for all of 18 years. (Shutterstock)

bench and remarked, 'The last time I sat here was 1943.'

He then recalled how, having been shot down as a bomber pilot, he had escaped a Nazi prisoner of war camp and made it to Berlin.

The series also took us to the first country to go communist in Africa, the former French Congo, Brazzaville. To film there required a quire of permissions, including from the Chief of Police who, it transpired, resided in the Brazzaville prison – an old stone, star-shaped penitentiary built by the French.

As we loitered outside the Chief's office, we saw a distant white man in Hare Krishnan orange being escorted down the corridor towards us, accompanied by two guards.

'Êtes-vous Francais?' he whispered.

Arthur C. Clarke was born in Minehead in Somerset in 1917. He spent his early years in England (he served in the Second World War as a radar operator) but moved to live in Sri Lanka in 1956. His writing explored the unexplained phenomena and the paranormal puzzles of the world with enormous imagination. Among his famous sayings was: 'The only way of discovering the limits of the possible is to venture a little way past them, into the impossible.' (Charlie Flynn)

'No.'

'Can you tell the French ambassador I am here?'

Then he was hustled away.

Back at the hotel, we rang the ambassador. It turned out his young compatriot had already been in prison a year, without anyone knowing, after getting off the plane with missionary intentions but no money. He was duly sprung. Who knows? Perhaps we saved him decades of incarceration.

Another hardship station was being in stunning Sri Lanka with the great science fiction writer Arthur C. Clarke, doing what became the *Mysterious World* series, which eventually ran to 52 episodes and still plays all around the world. The privations were unique. One morning we were filming on Unawatuna beach when a statuesque blonde in a bikini wandered up and enquired what we were doing.

'Isn't this the most beautiful beach in the world?' I suggested, by way of chatting.

'No,' came the response. 'The second most'.

I have still never made it to the Philippines, where Number One is, it seems, to be found.

By now, Paul Fox had taken over from Baverstock and was the point man in the weekly Monday morning warfare during which the ITV schedule was hammered out. One day he came back and announced that we were to produce a documentary on the first Tuesday of every month – starting next month. Thus began *First Tuesday*, which was arguably the most influential series ever made by ITV. John Willis and Grant McKee write about it later in this book.

Soon Paul Fox became Managing Director, and I became Director of Programmes.

Vernon Lawrence surrounded by a galaxy of YTV stars of Light Entertainment. (Shutterstock)

Straight away I had to confront the fact that the other ITV companies – particularly Thames – were gunning for *Emmerdale*. Its ratings were on the slide. Phil Redmond, creator of *Grange Hill* and *Brookside*, and later *Hollyoaks*, was an old Liverpudlian mate. I asked him – paid him, indeed – to look at *Emmerdale*. A few weeks later, he wandered across the Pennines to give me his rather gloomy analysis: we needed to get rid of a load of failing characters and get the nation's attention back. Oh, yes. How do we do that? 'Crash a plane on the village', he said, 'And start again.'

This was not long after Lockerbie, and trying to persuade the Yorkshire Television board, let alone the Independent Broadcasting Authority, that it was acceptable was an uphill task. But we did it, in five dramatic days. And *Emmerdale* has never looked back.

A truly strong thread in Yorkshire Television was its comedy and entertainment. Vernon Lawrence writes about this later in the book. But Vernon's mantra was always, 'In the beginning was the word.' And so he corralled some of the great comedy writers for us: Eric Chappell, sweating away in a shed in his garden in Grantham; David Nobbs in Harrogate; Marks and Gran in that most memorable series with Alan B'stard, *The New Statesman*. Who can forget the great moment when B'stard MP, needing some Prime Minister's notepaper, sneaks into her office, opens her desk drawer and finds there a picture of the inordinately handsome and appealing Cecil Parkinson.

There were some other great moments. There was the realization of our ideas about a real-life soap opera, *Jimmy's*, about the eponymous Leeds hospital, forerunner of so many subsequent real-life soaps.

Then there was *The Indoor League*, with Freddie Trueman, and produced by Sid Waddell, who went on to be the famous Geordie voice of darts. And all the sport, including great days with Leeds United, which was the basis of a terrific feature film, and the tragic Bradford City fire, which John Helm covered with such sympathy and sensitivity. Robert Charles writes about all that later in the book.

There was *Darling Buds of May*, which launched Catherine Zeta-Jones into the Hollywood world; and *Touch of Frost*, with David Jason.

Hopefully, our readers and viewers will find all this worth remembering. For those of us who were there, they were truly golden days.

Heartbeat, which was to become the ultimate Yorkshire television drama series, running to more than 100 episodes, was actually conceived in a jacuzzi on the roof of the Beverley Wilshire hotel in Los Angeles.

The iconic opening shot of *Heartbeat*, YTV's immensely popular Sunday night police drama set in the glorious countryside around Goathland, near Whitby in the 1960s. Based on the novels by Nicholas Rhea (in fact, Peter Walker, a serving policeman with a passion for writing) it was created by Keith Richardson, the Head of Drama. The first episode was screened in April 1992, in what was to become an 'appointment to view' Sunday night programme. It ran for 18 series, a total of 372 episodes, which drew an average of 10m viewers per night, making it one of the most popular in the country. (Shutterstock)

The Goathland Hotel, near Whitby, is about to undergo a change of identity, to become the 'Aidensfield Arms', the centre of all social life in the YTV series. (Goathland Hotel)

Greg Dyke, then Director of Programmes at London Weekend Television, and I, were in LA looking to buy Hollywood TV shows for ITV. But we had seen little we liked. We sat being cosseted by the jacuzzi and bemoaning the lamentable performance of the ITV weekend schedule, particularly Sundays. We promised each other we would go home and do something about it. Thus was created what became known in the trade as the 'jacuzzi schedule'. Greg went home and produced *London's Burning*. And I knew that I had an initial blockbuster simmering away in Leeds – *Darling Buds of May*. A good

start, but we needed quantity. Back home, we started to concoct the only drama I was ever involved in which was entirely written to a formula. First, the location. Well we had done some beautiful documentaries on the North Yorkshire moors – *Children of Eskdale* and *Sunley's Daughter* – so we knew where to go. Then we knew that the audience loved cop shows and doctor dramas. So we would marry a copper to a doctor and kill two birds. Then we knew 1960s music had an eternal pull. So we had a setting. It was Grant McKee, sitting round with us at lunchtime while we maundered on about our project, who came up with the obvious title. Doctor = Heart, Copper = Beat. 'Geddit?' he said. We got it.

A professional writer, who, for reasons to be explained shall remain anonymous, was engaged to construct something round our brief, and then the crew set off for what was to be a decade enriching the inn-owners of Goathland. A few weeks later, with gleeful confidence I took the first episode rough-cut home to view, knowing Greg had already scheduled it on Sunday nights. It was absolutely terrible. Unwatchable. And I could see no way of mending it through the usual tricks of editing and dubbing. I went back in the next morning and told them to scrap the whole episode, find a new director, rewrite the script and start again. I am afraid I also made the delicate suggestion that we should see a little more of Niamh Cusack.

All this was done, and *Heartbeat* was launched to a huge and appreciative audience and a career that was to last eighteen years (1992–2010). Fortunately, in those affluent days of commercial television, I did not have to tell any of the YTV hierarchy that I had quietly junked about a quarter of a million of their pounds.

Chapter 2

Clive Jones

Clive Jones joined the *Calendar* Newsroom from the *Sheffield Morning Telegraph*. He moved to London to help rescue the morning franchise, and began a meteoric rise through the upper ranks of ITV to the chairmanship of several leading industry companies. He was awarded a Fellowship by the Royal Television Society in 1995 and its Gold Medal in 2007, the year he was also awarded a CBE. Clive was always the man for a crisis. (Clive Jones)

It was a secret hothouse. A regional forcing ground mirrored by, and in endless competition with, its counterpart over the Pennines.

The local newsroom doubled as a talent conveyor belt that spawned three managing directors of ITV companies, a managing director of the ITV network, three directors of programmes, endless heads of department, national editors, news editors, BAFTA-winning directors and producers, award-winning indies, presenters galore that graced our national screens, and Channel 4's longest running series, plus a Police and Crime Commissioner, the odd MP and a national treasure.

I knew none of this when I was tempted away from the *Sheffield Morning Telegraph* in 1978 to join the news desk of *Calendar*, Yorkshire Television's regional news programme.

Within a few months I was news editor, and after just a few more months I was regularly producing the show, desperately learning my trade while being given endless support and encouragement by the most can-do set of creative technicians, cameramen, editors, journalists and programme makers I have ever worked with.

Richard Whiteley, he who became famous for being assaulted by a ferret and was loved by all presenting *Countdown*, was then the programme's anchor and for decades Geoff Boycott's only rival as the greatest living Yorkshireman. Richard's charm and passion for his native county, alongside the journalistic nous of Austin Mitchell, who went on to be the MP for Greater Grimsby for nearly forty years, were at the heart of the early *Calendar*.

Interviewing a trawler skipper for *Calendar*. Robert Hall (centre) with the Grimsby-based news crew, Ken Little (camera), Des Holmes (sound) and Paul Jackson (lighting). Robert was a graduate of Leeds University, set his heart on winning a job at Yorkshire TV and, after some experience at Channel Television, he succeeded. However, the only vacancy available was based in Grimsby, covering South Humberside and large tracts of Lincolnshire, none of which were the most newsworthy of regions, and he and the crew had to work hard to find items for ever-demanding producers in Leeds. The experience paid off in the long run. His intelligent approach to news, his easy style with interviewees and his excellent voice led him to a post with the BBC's national reporting team.

The driving ethos was set by the first three editors, John Fairley, John Wilford and Graham Ironside: cover every hard news story in the vast area we served from North Yorkshire down to King's Lynn, from the Lancashire borders and the Peak District across to Skegness … and then hit them with the story that everyone would talk about in the pub that night.

It was that 'pub' story that dominated the *Calendar* morning conference with which every day began. Covering the news was a given; the newsroom was full of superb hacks who had served their time on national newspapers, ITN, the BBC and the host of big regional newspapers and radio stations that served all our major cities in the days before the internet.

We had money, we had a helicopter, we had more crews on the road than any of our peers and we were pioneering opt-outs – bulletins to deliver even more local news to viewers from the Emley Moor, Belmont and Bilsdale transmission masts. But every day the holy grail was 'that story', usually run after the commercial break, the one which would seize the imagination in the local pub or ignite the conversation around the tea tables of York, Castleford, Chesterfield and Grantham. I emphasize the word 'tea', for that's what they still eat in the North in the evening, not dinner or supper, unless it's from a fish and chip shop.

Some of these stories were outrageous: Magnus Pyke being inadvertently blown up in a disused quarry near Halifax, when too much dynamite was applied and the Outside Broadcast scanner was knocked on its side … fortunately everyone survived, although there was the odd bruise; the DJ from Radio Hallam who was put in a cell, live on air, in front of baying fans for refusing to play Elvis records on the day the great man died; the hunt for the worst pub entertainer in the region that was so funny and outrageous that a visiting film star peed himself in the Green Room while waiting to be interviewed by Geoff Druett and the late, much-loved Marylyn Webb. I have never been able to listen to *My Way* since, without bursting into hysterical laughter.

Then there were scene hands climbing on top of the set and dumping endless baskets of fish over Whiteley's head when peace broke out in the Cod War; and the dustbin full of debris and fuller's earth that was dumped over his head when the Skylab station crashed back to earth in 1979. We forgot to warn him

about that. We had to buy him a new suit and promise not to do it again, as we nearly gave him a heart attack.

However, most days it was a human interest story: a *Calendar*-assisted tale of how a council house tenant won much needed repairs from the local authority; a celebration of community fundraising which enabled a young girl to get to the US for a life-saving operation; a lyrical film by John Willis, one of YTV's great documentary makers who went on to be Director of Programmes at Channel 4, on what was happening on the streets in the city when its two rugby league sides were battling it out at Wembley for the Challenge Cup; beautiful prelims of Barry Cockroft's haunting Hannah Hauxwell films. The best ever title was Grant McKee's *All Hull Let Loose*.

Sadly, I joined after the departure of Michael Wood, the first thinking woman's TV historian of choice, who apparently could knock out a heavy news report in the morning, dress up in Lincoln green for an afternoon feature on how Robin Hood was actually born in Sheffield, not Nottinghamshire, and still write a chapter of his doctoral thesis before the *Calendar* end titles dissolved into the YTV production slide.

The whole station was proud of *Calendar*, mind you, and everyone seemed to have worked on the programme at some time or other, whether they were now working on the first network satellite interview show called *Global Village* with David Frost, shooting great dramas for David Cunliffe, working as a PA on *Emmerdale*, directing light entertainment formats like *3-2-1* or vision-mixing comedies for Vernon Lawrence, later

Controller of Entertainment for the whole of ITV.

And it was not difficult to be proud of a programme that never seemed out of the Yorkshire Television viewing top ten, was often in the top three and occasionally took the number one spot away from *Coronation Street*. No wonder Mr Whiteley in his later years went on to be the Deputy Lord Lieutenant of West Yorkshire, and so many of us joined the massed congregation at the memorial service in York Minster following his untimely death in 2005.

Calendar's fascination with popular, as distinct from populist, journalism did not mean, however, that it did not report the news regularly and well. Alongside our news and feature crews, studio and down the line interviews, we had a network of stringer cameramen that we could put into the field every day.

In my time as both news editor and then full-time producer, the region lived in fear of the Yorkshire Ripper. We covered the hunt for this brutal killer in meticulous detail, and we did it fairly and responsibly but without,

Even sports commentators have their heroes. The production team of *Calendar Sport* demanded a souvenir photograph when Dixie Dean, the legendary Everton centre forward, appeared on the programme. Standing (L to R): John Wilford, Head of Local Programmes; Roger Greenwood, reporter and interviewer; John 'J.B.' Meade, producer; Robert Charles, programme editor; Fred Dinenage, presenter. Seated: Dixie Dean and Martin Tyler, commentator, now leading football coverage on Sky Sport. (Roger Greenwood)

I believe, scaring the populace of the region. We held the West Yorkshire police to account for their failings throughout the investigation. On the day of Peter Sutcliffe's conviction, *Calendar* mounted a superb one-hour special and delivered a network documentary that gripped the UK.

An industrial dispute over new technology, called by YTV's electricians' union, stopped most studio production, but not *Calendar*. We did not want to irritate our union colleagues who operated the lights, so we stayed out of the studio and presented the show from the central courtyard in YTV. A swirling wind blew the scripts everywhere, and Marylyn's famous blonde locks were plastered over her face during the news, but the show went on night after night until the strike was settled.

We had other weapons in our armoury too. *Calendar* was just the flagship programme, with every other local programme across a range of genres being produced under the general *Calendar* banner. I edited *Calendar Sport* for two years, with the likes of Fred Dinenage, still presenting the local news for ITV Meridian, Martin Tyler, who became the chief football commentator on Sky Sports, Roger Greenwood, an endlessly versatile presenter/reporter who could switch from news to sport in the beat of a second, and John Helm, who went on to be a star commentator for ITV and reported live, so heartrendingly sympathetically, on the tragic fire at Bradford City football club.

Calendar Sport went out on a Friday at 6.30 p.m., straight after *Calendar*. That meant a long evening the night before: a long time in VTR, with cumbersome 'quad' videotape editing machines in the 1970s, compiling the various inserts of soccer, racing and rugby league.

One memorable night in VTR for *Calendar Sport* was prompted by an errant researcher working on *Don't Ask Me*, the hugely popular network science programme based in the office just down the corridor from *Calendar*. Duncan Dallas, the programme editor, was notorious for bringing in ineffably bright, but very inexperienced, researchers each year who would dream up brilliant items but would then, with limited television knowledge and an apparent lack of common sense, cause chaos trying to bring them to the screen. That night, as we neared the end of the sports edit, a scream suddenly echoed through the building, quickly traced to the Outside Broadcast truck garage, off the car park at the back of YTV. Everyone still at the station ran towards the garage, led by security men, transmission staff and the odd programme maker not in the bar. Lights went on in the garage, where they found the petrified VTR supervisor being pushed against the wall by a very friendly, but very large, elephant.

Dumbo had been borrowed from a local zoo by *Don't Ask Me* for a studio item and a young researcher had been charged with getting it safely home, but somehow he had forgotten to book the animal transport and left the elephant chained up in the OB garage overnight.

There were also the weekly politics show *Calendar Sunday* and weekly afternoon magazines like *Calendar Tuesday*. Richard Madeley was scooped out of the newsroom to present a fashion show, before he headed over to Manchester and became a national star launching *This Morning*.

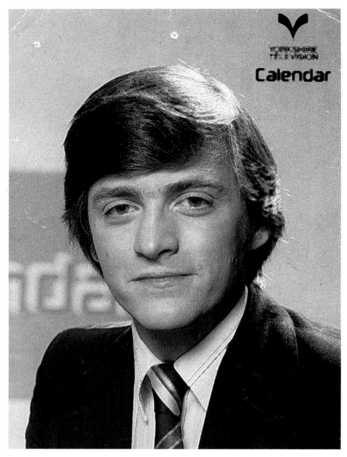

A first publicity photograph of a youthful Richard Madeley when he joined *Calendar* from Border TV in Carlisle. Although a Londoner by birth, Richard's ambitions quickly gave him a wide range of experience in local newspapers, local radio and local TV. In his few years in Yorkshire he built up a following as a fast-moving reporter who could never be given enough work. He also proved to be adept at dealing with the public and enjoyed every opportunity he was given to present programmes in the studio. His talents did not go unnoticed: Granada executives, looking for a team of presenters to front a prestigious new ITV Network programme, poached him to work, initially, on *Granada Reports*. An existing presenter, Judy Finnigan, was assigned as his mentor on his first day, and chemistry did the rest. They paired up to launch *This Morning*, transmitted 'live' from the Albert Dock in Liverpool which ran as an unchallenged success for more than 12 years, from October 1988. *This Morning* soon became better known as *Richard & Judy*, and Richard and Judy soon became better known as Mr and Mrs Madeley. (Shutterstock)

Calendar Carousel became our regular series on the arts, and vet John Baxter, or the 'Scots Omar Sharif' as he was known in the office, was tempted out of his surgery by his compatriot Graham Ironside to present an animal show that ran for decades.

Then, of course, there was *Countdown*. It was spotted on French TV by a vacationing head of department, and a *Calendar* team were sent out to see if they could convert what was a ratings hit across the Channel into something for YTV and possibly ITV as a whole.

The team included two colleagues sadly no longer with us: the chain-smoking, hard-drinking and wonderfully inventive producer, John 'JB' Meade and the gentle, funny, endlessly sardonic director, David St David Smith, whom we were to lose a few years later in a helicopter crash into the Humber, along with the brilliant cameraman Graham Barker.

JB harrumphed into the office after his trip to the French studios saying the programme was impossible and he was not certain it would translate to British screens.

David told of the French director rising from his seat during a live transmission of the programme to serve him and JB a glass of wine, and of how the female co-presenter chalked letters on a blackboard for the contestants, then nipped behind the set for a sneaky Gauloise.

Six episodes of *Calendar Calling* followed, to see how it worked. No one held their breath. And how wrong we all were. Richard found a new home from home, Channel 4 launched their schedule with *Countdown*, and Carol Vorderman became the co-host for 28 years from 1982. There was not a Gauloise in sight.

I was to leave in 1982, tempted away by the offer of becoming the Managing Editor of TV-AM, Britain's first breakfast television station.

'Do it', said one of my bosses. 'It will be the last television station launched in Britain and it will fail and then you can come back.'

It was the first of many launches in which I was to be involved. It nearly did fail, but we turned it around and it became a great success.

Sadly, I never went back to the station that gave me my first start in broadcasting and the programme that will always be my spiritual home. Grant McKee, who joined *Calendar* on the same day that I did, stayed on and became the station's very distinguished Director of Programmes. I envy him to this day.

Calendar is, of course, still alive and well, but they don't find elephants in the OB garage any more or blow up Magnus Pyke.

The production team are much too professional … but they may not be having as much fun.

Chapter 3

Graham Ironside

The name – *Calendar* – was the inspired choice of the Director of Programmes, Donald Baverstock, the man who had created *Tonight* for the BBC. Donald had assembled a team of producers and presenters for *Calendar* which, it could be fairly said, represented his somewhat erratic way of recruiting people. Among them were a top London model whose home was in Halifax, a tousle-haired writer who had been working on a political tome, an Irishwoman of deep intellect, a fresh-faced Oxford graduate he'd met on a train and a thrusting young political journalist, Jonathan Aitken, who was also the Conservative candidate for a local constituency. Jonathan was chosen as the main presenter – lots of intellect but a worrying lack of hands-on experience … Few of the prospective presenters had the slightest grasp of television 'language' or of the mechanics and practicalities of the medium – how to deliver a link, how to take

After a few months of technical hitches and equipment delays, the *Calendar* team moved into Studio 2, the dedicated News studio, near the end of 1968. Because of its limited size and flexible facilities it quickly became a hive of activity, recording a number of educational and other programmes like *Farmhouse Kitchen* in the mornings, before turning round to become home to *Calendar* in the afternoons. The founding fathers of *Calendar* were (front row, extreme left) John Wilford, News Editor and (second left) John Fairley, Editor. Others (L to R) are: Jonathan Aitken, the original if short-lived presenter; Paul Dunstan, newscaster and reporter; Peter Moth, presenter; Richard Whiteley, reporter and Simon Welfare, newscaster and reporter. Sid Waddell, then a producer, is in the centre of the photograph, and to his right is Donald Baverstock, Director of Programmes. The man in the white shirt is Peter Jones, studio director, and on his immediate left is Mr G.E. Ward Thomas, managing director. Second row back, far left, is Graham Ironside, Deputy News Editor. (Shutterstock)

Graham Ironside joined Yorkshire TV from Grampian Television (Aberdeen) in June 1968, as a News Assistant on the nightly news programme, *Calendar*. (Austin Mitchell)

A more serious complication arose on the Friday evening before Launch Day. As the technicians worked feverishly to complete the installation of the new, sensitive equipment in the Studio 2 Control Room, some wiring overheated and burned out most of their work. Luckily, the studio itself was untouched.

With three days to go, the prospect of getting *Calendar* on air looked remote, but with the quick thinking and flexibility which rapidly became essential characteristics of Yorkshire TV, an Outside Broadcast truck was found and installed in the car park, and the production team were left to cope, running up and down Studio Road, through wind and rain, with scripts for the studio and the OB truck.

After its first week of transmission, *Calendar* was floundering. The technical errors, quality of presentation and inconsistent quality of content earned it the dreaded description, 'Amateur Night'. At the end of the first week of 'live' transmission, the Head of News, although experienced and able, just could not cope with the volatile demands of the job. He went home to the North-East that Friday night and simply never reappeared, leaving the chicken apparently headless. The teething troubles continued for months: industrial strife, including a fifteen-week strike … the collapse of the iced-up Emley Moor transmitter in March 1969 … technical teams struggling with unfamiliar equipment … and production teams taking too long to gel.

But somehow the instinct to fight for life continued to flicker. Something Had To Be Done. Cometh the hour, cometh the man … although, in fairness, three men, rather than one, emerged in that hour of dire need. First,

direction through a floor manager, let alone how to cope with the everyday crises which haunt live programmes.

Even before the first day of transmission, *Calendar* seemed doomed to suffer more than its fair share of production problems. Unused to the bawling and shouting of journalists, one of the secretaries, an original staff member who had set up the first YTV admin office, took exception to their intemperate outbursts one hot and stressful afternoon and wreaked a dreadful revenge: the very next morning she had gone, and with her all the News Department typewriters, which she had assigned overnight to other departments.

John Fairley. Coming from BBC Radio, he at least knew more than most about fast-moving broadcast news and about handling presenters and their idiosyncrasies: his main presenter on *Today* was Jack de Manio, who famously never seemed able to read the studio clock.

Apart from possessing a formidable intellect and a daunting fount of knowledge, he was unflappable under pressure: approval could only be detected by a slight lifting of the eyebrows, and displeasure by a slight lowering of the eyelids. His lack of experience in television caused scarcely a hiccup. A junior member of the staff – still too fearful to admit to having been the source – said that he took over the responsibility for *Calendar* 'with an automatic assumption of effortless superiority'. That style he maintained with distinction throughout a stellar 40-year career in broadcasting. He certainly assumed the role of leader smoothly and with assurance, injecting those sterling qualities into the programme itself and some confidence into its producers and presenters.

Alongside him was the News Editor, John Wilford, another trained journalist and the son of a distinguished newspaper editor who had joined from ATV in Birmingham, where he had been an on-screen reporter. A keen sportsman, John had a clear vision for *Calendar* – to make it the No.1 popular choice for the early evening viewer – and a dogged determination to make it work.

The third man was Michael Partington. Appointed as YTV's political correspondent, Michael, born in Harrogate, had become editor of the *Pudsey News* at the age of twenty-three (in Yorkshire terms, the equivalent of climbing Everest at the age of three, possibly without oxygen). Later, he had joined the *Daily Express* in London, graduated to ITN as a reporter/newsreader and, before Yorkshire TV opened, had been political correspondent at Anglia TV. He knew the

Some of the original presenters and producers of *Calendar* at a reunion to celebrate the programme's 25th anniversary. (Back row, L to R): Barry Cockcroft, Director; John Wilford, Editor; Graham Ironside, Producer; John Fairley, Director of Programmes. (Front row, L to R): Michael Partington, interviewer/presenter; Liz Fox, interviewer/presenter; Richard Whiteley, reporter/presenter; Paul Dunstan, reporter/presenter; and Simon Welfare, reporter/presenter. (Shutterstock)

Richard Whiteley joined Yorkshire TV from ITN in London, where he became an editorial trainee after graduating from Cambridge. At the same time, Graham Ironside joined the new News team from Grampian TV in Aberdeen where he had been a researcher and News assistant. They worked together, more or less harmoniously, for 27 years and remained firm friends until Richard's death in June 2005. (Shutterstock)

Yorkshire region. He knew the business. He knew everyone worth knowing. And he knew how to select the news Yorkshire needed. He was also a gossip without peer.

On the subs' bench, as it were, sat two young hopefuls who joined YTV on the same day in June 1968, just four weeks before it went on air. One was Richard Whiteley, born in Shipley, educated at Giggleswick School in the Dales, a graduate of Cambridge and of the ITN trainee scheme in London. To his critics, and there were more than

a few, Richard had the physical build of an undernourished wimp, poor eyesight and asthma, and the dress sense of Worzel Gummidge. But he had passion – a passion for his native county, a passion for television since the age of eight, and a passion for his new company to succeed. He also had the passionate ambition – thought to be quite amusing then – to become a regular, if not a star, presenter on local television. Yorkshire Television, as he later declared, was his life.

As for myself, I had had three years' television experience at Grampian TV in Aberdeen and had moved house and home, young wife and baby daughter to Leeds, hoping to make a mark with a bright, new and bigger station.

Gradually, the London-based members of the production team faded out of the picture, not least, it was said, because they never quite grasped the concept of having to be available for duty in the Leeds newsroom every day from 9.00 a.m.

Donald had roughly four weeks to mould his raggle-taggle team of producers and presenters into a front-line fighting force; and it has to be admitted that his success was somewhat limited. Each morning, at about 9.30, the team gathered round a large table in a small hothouse of a room to decide which topics to develop for inclusion in that night's programme.

As fast as the team suggested ideas, the faster Donald shot them down with incisive and cutting comments. Eventually, a few projects would be accepted and reporters and producers dispatched to bring them to fruition. Then, every afternoon at about 5 o'clock, the team would reassemble to report what they had achieved, explain how each item would be presented and hear Donald's evaluation. It could be an unnerving experience for those unaccustomed to the ferocity (and accuracy) of Donald's criticisms. Careless work or loose thinking invited instant derision.

As one of the luckless victims, though already deputy News Editor, I once found myself floundering through an explanation of some financial feature of Yorkshire life and falling far short of Donald's expectations.

'Don't try anything like that before you've read Adam Smith's *Wealth of Nations*, boyo,' he said. 'Now – anybody got anything worth listening to?'

Alas, Donald had occasional blank spots too. When Barbara Hepworth, Yorkshire's most famous sculptor after Henry Moore, died in a fire at her studio in Cornwall, I tried to justify carrying a report in *Calendar*.

'Forget it, boyo,' rapped Donald. 'What's famous about her? I've never heard of her.'

However, under his forensic examination the new team came to realize that a programme like *Calendar* cannot rely on the events of the day to provide enough interest to fill a half-hour slot. It needs quick thinking and careful planning. In any case, news departments can only react after 'action news' stories – major crimes, disasters, etc. – take place, and they can only react quickly and effectively if they have had the benefit of sound training and experience. In that summer of 1968 *Calendar* was short of both.

However, the two Johns, Fairley and Wilford, knew enough to start building solid foundations, and they initially focused on the news element of the programme. The reporters were charged with producing a steady flow of ideas and information

The *Calendar* News Studio. Alan Hardwick (left), Marylyn Webb (right). (Yorkshire Post Newspapers)

which would make interesting items for the programme. Carefully, they built up a tight network of correspondents, contacts and 'stringers' (freelance cameramen) in the main cities and towns whose detailed local knowledge gave them enough information, contacts, events and topical ideas to create lively and informative programmes.

The News desk was charged with providing two self-contained segments of brief news items, one in each half of the programme, to be delivered to the studio properly prepared, rehearsed and timed. At least ten minutes of the programme would thus be reliably delivered to the viewer, leaving the rest of the production staff to concentrate on more complicated or in-depth reports which would reflect public interest in social issues and political events, as well as sport – of course – and, indeed, any topic which would interest most of the people most of the time.

Austin Mitchell, born and bred in Shipley, Yorkshire, was a brilliant student of history at Oxford and started his postgraduate career as a lecturer in New Zealand and as a Fellow of Nuffield College. In New Zealand, he started, and quickly learned to love, appearing on television. By chance, at a university dinner, Austin met Yorkshire's Deputy Chairman, Sir Geoffrey Cox, the man who pioneered ITV's *News At Ten*, himself a New Zealander and no mean judge of talent. Within weeks, Austin had been recruited to the ranks of YTV presenters. (Terry Ricketts)

Relics of the infamous "Calendar" football team – Austin Mitchell, presenter, and Graham Ironside, then an assistant News Producer. No 7 is John Willis, a key figure in the enormously successful Documentary department, then Channel 4, and now BAFTA.

Luckily their futures lay far from the football field: they were seldom troubled by scouts from Leeds United or indeed any football club, although their efforts were frequently supported by "ringers" like Bobby Collins, Billy Bremner and Jack Charlton.

Gradually, sanity was restored in the *Calendar* world: the programme gained in integrity, and the viewers, with Yorkshire's sense of fairness, gave the team some credit as a bunch of triers. They came to see the reporters and presenters as hard-working, approachable people trying to do an honest job, with no pretensions of becoming TV 'stars'. They lived in ordinary houses, shopped in the same shops, took their kids to the same schools and, generally speaking, became part of the social landscape. Austin Mitchell and Richard Whiteley were prime examples . They were stayers all, there for the long haul.

In spite of his Oxford education and his Antipodean travels, Austin Mitchell's Yorkshire accent remained undiluted, and his arrival a few months after the launch made an immediate impact. He took to *Calendar* like a duck to water, and the viewers took to him like a long lost brother. His effervescent presence lifted spirits in the office and in the studio, and he worked well with his fellow presenters, all strong personalities in their own right.

Liz Fox, a trained actress and a former presenter on Tyne-Tees Television, was the first woman reporter/presenter to star on *Calendar*. A bubbly personality with great ability, she could talk to nervous interviewees or tough MPs with equal charm, and loved to bring sparks of humour to the screen. Richard Whiteley used his ITN training and local knowledge as a busy 'on the road' roving reporter. Simon Welfare, an Oxford graduate in his first job, put his wide-ranging knowledge and silky voice to effective use as a reporter/newscaster, alongside Paul Dunstan, another late recruit, whose experience gave the news bulletins gravitas. Michael Partington, producing and presenting the 'heavier' subjects, carried out the main political interviews in the style and to the standard he had learned in his years at ITN. He thoroughly personified the mantra of the best political interviewers: 'No politician should leave my studio feeling happy.'

The producers and presenters gradually found their feet, and *Calendar* began to overtake *Look North*, the BBC competition – although it took more than two years to establish top ratings. The viewing audience, however, had to live with an unfortunately high level of on-air slips and trips, mostly due to the fact that the producers pushed the technical facilities and the technicians to the limits, not on an odd occasion, but night after night as a matter of course.

Simply producing scripts proved to be an enormous practical problem. For the normal nightly programme they would run to 40 or even 50 foolscap pages, and something like 30 copies were required – so ensuring the demise of at least one rainforest a week.

However, they were seen as fairly essential, except by one young manager who stopped production one afternoon and informed the producer of the day, 'You've already used up your allocation of paper for this year.'

For nearly ten months the Newsroom remained in the old trouser factory in Burley Road, a good distance up the road from the News Studio, Studio 2, in the main building in Kirkstall Road. That meant that all the scripts and paraphernalia needed for the programme had to be carried physically down the street, defying wind, rain, tea-time traffic and curious passers-by. Few nights passed when everything necessary arrived safely. For the fact that most items got there, thanks are due – 40 years overdue, perhaps? – to the patient hard work of the secretarial team of Eliza Seed, Diane Newton, Chris Shires and Julia Websdale, who all somehow maintained their sanity under pressure.

The logistics were frightening: Hull, for example, was a good hour-and-a-half's drive

Calendar reporters. (L to R) Paul Dunstan, Geoff Druett, Roger Greenwood, Richard Whiteley, Marylyn Webb. (Yorkshire Post Newspapers)

away, and meant crossing a toll bridge at Selby (price nine old pence and don't forget the receipt), where there were frequent delays. Grimsby was even further – the last train which got the film back to Leeds in time left at 10.10 a.m, and not much news seemed to happen in Grimsby before that!

An added problem was that the film processing labs, so vital to the news-gathering operation, were not actually on the premises – nowhere near Kirkstall Road, never mind the Newsroom. In fact, they were located three miles away, on the far side of the rush hour, so the processed films had to be carried through the traffic jams. Had it not been for the miracles pulled off by the lab technicians, usually under a barrage of abuse from stricken producers, and daredevil driving by two motorcycle dispatch drivers, Yorkshire viewers would have been treated to many a blank screen.

Even working at top speed, the film processors, or at least their machines, needed 45 minutes to process 100ft of film. It took 15 minutes, at least, to drive it back to the Studios. It would then take the film editors at least an hour to edit the films to the specific requirements of the programme and another 30 minutes to assemble all the edited film items in the order of transmission. Even then, they had to be loaded in the Telecine machines, which would convert the film into electronic pictures to transmit to the viewers.

With the programme on air at 6 o'clock (or, to be precise, 15 seconds past), rehearsals and timings needed to be completed by 5.45. That meant that the last film had to reach the labs by about 3.00 p.m., to be on the safe side. This may have happened on the very odd occasion, but no one who ever worked on *Calendar* can remember if ever it did. More often than not, film would be arriving at the labs at 5 o'clock … getting to the picture editors as the programme was starting … and be scrabbled on the air somewhere before half past six. Exciting times.

The only people who really enjoyed those days were the dispatch riders, who slithered through traffic jams on their motorbikes like eels and revelled in tales of 'near-misses' in dicey situations. From the car park to the editing suites they faced a 200yd run, on foot and in biker boots, to the back door of the building, then another 200yds of corridors and two flights of stairs (best recorded time 3 minutes 35 seconds) to deliver the films by hand to the film editors. So, in that age of the 'white heat of technology' (Harold Wilson's famous phrase), they came up with an effective, low-tech time-saving device. A battered wastepaper basket lowered to the car park on a long piece of string, then quickly hauled aloft, was the answer, and remained so until film was eventually replaced by videotape at the end of the 1980s.

Even collecting the raw material for the news was subject to the limitations of the technologies available at the time. There were no fax machines, no Telexes, and no computers. In fact, the only way the programme's freelance correspondents around the region could pass on tip-offs and file stories, was to pick up the telephone, call *Calendar* and dictate their information word by word to a team of copy typists. In real life, of course, these were young girls, some in their first jobs and more interested in their social lives, which were often extremely lively. So lively, in fact, that late nights occasionally took their toll. By the middle of the afternoon – the busiest time of the day for them – concentration would tend to slip. Errol 'Bomber' Graham, from Sheffield, a champion boxer of the period, was misheard as 'Hero Bummer' Graham. The Mayor of Torquay, on a civic visit north, would have been surprised to hear himself described as the Mayor of Turkey.

If the wordsmiths from time to time derided the efforts of their colleagues in Props and Graphics, they quickly re-appraised their view when the Lofthouse Colliery disaster happened in the spring of 1973. Seven miners were trapped when a massive inrush of mud and foetid water burst into the seam where they were working 300ft below the surface. Rescue teams fought for a week to try to reach them in the hope they were trapped in an air-pocket, sadly unsuccessfully.

It was a horrifying event, and coverage was difficult for the News team. There was a great deal to tell about the ingenuity and heroism of the rescue teams, but no way to show what was actually taking place below ground – until one of the Props men showed up. Jim Sables, a man who usually went about his work quietly and unnoticed, revealed that he had been a Lofthouse miner until forced out by injury. On a blackboard which was wheeled into the studio he quickly drew out a brilliant, detailed plan of the colliery which showed exactly what the rescue parties were battling against and what our cameras were unable to reach.

Calendar's viewers, once over their initial pleasure at the arrival of YTV, wanted programmes of the quality to which they felt entitled. And whenever they felt we had failed to achieve that quality, they would call, or write, to express their opinions with all the forthright vigour for which Yorkshire folk are famed. Burning ears became something of an occupational hazard for those who dared answer the phones at the end of a *Calendar* transmission.

Pursuing the news and meeting the expectations of Yorkshire's viewers was a daily challenge, but as the need for additional local programmes became apparent, so did the weight of responsibility. The miners' strikes, first in the 1970s and fatally in the 1980s, simply because they lasted so long, tested the strengths of the production teams to the full. Early starts, late finishes and constant pressure from both sides for fair and objective coverage meant serious demands on people's physical and mental capabilities.

As Marylyn Webb records elsewhere, the hunt for the Yorkshire Ripper, over five years, day and night, took a similar toll, with the added stress of real fear on the part of the women who were key members of the reporting and production staff.

Faced with tricky tasks, they never flinched and never spurned the chance to work on network series, create new local series and produce one-off documentaries, as the need arose. Gwyneth Hughes and Petrina Rance were dedicated and accomplished producers; Ruth Pitt, Jane Beckwith, Sita Guneratne and Marylyn, energetic and thoughtful reporter/interviewers, comfortable both on location and 'live' in the studio. No surprise that they all went on to other successes after YTV.

Under Richard Gregory and David Lowen, programme editors, Andrew Darling and Andrew Sheldon, producers, and Robert Charles, Head of Sport, the department kept up an enviable flow of programmes. Although they may have walked in the shadow of the

Marylyn Webb, with Bob Rust (left, in hat) and Richard Whiteley (right, in hat) trying to work at the Great Yorkshire Show. The Show is one of the biggest annual events in the Yorkshire diary and must be given thorough coverage. However, such was the popularity of the presenters that their preparations had to be combined with public relations activities, mainly signing autographs on odd pieces of paper. This was in olden days, of course, before the selfie was invented. (Terry Ricketts)

'big guns' in Drama and Entertainment departments supplying ratings winners to the ITV network, there is no denying the abundance of their output. Producing in excess of 500 hours of programming a year, they created more television hours than the network producers provided to ITV and Channel 4 combined.

What's more, it was a *Calendar* team which took on the format of the French gameshow *Des Chiffres et Lettres* and devised a production style for British TV which became *Countdown*, the first and iconic 'numbers and letters' programme on Channel 4.

The gifted if erratic John 'JB' Meade as producer, with David St David Smith and Peter Jones as directors, took on the task. Richard Whiteley, *Calendar*'s main presenter and television's most enthusiastic student, loved the idea and slotted into the presenter's chair as to the manner born.

To Richard's eternal delight, his was the first face on Channel 4, and Yorkshire TV – the *Calendar* team, in fact – contributed its first programme. But to my eternal pleasure, I can claim that Channel 4's *Countdown* first saw life as '*Calendar Countdown*'. Only six experimental programmes, and only shown locally, but nevertheless …

Chapter 4

Kathryn Apanovicz

YTV was always a special place for me. I remember, when we lived in Farsley, that the bus to Leeds stopped outside the studio on Kirkstall Road. Little did I know at that young age the difference it would make to my life.

I auditioned for a programme called *Junior Showtime* after having won the Yorkshire Top Talent competition. At the aforementioned competition I met a wonderful lady called Jean Pearce. She was credited as being the choreographer of the programme, but in all honesty she was responsible for putting the whole thing together, along with a director called David Millard. Jean ran a dancing school in Leeds. She asked my mother to bring me along for lessons and also suggested that I audition for *Showtime*.

What seemed like a few weeks later, I did, and met the notorious Jess Yates. I can't honestly say I was nervous, but Jess wasn't the easiest person. He always insisted on playing the organ to accompany you – though not very well, I'm afraid.

At my audition, he suddenly banged the keys and shouted, 'Can't you hear the bloody organ?'

'Yes,' I said, 'but you're not playing it properly' – fairly gutsy for a 9-year-old!

I found out later that this was one of Jess's little tests: he didn't like kids who burst into tears.

Time passed, and we went off to visit relatives in Poland. When we got home, a telegram was waiting. I was going to be recording my first appearance on television!

Junior Showtime would never be allowed to be made today. Picture this: children, all under the age of sixteen – this was always pointed out to the viewers. Of course, sixteen was the cut-off point, as after that Jess would have had to pay us the full equity rate!

Richard Whiteley in his pomp and his element, surrounded by the most important women in his professional life. (L to R) Kathy Apanowicz, his long-term partner; Carol Vorderman, his on-screen *Countdown* partner of 23 years; and from *Dictionary Corner*, Susie Dent. Richard became a national treasure after *Countdown* became a ratings hit on Channel 4, but was already a Yorkshire icon as presenter of *Calendar* and other regionally-based programmes. His old school, Giggleswick, where Russell Harty taught him English, has named its new theatre after him. (Kathy Apanowicz)

Sir John Gielgud. (Shutterstock)

Once Grace Kelly of Hollywood, then Princess Grace of Monaco, and a contributor to YTV's *Stars on Sunday*. (Shutterstock)

Anyway, there we were, all under the age of sixteen, some teenage girls, some youngsters like myself, singing show tunes and telling terrible jokes, almost what could be described as music hall turns. It was a sort of end-of-the-pier show.

Jess's involvement, from my point of view, was minimal. He left the day-to-day running of the programme up to Jean and David. He would appear occasionally on set, always with the same note: 'It's good, but can we pick up the pace a bit.' Everything was sung at breakneck speed!

I think it was a successful show because, to me, it seemed to go on for years. I appeared on the last show. We didn't know it would be the last, but honestly there has never been anything like it since.

Jess was always a bit of a distant figure, but I did hear stories of his ability to be very, shall we say, economical with the budget when producing his programmes. Years later, when I was acting in a series called *Angels* for the BBC, I came across a director who remembered me from my *Junior Showtime* days. He had then been working on a series called *Hadleigh* with Gerald Harper, a very glamorous drama, and he told me of the time the directions in studio were for the leading man to step out on to the balcony of his mansion. When he tried, he found it had disappeared! The missing balcony was discovered later in another studio with Ronnie Ronalde, a very entertaining whistler, standing on it and whistling 'In a Monastery Garden' for Jess's show *Stars on Sunday*!

Another tale was of Jess hearing that the great Hollywood star Gregory Peck was in the UK. He somehow managed to get through to him and offered him a chance to do a bible reading on *Stars on Sunday*.

Surely he'd jump at the chance? Sir Ralph Richardson and Sir John Gielgud, along with Princess Grace of Monaco, had already been on the show. Gregory Peck seemed quite open to the suggestion.

'What about a fee, Mr Yates?'

'Well, Mr Peck, can I call you Gregory', was the reply. 'We were thinking £25.'

'In that case, no thank you. My chauffeur has already had his hair cut!'

I love stories like that. They don't make them like Jess anymore. He was an old fashioned end of-the-pier impresario. He got things done. Who else would have got Bing Crosby to Leeds? I miss the likes of him and, let's face it, he saved YTV a helluva lot of money!

Junior Showtime started my career, and from that Mark Curry and I were seen by Alan Parker, who cast us, albeit in small roles, in the film *Bugsy Malone*.

I went back to YTV when I was seventeen. I had the most peculiar interview I think I have ever had for a job, with John Wilford, the then executive producer of *Calendar*. He just met me in the canteen and stared out of the window, whilst I gabbled away. I went home and was saying what a waste of time it had been, when the phone rang and I was offered the job of presenting *Calendar Kids*, with my best friend Mark Curry. He had had a similar experience. *Calendar Kids* was significant

Bing Crosby. (Shutterstock)

Mark Curry of the cheeky grin was only seven when he passed an audition for *Junior Showtime* in 1969. Brought up in Allerton Bywater, near Castleford, he was stage-struck from childhood and attended the Jean Pearce School of Dancing in Leeds. In the 1970s he teamed up with Kathy Apanowicz to present a local children's programme called *Calendar Kids*, and both went on to busy careers on stage and television. Most recently, Mark was appearing in the West End as 'Wizard' in *Wicked*.

Carol Vorderman and Richard Whiteley, whose on-screen chemistry created high ratings and long life for *Countdown* on Channel 4. To the delight of Richard, he made history as the first face to appear on Channel 4. It also made Carol a star. Here Richard introduces Carol to a racehorse which Richard bought for 'a bit of fun' after he was appointed honorary Mayor of Wetwang, a lively if little known village in the Yorkshire Wolds. Richard named his purchase 'Mare of Wetwang'. She did not prove to be a great investment: in her 19 starts on the flat she achieved one win and one second place. (Kathy Apanowicz)

to me because, although I had come across Richard Whiteley in make-up, I can't say that I knew him. He later became the love of my life …

Working in *Calendar* as a teenager taught me so much. I can remember having to read the news once, as nobody else was available. Not something you'd expect to see every day. But it set me up, and even today I think about the wonderful lessons that I learnt – and boy, did I grow up quickly and have great fun? TV is just not run like that anymore.

I will always consider YTV as a kind of family. I grew up on the corridors of YTV. I still feel that if you were to cut me in half like a stick of rock you would find Yorkshire Television and the chevron written there.

Dick and I were driving along Kirkstall Road when they were taking the chevron down outside the studio.

He turned to me and said, 'I think I had the best of it.'

And, do you know, I think he was right.

Chapter 5

John Wilford

John Wilford

Paul Fox came to Yorkshire in the summer of 1973. At that time, the three best contact books in London were held by Jonathan Aitken, David Frost and Alan Whicker. And it was the ubiquitous Whicker who picked up on the fact that Fox had fallen out with his BBC boss, Director General Huw Wheldon. This was ostensibly over the Beeb's refusal to replace Paul's ailing company car, but just as likely a reason was the imminent arrival of Alastair Milne from BBC Scotland as Director of Television. The two had crossed swords when Milne worked for Donald Baverstock's *Tonight* programme.

Whicker brokered a meeting between Fox and Yorkshire's MD, Gwyn Ward Thomas, who could scarcely have believed his luck: having fired Donald Baverstock for his erratic behaviour, he had landed one of TV's Big Beasts. Here was the man who had started *Sportsview, Grandstand, Sports Personality of the Year, Dad's Army* etc. The BBC ought to have hung its head in shame at letting him go!

Before he arrived in Leeds, Ward Thomas held a cocktail party for his senior executives in the YTV London office. I was on holiday abroad when this happened but, eager for news, had an arrangement with John Fairley to call him from the beach front.

'What's he like?'

'Well, he's just like the photograph.'

The picture he referred to was a black and white studio shot of a burly, somewhat forbidding looking individual, as indeed on first acquaintance he appeared to be.

Our first meeting followed not so much an invitation as a summons.

After a perfunctory greeting he said, 'I gather you're about to transmit a documentary in favour of warmongering.'

The film in question was about RAF V-bomber training in Canada, produced by one of our best news journalists, Paul Dunstan. It transpired a complaint had been made to Fox by the Head of Presentation,

Neil Bramson. He hadn't seen the film – only the promos.

'Well, the film hasn't been edited yet so it's a bit early to pass judgement,' I said.

Oh dear. Fox was not amused. He did not like being given duff information. Mr. Bramson, I fear, would have received a severe 'horning' (Fox was soon nicknamed 'The Rhino').

After that unsteady start, Fox and I developed a sound working relationship. He didn't always approve of things we did on *Calendar*, but we didn't make the programme for the benefit of the management. And I found him easier to deal with than Baverstock, who disliked me and didn't hide the fact. There were several reasons for this: I wasn't Oxbridge, I wanted *Calendar* to be populist, and popular, rather than the intellectual northern *Tonight* he craved.

We often clashed, and never more than when, in conjunction with our Head of Publicity, Alec Todd, a former Tory Party PR chief, and the Yorkshire Conservative Agent, Graham Macmillan, he handed me a list of senior Tories who, he announced, would appear on *Calendar* and when. It was my view that the editor of the programme should decide these matters and that it was quite wrong to have leading politicians imposed on us.

Incredibly, the matter was raised at board level, and the vice chairman, Sir Geoffrey Cox, was deputed to tell me to accept Baverstock's instruction. All television journalists have the greatest respect for Sir Geoffrey and, indeed, it was he who had first offered me a job at YTV. I suggested to him that it was not something he would have accepted when he was editor of *News At Ten*,

Sir Paul Fox being awarded a Fellowship of the British Film and Television Academy by Princess Anne in 1990. Sir Paul joined Yorkshire Television as Director of Programmes in 1973 and rejoined the BBC fifteen years later. (Shutterstock)

and he agreed. He said a compromise had to be found, and it was decided that we would allow the first name on the list to appear and then the rest would be forgotten.

That first name belonged to the then Welsh Secretary – not a man we would have normally considered, but a deal is a deal. I asked our senior political interviewer, Michael Partington, to delve into his past and see what could be found. The hapless minister, a charming man as I recall, was duly questioned about incidents which he could scarcely remember. I almost (but not quite) felt sorry for him. Baverstock was furious.

So Paul Fox was a positive appointment for me. And, as the years went by, I found him to be intensely loyal, thoughtful and generous.

Editing *Calendar* was like riding a bucking bronco. Deliberately so. We started at a huge disadvantage, since the BBC's *Look*

North, ably fronted by David Seymour and Barry Chambers, was well established and had a decent audience. We had unknown presenters, and many viewers resented the fact that they had lost the Granada TV evening programme *Scene at Six Thirty*. But our biggest problems were of our own making. We had a production team who lacked experience and, in some cases, was downright incompetent. The technical equipment, hastily installed to meet deadline day, was unreliable, and we were plagued by breakdowns. John Fairley and I read the news. Badly.

But things could only get better. We poached ATV's *Midland News'* excellent newsreader Paul Dunstan. We took on a first class studio director, Peter Jones. And then, through the door, walked Austin Mitchell. A rumbustious Yorkshireman with outrageous intelligence and personality, he really was a gift from the gods – well, New Zealand actually, where he had held a university chair in politics and presented a weekly TV show.

He had the rare ability to grill a politician until you could smell scorching flesh, then cavort around grilling sardines on Scarborough beach.

Alongside Richard Whiteley, Michael Partington and Liz Fox we found we had a strong on-screen presence. And behind the scenes, some imaginative producers – Sid Waddell, John Meade and Kevin Sim. But the essence of *Calendar* was the news team, led by the reliable and accomplished Scotsman, Graham Ironside. News took precedence over everything in the programme. In a decade we had some of the biggest stories in Britain: the Yorkshire Ripper, the Black Panther, two national miners' strikes, the Lofthouse Colliery disaster, the Flixborough chemical explosion.

As *Calendar* became successful (at one time we had four programmes in our top ten – unprecedented for a network company) Paul Fox allowed us to spread our wings and make our own spin-off programmes. Two stand out for me – mainly because I produced both! *It's No Joke Living in Barnsley*, with the late Brian Glover, won the RTS award for Best Regional Programme of the year.

And on the night Brian Clough was sacked from Leeds United after 90 days as manager, our live studio confrontation between Clough and former Leeds manager Don Revie was reprinted verbatim in the next day's *Daily Express*. That doesn't happen very often! Paul Fox was instrumental in talking Revie into the studio, though I suspect Don was itching to confront his long-time nemesis face to face. A big story that led to a feature film and even a stage play.

But it's the little silly things that I remember best, and which won our audience over in the seventies. The Mayoress of Batley, for example, clad from head to toe in pink chiffon, playing a pink piano and singing 'Tiptoe Through The Tulips', while her poodle (dyed pink of course) strutted up and down on the piano lid.

You get the picture.

Chapter 6

Keith Richardson

(Keith Richardson)

Dylan Thomas was all for beginning at the beginning, but I am pretty sure that the trials and tribulations of the transmission mast falling down and the like have been well documented. However, it is probably worth pursuing some of the reasons that Yorkshire Television became the amazing programme company that it did. And although my experience was mostly in drama, I think my thoughts also apply to all the other production departments.

Television was still a very young industry and there was a lot of learning to be done, even as the first colour studio was being built. Disparate types crossed the Pennines, hordes made their way up from Rediffusion and a smattering of canny Scots invested their all in the rail fare to Leeds. I abandoned my job cleaning houses for rich ladies in Hampstead.

So now we had different tribes with different skills all in the one place.

What was the key ingredient, apart from talent and enthusiasm, which created such a powerhouse in Yorkshire? The great Yorkshire writer David Nobbs once boasted that we were the last generation that drank at lunchtime, and lamented that alcohol now played less of a part in working lives than it did in his heyday. That got me thinking. It's a theory, and only a theory, but I'm certain that having a bar on the premises helped to create a good atmosphere. The disparate tribes were all able to mingle over a glass of ale, and frequently problems were solved in this way. Of course, I recognize that a few problems were started this way as well – possibly. But I think the good outweighed the bad. The thing about the bar was that it was a meeting place when the day was over, a chance to relax; and because the visiting directors and actors only had hotel rooms to look forward to, they were only too happy to share a jar and experiences.

I can, however, remember that there was at least one occasion when alcohol didn't help. A famous director, who shall be nameless, came in to do a drama, and the excitement was tangible. Everybody loved this man, and he was one of the most highly respected of directors. I was then Assistant Floor

Manager and delighted to be asked to attend a production meeting. First time to see how the top guys did it. Remember Production Meetings? That was when we all gathered and the designer produced the studio plan and the lighting director instantly said, 'We can't have that ceiling piece in there. I'll need to get my lights in there.' And there would follow four hours of conversation about how to adapt the ceiling piece for lighting. So, we've all travelled to London for this meeting. Famous director arrived an hour late, walked in, sat down and promptly went to sleep. He was, I think the expression is, 'suitably refreshed'. Amazingly, the meeting took place around him, and when it was over he woke up and went home. As I said, he was very famous and much loved – but it wasn't for his conversation.

Booze certainly played a role in my training. I was fortunate enough to work on an American co-production which starred Robert Shaw and his then wife Mary Ure – both fairly well known imbibers. For some reason it was deemed that I was the best person to accompany them on the train from London to Leeds, to make sure that they didn't drink too much and did arrive in time for the technical walk-through in Studio 4. Remember them? Technical walk-throughs? Grand days! Well, we ate lunch on the train and Robert had a few beers and Mary drank port all through the journey. We arrived in Leeds and taxied to the studios, where they insisted that there was ten minutes available to have a quick one before going into the studio. Robert ordered a triple whisky and Mary a pint of lager, which she downed saying all would be well, as she'd only had wine and no spirits on the train. Robert

had to point out to her that port was a wine fortified with spirits. She still finished the pint of lager before he'd downed his triple whisky. They strode into the studio and, as film actors, were dreading the walk-through – an unusual practice in the film world. Both were perfect. Maybe the booze helped? Who knows? Anyway, I didn't get the rollicking I was expecting, and Robert introduced me to Stolichnaya vodka, which was posh and new then, and it's been my tipple ever since.

One of the most important lessons of my training was imparted directly by a wonderful Scottish director who was an alcoholic. Sadly, sometimes after lunch the day did not pan out well. In fact, I frequently ended up having to work out the camera scripts. That was fine until we got to the studio and none of the shots worked. Then I got blamed. Sounds bad, but it was the most amazing way to learn how to get things right. On one occasion I was invited to go to the VTR editing suite to see how it was done. In those days editing suites were rather dark, dingy places without windows, buried deep in the building, and VTR editors were strange, lonely people, who usually only made contact with the rest of the world through talk-back. They also had long periods of inactivity and, judging by the magazines around, also a lot of time for reading. This was the pornography of the 1970s, and actually consisted of rather tame glamour shots rather than the clinical stuff of today.

Anyway, the director started flicking through one of these magazines, then stopped, held it out to me and said, 'Well, what do you think?'

I wasn't sure what to think, so I said I thought she looked very nice.

'No, you fool,' he said. 'Look at her feet, they're filthy. You must always take in the whole picture. Notice everything.'

Sounds a bizarre way to learn, and it was, but it's also something I've never forgotten. 'Of what use are lens and light, to those who lack in mind and sight.' A salutary lesson learned from a Brunswick Thaler dated 1589. And a Brunswick Thaler is a silver coin, not a German who went to sea. For me this is the key maxim for television, and it existed over 300 years before television was even invented.

Enough about drink and its capacity for bringing people together, but it must be said that the spirit is often boosted by a tot or two of an evening, particularly if you have a hard day ahead of you. I read an interview with Jeffrey Piven, star of *Mr Selfridge*, who said, 'One of the things Brits do so well is go out, experience everything, have very little sleep and do the best work of their lives. For some of the young assistant directors, it was a badge of honour that they'd be viciously hung over and still do a brilliant job.'

However, alcohol wasn't always involved in these early times. One director (and remember, most people then came to television drama via the theatre) – insisted that sets were built on a small rostrum to replicate a stage, which then meant cameras could not get into the sets, and he even told actors to ignore the cameras! Now this didn't make for the best television but it did help actors new to the medium concentrate on their performance, the performance being the thing that, after the script, was most important. Another director had the opposite approach and created sets made entirely of glass – producing an extraordinary situation in which the cameramen had their work cut out not to shoot pictures of themselves.

David Cunliffe, Yorkshire Television's second Head of Drama, with Charles Dance in Athens in 1988, taking a break from filming *Out of the Shadows*, a made-for-television movie in which a member of the American embassy staff is wrongly accused of a murder in Greece. (Rod Lofthouse)

A peaceful scene in the Yorkshire Dales, fictitious home of one of the world's longest-running soaps. *Emmerdale Farm* was created by the writer Kevin Laffan at the request of Donald Baverstock, YTV's Director of Programmes. (ITV)

These early days of Yorkshire Television drama were overseen by Peter Willes, an exotic gentleman who had had an early career as a Hollywood actor and also served time as Vic Oliver's manager; but he had the most extraordinary connections, with all of the top writers and actors, and it was he who really laid the foundations of the Yorkshire Television Drama Department with the sheer class of the talent that he persuaded to make their way to Leeds. It is remarkable that in the fifty years of Yorkshire Television drama production, there were only ever three Controllers of Drama: Peter, David Cunliffe and myself.

We oversaw an extraordinarily diverse output: classic adaptations, drama-documentaries, costume drama, thrillers, comedy-dramas, continuing series and television movies. I think it is invidious to mention individual names or highlight particular productions from such an exalted list, but obviously there are moments and people that stand out. I was particularly thrilled to assist a director in persuading Dirk Bogarde to star in his first film for television, and even more so when he agreed to write the screenplay of the Graham Greene novel, *May We Borrow Your Husband?* Dirk was a consummate actor, and it transpired that

A souvenir photograph of a Yorkshire TV production team posing near the real Berlin Wall in 1987. The programme they were working on was *The Contract*, an East-West spy drama in which a British agent was attempting to arrange the escape of a defecting Russian missile manufacturer. With some ingenuity, YTV recreated the Berlin Wall near Blubberhouses in West Yorkshire, a German autobahn on the Stanningley bypass in Leeds and a German checkpoint in Leeds Market. (Danuta Skarszewska)

his reason for previously rejecting television offers was that he felt that shooting in 16mm was less familiar to him than shooting feature films in 35mm. As an actor, Dirk would use his knowledge of lenses to force the director to get closer and closer, and he usually held back his performance until the camera was very close. When he saw the 16mm equipment actually in use he was very relieved, realizing that the filming technique was exactly the same for television as for film. Another anecdote from that film: the director and I were in a pub (again!) discussing the fact that Dirk had written a fifteen-page dialogue scene between only two characters; the director was really nervous about how to make it interesting and visual.

A Scottish documentary maker was with us at the time and he simply looked at us and said, 'Never forget the landscape of the human face, laddie.'

So the scene was shot by slowly moving the camera closer and closer on the two characters whilst at the same time going through 360°, and the dialogue came alive. Another valuable lesson.

Another highlight for me that I think warrants a mention was a film on the miners' strike, called *Scab*. It was a Yorkshire-based production, incorporating actual news footage to recreate some of the stories of the miners' families during this difficult dispute. This was an innovative style of production and it collected the RAI Prize at the Prix Italia Festival.

In the early days we were obviously more studio-bound, but slowly location work started to emerge, taking full advantage of one of Yorkshire's great assets – its scenery. The most renowned of these productions was *Emmerdale*. The opening image was a huge long shot of a hearse making its way through the Dales – communications being not what they are today, I was squashed on the floor communicating with the camera via a very dodgy walkie-talkie. It was Sod's Law, of course, that despite going on to location in a beautiful summer the script called for rain, so we had to import truckloads of water, to the bemusement of the people of Arncliffe.

We continued to shoot a lot in Yorkshire: a huge section of the Berlin Wall was recreated on Blubberhouse Moor, the city of Leeds was turned into war-torn Belfast, the River Thames was reproduced in York. Then the tentacles of production spread. We filmed in France, where virtually everyone contracted salmonella poisoning and the unfortunate camera crew had to spend long hours with upset stomachs filming from, of all things, a hot air balloon. My function there was less that of a producer, more a courier of carrier bags full of desperately needed medication. Things got so bad that the leading man and lady both required rehydrating with saline drips before they could make it on to the set in the morning.

In Hong Kong it was constant negotiating with the Triad gangsters, regardless of which street or area we were filming. In South Africa we reconstructed the Tower of London and filmed on a reproduction of HMS *Endeavour* as she made her maiden voyage from Australia back to Whitby. Due to her shallow keel, most

Ray Lonnen and Gary Payne filming the series *Yellowthread Street* in Hong Kong in 1989. The production manager, Tim Dowd, is on the left and, checking the shot is Dave Carey, camera assistant. *Yellowthread Street* was based on the novels of William Leonard Marshall about the work of fictional detectives in the Hong Kong police. The series ran to thirteen 1-hour episodes and was screened on ITV in 1990. (Danuta Skarszewska)

The Dingles of *Emmerdale* in Venice, a long way from their native heath of Beckindale, shooting a scene for a one-off special episode. (Tim Fee)

of the sequences shot on the ship were filmed between bouts of seasickness – affecting both cast and crew. In Venice we paid homage to the film *Don't Look Back* by including a small person in red in the background of *The Dingles Do Venice*. We had many equally glamorous experiences filming in Holland, Germany, Greece, the Seychelles, America, Australia and Canada, to name but a few.

It was after returning from Hong Kong, flushed with success at having achieved a remarkable police series, that John Fairley, the then Director of Programmes, cautioned that we 'ignore our own back yard at our peril' – words which certainly resonated. Thus came the creation of the first *Heartbeat*, and the 371 episodes which followed.

Naimh Cusack and Nick Berry on a picnic. Naimh became pregnant in real life and decided that the demands of motherhood were incompatible with the demands of a challenging shooting schedule in North Yorkshire. (Shutterstock)

The first couple of *Heartbeat*, PC Nick Rowan (Nick Berry) and his wife, Dr Kate Rowan (Naimh Cusack), in an early scene from the programme. (Shutterstock)

The disparate hordes that all those years ago descended on Leeds became a close-knit family, all working together with a common goal. The constant opportunities on film and in studio created a lineage of really talented, enthusiastic practitioners, both behind the camera and in front. Designers, cameramen, sound, sparks, chippies, make-up, wardrobe, scripts, and all of the other unsung heroes. Making the best of programmes. And that is what we did.

I'm immensely proud of the work that we all did because, remember, we were all in this together. I know that it is almost de rigueur for people of a certain age to say that there was a Golden Age of television and that it's past, but I do think that those of us who were there – and they know who they are – did have the best of times, and that's because we created them.

Chapter 7

Alan Plater

Alan Plater, creator of the Beiderbecke series, with James Bolam and Barbara Flynn. (Shutterstock)

The first work I did for Yorkshire Television illustrates the audacity, or maybe the recklessness, of the industry at the time. I wrote three half-hour plays for Les Dawson under the overall title *The Loner*.

Les played a man living alone in a house halfway up a hillside in the Dales. In each story he walked down the hill, into the town nestling in the valley and into a small adventure. The most successful was called *Dawson's Brief Encounter*, a story of unrequited love based on his occasional lunchtime meetings with an enigmatic woman played by Gillian Raine in a little self-service caff, where I seem to remember the woman behind the counter saying, 'Don't worry about the skin on the custard. That's the goodness floating to the top.' I also recall they go to a pub where the juke box plays Gregorian chant. I suppose I was already into my preferred territory of gritty Northern surrealism.

Les was beautiful to work with – a dedicated professional, word-perfect from day one of rehearsals – and it's still a matter of regret that we never managed to work together again. We often talked about it, but sadly it never happened.

What did happen was a phone call from Peter Willes. He had commissioned the Les Dawson trilogy and took some departmental pride in having poached Les from the light entertainment people.

What Peter said was: 'You haven't told me enough about the woman Les met in the play. I'd like to know more about her. Write me a play about her.'

Peter's method in commissioning plays was unique in my experience. He hated written outlines, treatments or synopses. When you thought you had an idea he would invite you to dinner at the Queen's Hotel and ask you to tell him the story.

Fairly soon in the narrative he would hold up his hand and say, 'Stop! If you tell me any more it will spoil the surprise when I read it.'

The play I wrote was called *Willow Cabins*, a slightly offbeat love story with Dorothy Tutin and Michael Bryant, and it produced a nice little anecdote. Peter Willes was a great friend of Harold Pinter – indeed, he was the first man to put his work on television, at Associated Rediffusion, when the writer was desperate for paid work of any description. Pinter paid handsome tribute to Peter after he died.

The play in question, incidentally, got the highest ratings ever recorded for a television play up to that point. So Peter decided to watch *Willow Cabins* at Pinter's house, with Lady Antonia. Apparently, at the first commercial break, Harold turned to the other two and said, 'It's a little obscure, isn't it?' They thought this was a bit rich coming from him.

Soon after *Willow Cabins*, Yorkshire hired me to write my one and only sitcom – a little number called *Oh No It's Selwyn Froggitt!* – and again, in the spirit of the times, the whole thing began in a bar, this time at the BBC's Pebble Mill studios. Bill Maynard had played in a series called *Trinity Tales* – an updated version of Chaucer about a group of rugby league supporters on their way to Wembley. Bill told me he'd shot a pilot episode of *Selwyn*, written by Roy Clarke of *Last of the Summer Wine* fame – but Roy wasn't available to write the series. Did I fancy it?

'Yes, all right, Bill,' I said.

I wrote fifteen episodes over three series, and a couple of things linger in the memory. First was Bill's brief to the writer which ran: 'I want three (expletive deleted) big laughs on every page and if they're not there I'll put them in.' Second was the fact that it was the only time in a long career that a show of mine was number one in the ratings. Selwyn became a national celebrity. One year I sat with Bill in the VIP seats at Wembley for the rugby league Cup Final – it was our bit of payola for *Trinity Tales* – and we suddenly realized hundreds of supporters all around were on their feet, looking at Bill, thumbs in the air, chanting 'Magic'.

Yorkshire Television, having given me my one and only chance to write a sitcom, then made me another unique offer I couldn't refuse. This was to write a children's serial – or perhaps more accurately, a Sunday afternoon family serial. It was called *Flambards*, from the book by Kathleen Peyton.

The outstanding thing about *Flambards*, in retrospect, was the amount of money we were allowed to spend on it. It's essentially a tale of young people growing up in the early part of the twentieth century, and it's chock-a-block with horses and aeroplanes. We were able to construct an aerodrome in a field near Harrogate, with several full-size replica aeroplanes of roughly Blériot vintage and matching scale models for the flying sequences. There was nothing digital about it. What you saw was really there on the day.

In 1979 I was asked to dramatize J.B. Priestley's *The Good Companions* for television and, as a companion piece, to interview the great man and present a documentary about the making of the series.

An anxious moment for Barbara Flynn and James Bolam, filming Alan Plater's comedy drama, *The Beiderbecke Affair*, in the less than glamorous surroundings of a Yorkshire power station. Bolam plays Trevor Chaplin, a woodwork teacher and jazz fanatic who becomes entangled in a murky mystery when some records he has ordered fail to turn up. He and Jill Swinburne (Barbara Flynn) drift into a quirky relationship when he starts giving her a lift to school, where she is an English teacher. (Darren C. Miller)

If the dice had fallen differently I could have turned into Melvyn Bragg or Alan Yentob. Whether this is a good thing or not depends on your point of view. I interviewed Priestley at his large house near Stratford. It was called Kissing Tree Cottage, and when I asked him whether it was a nice place to live he said, 'Good enough for Shakespeare, good enough for me.'

There are many strange quirks and eccentricities in my YTV story. One is that if it hadn't been for *The Good Companions* there wouldn't have been a *Beiderbecke Trilogy* – and *Beiderbecke* is the work that seems to have lasted longest in the public memory, judging by the letters, and now the emails, that I still receive frequently, with unanswerable questions about the minutiae of the series.

Head of Drama David Cunliffe originally wanted *The Good Companions* in thirteen episodes. I read the book and concluded we could do it more neatly in nine.

'But we've promised the network thirteen weeks,' said David. 'What are we going to do to fill the other slots?'

'Easy,' I said. 'I'll write you a four-part original.'

'Fine,' said David. 'Let me know what it's about when you've got a minute.'

It really was as casual as that.

The four-parter was called *Get Lost!* and was about two teachers from a comprehensive school in Leeds solving a mystery. It starred Alun Armstrong and Bridget Turner, had a jazz score in the style of Duke Ellington and was well enough liked for me to be commissioned to write a sequel. It was called *Get Lost Revisited*, but when we were into pre-production it emerged that Alun was starring in *Nicholas Nickleby* on Broadway and wasn't available.

The solution – and this is strictly an edited highlights version of what happened – was to rewrite it, take out the back references, change the title to *The Beiderbecke Affair* and re-cast it, this time with the peerless James Bolam and Barbara Flynn. For the record, I am in love with Barbara. Her husband knows about this, but please don't tell Anne Stallybrass.

There were three Beiderbecke series – the *Affair*, the *Tapes* and the *Connection*. Frank Ricotti won a BAFTA for the music, and over the years the series provoked some remarkable fan mail.

I was told by teachers, 'Our school's just like San Quentin High.'

I was told by policemen, 'We've got a graduate cop just like Hobson.'

I had a letter from a young couple who said, 'We're just like Jill and Trevor. I teach English, my husband teaches woodwork and once a week we read aloud from the novels while getting smashed out of our heads on Frascati.'

Probably best of all, I had an email from a man in Moline, Illinois, who told me he lived across the river from Davenport, Iowa, Bix Beiderbecke's birthplace. Why was this remarkable? Because my correspondent's name was Christopher Beiderbecke, and he was Bix's great nephew. When you think about it, it's like Samuel Beckett getting a postcard from Godot.

Chapter 8

John Willis

In 1983, John Willis, then a young director at Yorkshire Television, travelled to China to record the astonishing story of a man called David Young from Newcastle. His film, *The Chinese Geordie* described how and why Young deserted from the Royal Navy to spend 34 years in a Chinese commune. (Grant McKee)

One of the most important roles of the major ITV companies outside London in their heyday was to sympathetically reflect the people, landscape and culture of their region back to the nation at large.

For all the magnificence of its dales and coasts, and despite the defiant individualism of its citizens, Yorkshire had been largely forgotten by an ITV in the north led by Granada from their Manchester HQ. The arrival of YTV was an opportunity to change all that; to dig out stories from Yorkshire that would delight, surprise or shock viewers, not just those living in Hull or Huddersfield, but the ITV audience all the way from Land's End to John O'Groats. No documentary fulfilled that ambition better than *Too Long a Winter* (1973). Its central character, Hannah Hauxwell, lived alone, scraping a hard living at Low Birk Hatt Farm high up in the Dales, without any of the absolute basics of modern life, including electricity, let alone any of the comforts.

Hannah's gentleness, her winning smile and her guileless authenticity stole the nation's heart in an instant. Thousands of well-wishers sent messages to Hannah via YTV, and enough money was sent in by viewers to finally connect electricity to Hannah's farm. The director of the documentary, Barry Cockcroft, was not even from Yorkshire; even worse, he was born in Rochdale, Lancashire. Yet his early years on the *Rochdale Observer* had given him an intuitive and fundamental understanding of how a local story could have wider resonance.

Barbara Twigg, a colleague of Barry's regular researcher, Julie O'Hare, had come across Hannah while walking in the Dales. When Barry made his way up to Low Birk Hatt for tea with Hannah he knew immediately that she was special, that Hannah had a clarity of purpose, an innocent charm, that would cut through all the noise and clutter of modern life and appeal to millions watching television.

Barry, despite his devotion to words and language and his origins on a local newspaper, also understood the power of pictures to the television viewer. With his favoured cameraman, Mostafa Hammuri, who was nearly always clad in an immaculate white suit even in the dirtiest of locations, Barry would spend hours lining up 'the big shot' from the top of a dale or moor. The spectacular landscape around Hannah Hauxwell's farm was the perfect environment for Barry and Mostafa to work their magic in.

As a young researcher, I worked on several science films with Barry. On his orders I once found a white horse with a female rider to gallop endlessly across a reclaimed slag heap in Wigan for take after take. The link between the white horse and the science of land reclamation was hard for me (and for Barry too) to discern, but the white horse was the perfect visual contrast to the black coal waste of the slag heap. Barry had pulled off his 'big shot' once again.

Barry also understood two other important things. First, keep your film crew happy, and this meant his long-suffering PA, Kathy Rooney, or researchers like Julie O'Hare, ensuring that somewhere was booked for a good lunch. Indeed, lunch sometimes felt like it was the most important event in Barry's day. Secondly, Barry worked out that too often television reflected an urban world and that too many documentaries were set in cities. Supported by his executive producer, John Fairley, Barry embarked on a string of beautiful rural films, from a delightful Yorkshire moors family in *The Children of Eskdale*, to the fishermen of the Wash in *The Linehams*

Hannah Hauxwell, the North Yorkshire farmer whose story was told by director Barry Cockcroft in his documentary, *Too Long A Winter*. Her plight, wresting a lonely and sparse living from her smallholding, caught the public's imagination, and she went on to make many more appearances on Yorkshire TV. (Shutterstock)

of Fosdyke, eventually returning to Hannah Hauxwell in *A Winter Too Many* (1989).

Yorkshire's reputation as a centre of excellence for documentaries did not come fully formed with the arrival of Hannah Hauxwell. Under the leadership of Tony Essex, who had made his name on the series *The Great War*, YTV quickly attracted some of the best documentary talent around. Early on, Tony's team, led by directors like Duncan Dallas who were poached from the BBC, delighted national audiences with some gentle but delightful films. They included

Mostafa Hammuri, film cameraman. (Charlie Flynn)

Beatrix Potter: a Private World (1972) and
It Never Seemed to Rain (1970), a nostalgic
portrait of holidays in Scarborough.

At the same time as Barry Cockcroft was
shooting *Too Long A Winter*, I was in Japan for
several months working as Assistant Producer
to Antony Thomas on *The Japanese Experience*.
Antony was another director brought in by
Tony Essex, this time not from the BBC but
fresh from South Africa. Here was a very
different approach to documentary making,
showing immediately that YTV's factual
ambitions were not confined to telling local
stories to a national audience. Antony is a
documentary essayist. If Barry was instinctive,
often working out his route through a subject
in the editing room, Antony meticulously
researched and planned every sequence.

For me, four months in Japan, away from
my young and growing family, was tough, but

I learnt an enormous amount from Antony's
rigour. When I eventually made my own films
they were very different from *The Japanese
Experience*, but Antony instilled in me the
importance of sequences and the essential need
for them to have a dynamic of their own. I also
learnt from Antony just how deep a director's
commitment needed to be. We filmed with
itinerant day workers in Osaka. Like a scene
from *On the Waterfront*, some days they were
employed and others they weren't. Violence
and disputes were frequent. To win the trust of
this group of tough and extremely suspicious
men, Antony and our interpreter spent the
night before filming sleeping in their crowded
dormitory with scores of day workers.

On another occasion, Antony and I dined
with some of Japan's most brutal gang
members, the Yakuza. Bizarrely, the venue
was a temple in Tokyo run by the local Abbot.
You could tell who the Yakuza were by their
suits and ties and armed bodyguards. Outside
the temple, the gangsters had a line of Lincoln
Continental limousines being minded by
their chauffeurs. The Yakuza hosts generously
offered us *fugu* fish, the famous and expensive
Japanese delicacy which unfortunately can also
be poisonous and is known to be as deadly
as cyanide. Only licensed chefs can cook this
scary dish, but even so several *fugu* lovers die
each year. Faced between risking the fish or
angering murderous gangsters we wanted to
film with, I took my lead from Antony and ate
the *fugu*. We survived.

If many YTV documentaries marched to
an international beat, my own instincts when
I started to direct documentaries were more
domestic and journalistic. I watched and
admired from afar Antony Thomas's next series
The Arab Experience, or the work of Jonathan

Dimbleby or Robert Kee, but I wanted to make my own films closer to home. YTV was an outsider, a blow-in as Yorkshire folk might say, compared to the well established companies like Thames and Granada, so Yorkshire Televison had no choice but to take risks. Playing safe was not an option, if YTV was to truly become one of the 'Big Five' of ITV. So young directors like me were given a chance that might have taken years of waiting for at one of the better known ITV companies.

Executive Producer Michael Deakin was once cutting a documentary in a Soho edit suite. Emerging into the street late at night, he saw two young boys trying to sleep by the street-level vents of a basement bakery where the air was warm. They told Michael that they were homeless and that there was a growing army of young men and women like them. Many of the best ideas for documentaries spring from a moment of personal experience, and this was no exception. Michael was shrewd enough to know that there might be something interesting here. I was asked to direct the documentary, perhaps because being twenty-six years old was an advantage when making a film about young people only a few years younger. I had made one other modest film, but John Fairley and Michael Deakin were prepared to give me a chance on what was inevitably a difficult subject.

Working with researcher Di Burgess, we saw that there was a tidal flood of young people, mainly from Scotland and the North of England, who were arriving in London without money or friends, looking for a better life. To us, the provision for these youngsters seemed almost non-existent. In the front line, picking up young people on

the mainline railway stations and offering them places in his string of hostels all over London, was an extraordinary character called Roger Gleaves. Wearing what looked like an old RAF uniform, Gleaves, untrained and unofficial, was the best we as a society seemed to be able to offer. Gleaves agreed to let us film, confident no doubt in the quality of his hostels and unable to resist his moment in the spotlight. As Di and I got to know the young people in his main hostel in Brixton, and they grew to trust us, we began to hear disturbing stories about Roger Gleaves. Where was the money all going? Was he too interested in some of the young boys? Who were the charities he claimed to represent?

As we filmed, we determinedly dug deeper into a world where officials seemed only too happy to get the problem young people, the throwaway children, off their patch and into the hostels run by Gleaves, unofficial and certainly uninspected though they were. Perhaps they were convinced by the quasi-religious appearance of the organization run by Gleaves who claimed to be a 'Bishop' in the 'Old Roman Catholic Church'.

As our suspicions deepened, the story suddenly took on an ugly and deeply tragic turn. The body of a young man, William McPhee, also known as Billy Two-Tone, had been found by the side of the A23 close to Brighton in Sussex. Billy, a 19-year-old Scot, had twenty stab wounds, and the police pathologist likened the case to a gangland killing. McPhee had been living in one of the hostels run by Roger Gleaves' organization in Hounslow. We had not filmed at that particular hostel, focusing our research on the headquarters in Brixton where Gleaves himself operated.

However, we immediately understood that we had not just filmed runaway children being exploited but had filmed the background to a murder. Arrests were quickly made, and three men involved in the Gleaves hostel in Hounslow were charged with murder. A year later they had been sentenced to life imprisonment, and Roger Gleaves, in a separate trial, had been sent to prison for four years for buggery and assault occasioning actual bodily harm. The documentary had an enormous impact. ITV showed the first part, *The End of the Line* at 9.00 p.m. and then extended the film by a further hour to show *The Murder of Billy Two-Tone* after *News at Ten*. Over nine million people watched the programme.

In those days of limited channel choice, a television documentary could still become a debating chamber for the United Kingdom, knitting everyone together in a common viewing experience that they could talk about afterwards; it was not just the horror of the murder that sparked off so much concern among viewers but the way that Gleaves, with his thin façade of being a 'bishop', had managed to fool the authorities responsible for homeless young people. His housing empire was all our society had to offer them and it was based on financial corruption, a pseudo-religious cult and sexual exploitation. After the film, questions in Parliament forced the Department of Health and Social Security to report on the services for homeless youngsters. The *Johnny Go Home* report recommended many changes in the system. The Gleaves hostels had all been closed down, but new facilities were opened up as a response to YTV's film, including a walk-in medical centre in Soho for the homeless and a number of new hostels.

The programme also won the British Academy (BAFTA) Award for Best Documentary. I was filming with Alan Whicker in Australia at the time and flew back overnight for the red carpet ceremony. I had been on a plane for more than a day with little or no sleep and was so jet-lagged and tired that I now can't recall a single thing about the whole evening.

Johnny Go Home was photographed by Frank Pocklington. Frank was one of a number of superb cameramen employed by YTV. Some joined from elsewhere, but others lived locally, and having a network TV station on their doorstep gave them an opportunity to develop skills and experience without having to move to London. As a young director feeling his way, I owed a huge debt to all the cameramen at YTV, especially the brilliant Mike Shrimpton and Alan Wilson, and Graham Barker, who sadly died in a helicopter accident on Humberside while filming. Less obviously recognized, but just as important, were the sound men like Don Atkinson and Terry Ricketts. Then, back in the edit suites in Leeds, were an exceptionally talented group of film editors. I worked a

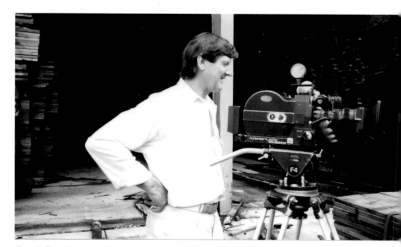

Frank Pocklington, film cameraman. (Terry Ricketts)

Mike Shrimpton, film cameraman. (Charlie Flynn)

great deal with John Watts and Barry Spink, both masters of their craft. Other first class editors included Clive Trist, Graham Shrimpton and Terry Warwick.

In 1976 one of YTV's best reporters, Paul Dunstan, came up with a story that originated on the local programme *Calendar,* and I agreed to help him turn this into a television documentary which was eventually called *The Bradford Godfather.* It was another good example of how the deep roots of the ITV regional companies could produce stories that were unreachable by the London media.

Mohammed Faisal Hussain had been one of the first handful of immigrants in Bradford when he arrived in 1927. Now aged seventy-three and the personnel officer in a local foundry, Mr Hussain was the elder statesman and all-round Mr Fixit of Bradford's sizeable Muslim community. He was often, in a respected way, called 'The Godfather'. Paul's documentary journey took us back to the Bradford Godfather's home near Lahore, where he received a hero's welcome on his return. It was a warm-hearted , sometimes amusing, sometimes sad, celebration of family, community and difference. It was a rare insight into the Muslim community that had developed in Bradford over many years.

Following the impact made by *Johnny Go Home* I spent the next few years making a number of social and investigative documentaries that used the same template, part social exploration and part investigation.

It began when a man called James Cutler, who was a squatter in East London, virtually stalked me with two carrier bags full of documents. His claim was that as the old East End was being boarded up and its inhabitants decanted to new houses in Essex, unscrupulous landlords were moving into the area, ripping off local authorities over short-term lettings. James proved to be not only fiercely determined but a brilliant investigator, so brilliant that we later employed him on several other documentaries. *Goodbye Longfellow Road* (1978), as the film was eventually called, was based on a single street in Tower Hamlets that had been earmarked for demolition back in 1943 but had provided solid and happy family homes in the nearly forty intervening years.

Researcher Di Burgess found a marvellous East End family, the Morters, who were saying goodbye to their longstanding home and moving out of Longfellow Road in Mile End. We filmed them as the family were casually loaded on to the back of the removal van, as if they were sideboards or beds, and driven off to Essex. Needless to say, we were accused of setting this powerful and emotional scene up, but in fact the removal men were just very late and we merely observed and filmed their hurried indifference to Mr and Mrs Morter.

Goodbye Longfellow Road caused a furore, with the London *Evening Standard* and local media all very exercised. As with *Johnny Go Home*, the film showed that when ordinary citizens were disregarded and disenfranchised, fertile ground was created for profiteers and conmen to move in. The post-transmission fuss led immediately to the exploitative housing associations being closed down, but

the Morters' sturdy little house in Longfellow Road remained unoccupied and the street undeveloped long after they had been removed to the bleak suburbs of Essex.

On the other side of the open plan office in Leeds, a different kind of documentary was being developed. Springing out of an historical series called *Women of Courage*, Kevin Sim found a story about a remarkable woman called Kitty Hart who had survived Auschwitz. Teaming up with distinguished director Peter Morley, in 1979 he made the hugely powerful and successful documentary *Kitty – Return to Auschwitz*. No doubt Peter's own personal history as a young boy from a Jewish family who had fled Berlin in the 1930s gave the film an extra dimension. But it was Kitty herself, emotional but tough, fragile yet resilient, who gave a powerful human face to the horrors of that camp.

In that same year, 1979, YTV made another two-part documentary, this time called *Rampton – the Secret Hospital*. I had read in a social work magazine about a hospital near Newark in Nottinghamshire that had a unit, the Eastdale, which acted as a halfway house for patients from the top security hospital Rampton, often called the 'Broadmoor of the North'. The staff, led by the consultant Harry Hunter and psychologist Peter Thornhill, were cautious but also open and honest. For a start, we were astonished to find that, alongside patients who had committed murder or rape, were men and women who had committed very minor crimes or no crimes at all but were, in the language of the time, mentally handicapped.

As we started to film at Eastdale, we heard more and more stories about the often brutal regime at Rampton. As James Cutler started investigating those allegations, we filmed the former Rampton inmates preparing for their first footsteps for years into the real world. We filmed a busload of patients going to a local dance. Afterwards we received several complaints from women at the dance, not worried about having danced with men with serious convictions, including murder, to their names, but frightened that their husbands would see the film and discover that their wives liked to stray from the married path every other Monday.

Our long and detailed investigation into Rampton uncovered hundreds of allegations of abuse and assault by staff on patients. Not every single one was provable, but they showed a pattern, a system: women patients who were throttled with wet towels to hide any marks of abuse and assault, and male patients, often the most vulnerable, who were just beaten up. One elderly man in his seventies had been kicked until he was 'black and blue'. He had been in Rampton for over 25 years after stealing a woman's handbag.

The government was forced to set up an inquiry under the leadership of Sir John Boynton that recommended scores of improvements in the running of Rampton, including an assessment that there were 130 patients who should not be in a top security hospital. Of course, the programme sparked off tension as well as debates. The local MP rushed to the hospital's defence. Some nurses were charged and others dismissed. I received a number of threatening calls on the family telephone at home in rural Yorkshire.

Other high profile projects included Paul Dunstan's thoughtful film about the Yorkshire Ripper in which some of the victims, so often demeaned in the press, were sympathetically shown to be ordinary women who had been forced reluctantly into prostitution by economic or family circumstances.

In a totally different sphere, another YTV film, *Churchill's Few*, was a human story about the Battle of Britain, but credited, at last, the Poles and the sergeant-pilots who had flown so courageously but whose contributions had been undervalued. For the first time, too, this documentary told the story of the battle from a German perspective, through the eyes of a Luftwaffe pilot, Ulrich Steinhilper, who the film showed to be clearly cut from the same heroic cloth as his RAF enemies. In a moving scene he met and shook hands with the RAF pilot who had shot him down over Kent.

However, the call to continue with those long and painful social investigations could not be ignored. In 1982, with researchers James Cutler and Peter Moore in the front line, I directed *Alice – a Fight for Life*, a two-hour investigation of the asbestos industry. Again, it was screened before and after *News at Ten* and, despite the news being extended until 11.00 p.m. because of the IRA bombing in Hyde Park, millions of viewers stayed up to watch. The film's heart was a Yorkshire woman, Alice Jefferson, who was dying of asbestos-related cancer following a brief stint working as a young girl at an asbestos factory in Hebden Bridge. Alice's courage and her spirit shone through the screen. She was one of the most remarkable and courageous people that I have ever met, ordinary but extraordinary at the same time. Her battle for compensation to help support her young family after her death was the spine of the film, but our journey to discover how asbestos was still being used, given that the mineral's dangers had been first revealed back in 1898, stretched from Canada to India.

On transmission, the response was instant. Overnight, shares in asbestos companies fell by £60m, and quickly the government acted to reduce dust levels in factories. In effect, this was the end of the industry in the UK, but not before thousands of workers had died unnecessarily. Yet the story never goes away. The asbestos industry has now shifted from Europe and North America eastwards, with the major mines now in Russia. Asbestos is commonplace in the developing countries of Asia, like Vietnam and India. Decades after *Alice – a Fight for Life*, workers and the public are still being told the 'magic mineral' is safe. And their health is still being put at serious risk.

In the developed world, *Alice* still saved lives by sparking off significant improvements in the way asbestos was being dealt with. It was a reminder that television could, just occasionally, use its power, its ability to reach right into the sitting room of the viewer, for a social good. For me, looking back now from a television landscape of risk-averse channels and slow decision making, I realize just how lucky I was, how lucky we all were, to enjoy the liberation of making programmes that we believed in, supported all the way both financially and editorially. Yorkshire Television at that time was a wonderful place to make television programmes. Supported at the very top by Paul Fox and John Fairley, all YTV's documentary makers were expected to be ambitious and to take creative risks. Sometimes we failed, often we succeeded, but we were always encouraged to try. That was a rare privilege.

Chapter 9

Grant McKee

Cameraman Mike Shrimpton (left), sound recordist Lindsay Dodd (centre) and Grant McKee, the producer/director, carrying out reconnaissance of a location in Ethiopia for *The Unofficial Famine*. (Grant McKee)

John Fairley telephoned me at a crossroads in my working life. It was 1978 and I was a young feature writer on the *Yorkshire Post* juggling two possible career moves. One was to become a parliamentary correspondent for the United Newspapers group; another was to join the *Financial Times*' tiny sports desk. Now there was a third option: over lunch in the YTV canteen, John, who would become one of the three great influences of my working life, told me he had enjoyed some of my writing, so why not move half a mile west from Wellington Street to Kirkstall Road and come into TV?

A new medium, and the prospect of international travel as a documentary researcher was the clincher. Sitting in the box for *Calendar* on my first day was a rude awakening to the demands and excitement of live TV. I never sniggered at its mistakes again. The coolness under pressure of PA, vision mixer and director was daunting. My own first feeble attempt at doing a piece to camera meant that Graham Ironside never considered me worth persevering with as a *Calendar* reporter, and after six months learning the difference between stripe and sep mag film stock I manoeuvred my way into documentaries.

Jonathan Dimbleby arrived and made a pertinent and provocative series of films: *The Police: a Force to be Reckoned with*, *The Bomb*, *The Eagle and the Bear* and *The Cold War Game*. As his lead researcher, I got the foreign travel I wanted, a brief spell in Kuwaiti detention for illegally photographing a military base and a sustained lesson in journalistic rigour from Jonathan, second of the great influences on my working career. *The Bomb* was a definitive critique of the folly of the nuclear arms race at the height of the Cold War from Hiroshima survivors to US silos, with soldiers chillingly ready to launch their ICBMs.

But for prescience I fondly recall a sequence in *The Cold War Game* which we shot in

(L to R) Jonathan Dimbleby, Francis Gerrard, Frank Pocklington, Steve Pettinger and Big Stan Spencer. (Terry Ricketts)

David Frost preparing a 'piece-to-camera' on the lawn of the White House, assisted by Chris Edmondson, the production assistant. (Chris Edmondson)

Communist East Germany at a Lutheran church service, where we had been told there would be an unprecedented demonstration against Soviet SS 20 missiles as well as American Cruise missiles. Our minders did not stop the filming. This was history in the making. It would be the protests emanating from the Lutheran church that duly emboldened East German citizens to bring down the GDR and the Berlin Wall.

David Frost was another big name to come to Kirkstall Road. His prime-time live series *David Frost's Global Village* exploited the latest satellite technology to beam the world into Studio 4 on a giant screen called an Eidophor, developed by NASA but long extinct. It was hair-raising stuff; the high price of satellite feeds meant that the line was booked only a minute or so before going live, so the relief and thrill of a fuzzy image materializing from the other side of the world was enormous.

Memorably, at the height of the war that would turn Rhodesia into Zimbabwe, the first ever live pictures out of southern Africa brought the warring leaders Ian Smith, Joshua Nkomo and Robert Mugabe head to head, albeit from different studios. No peace treaty emerged; indeed, it was a hard job keeping order between the rowdy rival ZANU and ZAPO supporters who had been bussed into Leeds.

Another electrifying live moment came in a David Frost debate on the Northern Ireland 'Troubles' during Mrs Thatcher's much derided ban on Sinn Fein/IRA speakers being heard on British TV. In an attempt to circumvent the ban, the Sinn Fein president (and IRA veteran) Ruairi O'Bradaigh was rushed around foreign studios in Dublin, Paris and Brussels, before a Hamburg studio was found prepared to house him. No sooner was he introduced by Frost than the Tory MPs walked out. Ironically, there was a sound problem in Hamburg, and O' Bradaigh was never heard.

Jimmy's, the documentary series set in St James' Hospital, Leeds, was a success beyond our and ITV's wildest dreams. Starting in daytime, it ran for some 150 episodes in peak time, usually against *EastEnders*, sometimes twice a week, with audiences rising to 10 million. While hospitals have always been fertile ground for television, this was something else. It can lay fair claim to being the original docu-soap, a forerunner of *24 Hours in A & E*, *One Born Every Minute*, *Children's Hospital* and many more.

It was a soap, too, in the sense that it cut regularly between running stories with cliff-hangers and familiar characters. There was no commentary, and producer/director Irene Cockroft, who worked on every single episode, recalls how some of the audience believed so firmly it was a drama that nurses were asked for their autographs at supermarket check-outs.

There were births and deaths, joy and tears, old and young, stunning recoveries and necessarily some sad outcomes. Every corner of Europe's biggest teaching hospital was covered. Despite the 7.30 p.m. transmission time, there was no squeamishness about the blood and gore in Accident and Emergency or the operating theatres, exemplified by the riveting case of twelve-year-old Jamie, whose hand had been severed in a launderette accident. We watched his hand being sewn back on by surgeon Simon Kay (with his conveniently handsome Dr Kildare looks and bedside manner) and followed Jamie's gradual

(Back row L to R): Dave Barratt, camera assistant; David Frost; Alan Pyrah, cameraman; David Green, producer. (Front row L to R) Rod Lofthouse, sound recordist; Mick O'Grady, driver. The sound recordist, Don Atkinson, has almost squeezed into the picture at the top left-hand corner. (Rod Lofthouse)

recovery of the use of his fingers. It was a pioneering piece of surgery. Simon Kay made the news again in 2016 with a double hand transplant.

Equally heart-melting was the story of Ramona, a young Romanian girl with a frightful cancerous growth on her neck which would certainly have been terminal had she not been rescued from Romania by Andrew Batchelor, a plastic surgeon at St James's. Ramona's and her mother's stoicism through long chemotherapy was one of *Jimmy's*' most potent storylines. It was not until many years later that I discovered the production team were making extravagant mileage claims on expenses and siphoning off the proceeds to help fund Ramona's mother's stay in England in support of her daughter.

Other, shorter, peak-time series on the network included Peter Gordon's *On the Manor*, set in one of Sheffield's toughest estates left behind in Thatcher's Britain; it had more than a touch of *Shameless* about it, but also great humanity. There was *Power in the Land*, on the changing face of the British countryside, and *Scales of Justice*, a critique of the British justice system, which had an unforgettable moment in Peter Moore's episode on barristers, when he persuaded Gray's Inn to let the cameras in for one of their formal dinners. It was a bad mistake on their part. As the drink flowed, the scene began to resemble one's imagining of the Bullingdon Club, braying barristers standing on their benches and throwing bread rolls around the ancient hall. Frank Pocklington, the cameraman, a veteran of *Picture Post* magazine and a maestro of framing and lighting, but no fan of hand-held work, railed against the inclusion of one key shot on the grounds that it was fractionally wobbly and out of focus. It stayed in.

Peter Moore revelled in upsetting the barristers. He had a fine sense of mischief as well as being an excellent investigative journalist. He went on to become, under John Willis, the best documentaries commissioning editor at Channel 4, launching *Cutting Edge* and later, for the BBC, *The Apprentice*, where he was revered as the only executive producer who could work with Alan Sugar – and vice versa.

But one factual series above all will always be associated with Yorkshire Television: *First Tuesday*. The strand had a fairly short life, a little over ten years, before it was swept away by the arrival of ITV's central scheduling, but at its best it made some of the most distinguished documentaries in the history of British television. It would be tedious to list its awards but they included a full sweep of the most cherished: Emmy, Prix Italia, Prix Europa, BAFTA, Royal Television Society and more, both for individual documentary and best series.

Its prosaic title was lifted from the United States, NBC's monthly response to CBS's *60 Minutes*, and was justified by Paul Fox – correctly – on the grounds that the ITV schedulers would never shift it from its slot; nor did they. Launched in 1983, John Willis was its first editor; I was his deputy, then editor, for five years; Jonathan Dimbleby was the lead presenter alongside, briefly, Jane Walmsley. Olivia O' Leary took over for the final five years. Above all, it was John Willis's programme. He was hugely respected both as editor and as the outstanding documentary maker of his generation, compassionate, determined, funny and the third of my three great inspirational mentors. He assembled a wide-ranging team based in Leeds and London; there were grizzled veterans and raw, emerging talents, existing staff and new contracts. It worked; there was a tremendous *esprit de corps*, and the docs unit grew from a cramped office behind *Calendar* to a 40-strong team in Leeds and London.

John also directed its very first film, *The Chinese Geordie*, still fondly remembered for its poignant story of a Geordie who jumped ship to live under Communist rule. Some 200 films followed, from ten-minute shorts to Peter Kosminsky's masterly and unflinching two-hour *The Falklands War: the Untold Story*. The films ranged in technique and subject matter, from the investigative to the elegiac, but invariably they held up a mirror

Peter Moore, producer, and Jill Turton, production assistant, in a Palestine refugee camp, preparing to film for *First Tuesday*. (Grant McKee)

All in a day's filming. Andy Hartley, a camera assistant, rehearses a tracking shot with a young Buddhist monk not in an exotic location in Nepal or Sri Lanka. In fact, the location was Eskdalemuir, near Lockerbie, in the Scottish Borders, where Buddhist monks had decided to create a new community in the middle of nowhere. (Terry Ricketts)

to Britain and the world with human stories that illuminated the issues of the day, from the flamboyantly, arrogantly rich, like Peter Gordon's delicious portrait of Rupert Deen, who had never done a day's work in his life and, drinking champagne in his Mayfair bath, suggested the country should be run 'by me and a few of my friends', to the dispossessed and voiceless at home and abroad.

One early film established *First Tuesday* as a programme of major impact, James Cutler's *Windscale: the Nuclear Laundry*, a devastating exposé of the (hastily-renamed) Sellafield nuclear reprocessing plant on the Cumbrian coast. It found startling levels of background radiation along the local shoreline, a catalogue of safety breaches and, most disturbingly, by trawling through death certificates, an abnormal cluster of childhood leukemias nearby. In the public outcry that followed, the Government set up an inquiry chaired by Sir Douglas Black, which was ultimately inconclusive as to causation; the epidemiological debate still rumbles on. British Nuclear Fuels, the then operators of Sellafield, were furious and attacked the programme not through the courts but through the Broadcasting Complaints Commission, citing seventeen significant instances of inaccuracy or unfairness. All seventeen were thrown out. In fact, with the expertise of Patrick Swaffer, libel specialist at Goodman Derrick (whose signature you can now see before every film in the cinema, as he became the chief censor at the BBFC) and the doyen of the libel bar Richard Rampton QC, *First Tuesday* was never successfully sued and never lost a BCC hearing.

It is no exaggeration to say that the British public's perception of the safety of nuclear installations was never the same again after *Windscale*. James Cutler was probably the most tenacious producer in YTV's documentary department. He followed up with *Inside Britain's Bomb*, a journey which literally followed Britain's nuclear warheads as they moved by night around the country and uncovered more accompanying health revelations at its assembly points. It was in its way a challenge to official secrecy at a time when it was seen as treasonable to show even the exterior of MI5, much less name its bosses, or publish nuclear secrets. We fully expected James to end up in a cell.

Other coups by James included an exposé of phone tapping in *The Buggist* and the discovery of babies being born with defects from thalidomide in Brazil. In sharp contrast, James also made the final film to be shown on *First Tuesday*, a rural idyll in tribute to an amateur wildlife film-maker on Exmoor, *Johnny Kingdom and the Pursuit of Happiness*. It led to a number of series for Kingdom with the BBC. James surprised us all years later by turning up as Jim from Cambridge, a contestant on *Who Wants to be a Millionaire?*, sadly losing in an early round.

Investigations were always at the heart of *First Tuesday*. Mark Halliley's damning *The Granny Business* was the first to expose cruelty to residents in old people's homes. As Mark remarked, the experience 'made me frightened of growing old'. Abuse in institutional homes is a scandal which persists to this day and continues to occupy film-makers.

It was Chris Bryer and Roger Finnigan's cool, forensic *Disaster at Hillsborough* that first laid the blame for the death of the ninety-six Liverpool fans on the failings of South Yorkshire Police and Superintendent David Duckenfield. The shot down the fatal tunnel, empty but set to the chants of the Liverpool fans, was much used and copied in subsequent films on Hillsborough. In 2016 the film-makers and I were interviewed by police for the protracted coroner's inquest which finally returned a verdict of unlawful killing. I asked whether they had found any faults in the film. No, it was fair and accurate, came the reply.

Chris Bryer, an ex-*World in Action* journalist and a rare import from Granada, with whom we had at best a wary relationship, was my successor as Controller of Documentaries and Current Affairs before he re-settled in France. In more personal and poignant vein, in *Return to Nagasaki* he took his father back to Japan; he had been a prisoner of war on the day the bomb dropped there, just a mile from the epicentre of the explosion, and had survived.

Other investigations and campaigns ranged the world: Death Row in the States; the Spanish 'cooking oil' disaster which caused 1,000 deaths; the Camorra's interception of relief money from an Italian earthquake. Julian Hendy's *Hostage to Fortune* exposed the scandal of private psychiatric homes in the States locking up harmless people for profit; at home, subjects included fatal farm accidents and the use of the 'liquid cosh' in mental hospitals in Britain.

There were illegal arms deals revealed in *The Bofors Affair* and the cynicism of the American cigarette manufacturers exploiting the developing world markets in Ros Franey's *Tobacco Wars*. The researcher on that programme was Richard McKerrow, whose independent production company Love Films would later give the nation *Benefits Street* and *Great British Bake-Off*.

Alongside the investigations came more filmic reflections of Britain: debutantes in London and housewife strippers in Gateshead, punks in Huddersfield, the last coal miners in Kent and a school for butlers. We went to Derbyshire's Calke Abbey to find a stately home in glorious decay and tracked down an old lady from Scunthorpe living alone in a jungle in Belize. One short film, *Last of the Little Mesters*, directed by Marilyn Gaunt, was an exquisite evocation of the Dickensian world of Sheffield's musty cutlery workshops.

Marilyn also made *The Swap*, our highest rating film at *First Tuesday*'s regular 10.30 slot, in which two families, North and South, exchanged lives and experiences. Perhaps we should have turned it into a series, as it was the forerunner of a slew of factual series like *Wife Swap* which became TV staples, all too often meretricious, while Marilyn's film was a social experiment with real purpose.

Access to institutions normally closed to public view is usually TV gold. Peter Gordon recorded life on board the world's biggest aircraft carrier the USS *Nimitz* and in playing Jimi Hendrix's distorted version of 'The Star Spangled Banner' was accused by one American complainant of 'crapping on

the flag'. His *Officer and a Lady* followed the first women Army officers to pass through Sandhurst alongside bizarre cocktail party etiquette and a white horse at the passing out parade being ridden up the steps and into the college.

Similarly, Jill Nicholls charted the rigours of the first women to become fire-fighters, and *Britannia Waives the Rules* watched the first women training to become officers at Dartmouth's Britannia Royal Naval college. The *Sun* newspaper rarely showed any interest in *First Tuesday* but when it heard that the women on their first sea voyage on HMS *Bristol* were being spied on in the showers, it dug out the headline 'All Aboard For HMS Bristols'.

TV documentary then travelled abroad much more freely than today's budgets and ratings demands allow. In *New York: the Quiet Catastrophe* Peter Kosminsky filmed a chilling final sequence of the unmarked coffins of the city's homeless being unceremoniously tipped into a mass grave on Rykers Island. *Subway City* found a colony of squatters living fearlessly in Manhattan's underground railway tunnels.

We met street kids in Mexico and Israeli settlers in the West Bank; went inside the US Army base at Guantanamo on Cuba; investigated zealous missionaries and 'the disappeared' in South America. Mick Czaky's *Killing the Dragon* followed heroin addicts to Thailand for a poison cure, which produced a startling sequence of mass projectile vomiting. Ian Stuttard and Ann Webber's *South Africa's Death Factory* reported on Pretoria's notorious central prison, where under apartheid, black prisoners were being hanged every other day. Happily, its death row is now a museum.

Even more daring was Roger Finnigan and Tim Tate's *Laogai: Inside China's Gulag*, which followed Harry Wu, said to be 'China's Most Wanted Man', as he travelled the country secretly filming the prisons of the nation with the highest rate of capital punishment. At one stage he even disguised himself as a prison guard to gain access. Wu, who had spent 20 years locked up as a political prisoner under Mao Zedong, died in 2016.

As Deputy Editor I did not make many films myself, but late in 1984 an aid worker called Jon Bennett alerted us to an unfolding famine in Ethiopia under Mengistu and his Soviet-backed Dergue regime, in particular in the rebel-held province of Tigray. In those days of ten-strong documentary crews, we persuaded the unions (at considerable cost; we paid an electrician the full rate to stay in Leeds) to cut the numbers to four: myself, Jon Bennett, Mike Shrimpton on camera and the resourceful Lindsay Dodd on sound.

There was a full-scale civil war under way, so we went in behind enemy lines via Sudan, under the protection of fighters from the Tigrayan People's Liberation Front. There were no roads through the Simien Mountains so we trekked on foot, often by night, sleeping under trees by day to avoid being seen and strafed by Soviet fighter planes.

The Dergue was allowing no food aid into the rebel areas, and we encountered terrible scenes of starvation and mass exodus, done maximum justice by Mike's exemplary photography – he was long the cameraman of choice for *First Tuesday*. We sent back one set of rushes on a donkey in the hope that it would make the news; but by the time it made it to Leeds, covered in African dust, Mike Buerk had beaten us to it with his historic report on the BBC. Even so, when *The Unofficial Famine* was broadcast, the Disasters Emergency Committee allowed an appeal at the end of the programme, approaching midnight, which raised more than £1m. In particular, one scene of an old woman, too weak to walk, being left by her departing family to die in a deserted village, touched many viewers.

There was an unnerving moment when we wanted to film Soviet planes flying in. To get close enough to the airstrip we were warned we would have to go through what was a suspected minefield. We made it there and back and thought no more about it, until the next morning when there was a shuddering explosion; a peasant farmer had been blown up.

A final footnote, on what was a horrifying privilege, was that the TPLF finally won their war and the first president of the new Ethiopia was Meles Zenawi, the rebel soldier who had been our escort.

Personally, my own most memorable day was 19 October 1989 at the Old Bailey, when

Grant McKee. (Chris Edmondson)

Gerry Conlon of the Guildford Four released at the Old Bailey. (Press Association)

the Lord Chief Justice of England allowed the appeal of the Guildford Four, convicted of fatal IRA pub bombings in Guildford and Woolwich in 1974. It was all over in five minutes. The Crown offered no evidence. Lord Lane made no apology for 14 years of wrongful imprisonment in what he called 'this regrettable affair.' He simply conceded, 'The police must have lied. You are free to go.' Paddy Armstrong, Gerry Conlon, Paul Hill and Carole Richardson turned and embraced me and my exceptional co-producer Ros Franey before walking to their freedom.

First Tuesday had played a fundamental role in the vindication of their innocence, and that of seven others in an associated case, beginning with *Aunt Annie's Bomb Factory* in 1984, followed by *The Guildford Time Bomb, a Case That Won't Go Away* and a book on the case. Before *First Tuesday* there had been no interest in a long-forgotten case, but the programmes unearthed new evidence and witnesses and sparked a campaign that brought in the likes of Merlyn Rees, the former Home Secretary, Lord Devlin and Cardinal Basil Hume.

On their release, the four gave us exclusive interviews which we lashed together through the night to transmit *The Guildford Four: Free to Speak*, a raw account of their brutal lost years of incarceration. Sean Day-Lewis in *The Listener*, rather over-excitedly perhaps, named it as one of his ten best documentaries of the century.

One light moment in a shabby saga was when Ros and I were on a live BBC programme with the former Master of the Rolls Lord Denning, who spectacularly defamed us by calling us fellow-travellers of the IRA. Regrettably, the presenter David Jessel smartly asked Denning to withdraw the smear, which he did, thus averting what might have been a highly entertaining libel suit against Britain's most famous judge.

Programmes on Northern Ireland never rated well, but there was a sense of duty to cover 'The Troubles'. We investigated the improper use of rubber bullets and documented the end of the notorious Divis flats. In *For Queen and Country* Geoff Druett and Jill Turton were embedded in a grim Army post off the Falls Road, where the imagery and the soldiers' description of shooting – 'Firing in anger, yeah, it's good fun, makes the job worthwhile … if you can't get a good conviction, then get someone slotted' – gave the Guardian cartoonist Steve Bell a week's material for his *If* strip. Nick Gray and Geoff Druett's *Peace People: the Dream that Died* examined the messy aftermath of the Nobel Peace Prize given to three campaigning Belfast women and Betty Williams' striking disclosure about the prize money, intended for peace work: 'I kept my half of the money. I needed it. I was broke … I don't apologize.'

My biggest regret was the low impact made by another film from Northern Ireland, Glyn Middleton and Mark Ackerman's *Hidden Hand: the Forgotten Massacre*, which sadly lived up to its title. It took an expensive year to research and then convincingly assert significant British collusion in the Dublin and Monaghan bombings of 1974, when 33 lives were lost in the worst single day of 'The Troubles'. Outside radical circles, it seemed nobody cared or wanted to know. After Yorkshire TV, Glyn was a co-founder of True North, the most prolific and successful of the independent companies making factual programmes out of Leeds.

Nick Gray was the first producer/director on *Jimmy's* and made more than a dozen films for *First Tuesday*. This is what *Edge* magazine said:

During a TV career of over 40 years, Nick Gray has made many programmes, from *Emmerdale* to *Left-Handed Arm-Wrestling*. He's been shot at in Belfast, the Peruvian hotel where he was staying was bombed; he's been threatened with summary execution in the Lebanon, jailed in Algeria, had Yemeni villagers stoning him, been stalked by a black bear in Siberia, faced a 4-metre anaconda in Venezuela, and narrowly avoided a brawl in Ethiopia.

You could add that he also made films about characters as diverse as Maria von Trapp (his film still plays on a loop in the Von Trapp family museum), Archbishop Milingo, Dirk Bogarde and *Born Free*'s George Adamson, and directed *Calendar*'s classic encounter between Brian Clough and Don Revie (the YouTube viewings are climbing towards the one million mark). But his defining film was *Escape from Tibet*. In it, Nick and Hugo Smith followed the trail of refugees from the Chinese occupation of Tibet over the Himalayas, a trail self-evidently full of danger and hardship. Among the refugees were two young brothers, Pasang and Tenzin. Their story so moved the public and Nick that the brothers were sponsored to come to London and are now British citizens. Nick has never stopped campaigning on behalf of them and

Kora National Park, Kenya, 1988. A Yorkshire Television crew with George Adamson, the expert on the lifestyle of lions. (L to R) Rod Lofthouse (Sound); Adamson; Nick Gray (Producer/Director); John Pinkney (Assistant) and Mike Shrimpton (Camera). (Nick Gray)

Tibetan refugees, writing two books and touring the world fund-raising with his film.

Kevin Sim has long been one of Britain's finest documentary directors. His career saw some quixotic diversions, like helping set up TV-AM with its ill-starred 'Famous Five' and giving the world Loyd Grossman and *Through The Keyhole*, before he returned to Yorkshire to make a string of outstanding films for *First Tuesday*. *Yanks Meet Reds* reunited American and Soviet soldiers at the Elbe, where the two armies linked up at the end of the Second World War; *Sonia's Baby* followed the agonising struggle of a woman to become pregnant from her dead partner's frozen sperm; *The Man Who Shot John Lennon* brought exclusive revelations about his killer Mark Chapman. But for most of us his masterpiece was *Four Hours in My Lai*, co-produced by Michael Bilton. Hearing from both perpetrators and victims of the massacre was harrowing in the extreme, but it also had a terrible beauty. I used to show new arrivals in the department the opening sequence as a master class in imagery and eloquent commentary. The film won just about every award going.

As did Peter Kosminky's *The Falklands War: the Untold Story* and *Afghantsi*, two more films that depicted war in all its horror and humanity and established Peter as a superlative film-maker. *The Falklands War*, co-produced by Michael Bilton, still holds up as the definitive television account of the conflict. Stripped of all jingoism, the interviews with soldiers and officers, British and Argentinian, survivors of the *Belgrano* and HMS *Galahad*, mothers and widows, are etched in the memory. This was Major Chris Keeble of 2 Para on the assault at Goose Green:

Peter Kosminsky, director, with Grant McKee. (Chris Edmondson)

It's dark. There's an enormous amount of noise. There's incoming fire to you. There's white phosphorus going off … There's tracer coming towards you and going away from you. There's fear running through you … You throw grenades. You fire your weapon. You bayonet. It's savage, gutter fighting. Everything you've ever experienced before is nothing like it. It is basic killing.

Afghantsi saw Peter and his crew embedded in a Soviet Army airborne division mountain outpost. The bewildered conscripts talked freely of the futility of their mission, of the loss of friends. There were, too, stunning filmic sequences as the sinister helicopter gunships swirled, the Antonovs took off firing decoy flares and the tanks pulled out of Kabul, retreating after 10 years of an unwinnable war, set to the haunting lament of a Bulgarian folk song ('Pritouritze Planinata' – The Mountain Has Collapsed). Of course, it all resonated when 25 years later British forces made the same retreat.

These were the days of *glasnost*, and Yorkshire TV took full advantage of the window of opportunity. In the same year Kosminsky made *Murder in Ostankino Precinct*, a *film noir policier* following a Moscow detective as he tracked down a seedy killer across Russia, gaining access to the whole process through to police cell interrogations in a way beyond any contemporary access in Britain.

Then when the Soviet Union fell three years later, we made three films for Channel 4 that could never have been made before. Clive Gordon's *Children of Chernobyl* detailed the terrible local aftermath of the nuclear disaster; Clive went on to film fearlessly in the most insanely dangerous theatres of war like Serbia, Chechnya and Rwanda. Kevin Sim made *Crime of the Wolf*, a disturbing, almost Dostoevskian, exploration of the mind of a notorious and manipulative serial killer, and *Letters from St Petersburg*, in which he spent the first snow-bound winter of the city's new freedom sending weekly film dispatches from the unravelling superpower.

The latter was a bizarre operation by British TV standards, where film was fast giving way to tape. In Russia, everything was shot on 35mm and edited in the sprawling movie studios of Lenfilm. Graham Shrimpton flew out to work on the clunking great edit machines, the epitome of crude but effective Soviet engineering. It was all paid for in hard currency (and fuelled by vodka and backhanders); when we realized that in the chaos of the day the Russian banks were liable to steal the cash, we decided it was safer and cheaper to fly in with thousands of dollars in the proverbial briefcase. The ensuing films were magnificent, even by Kevin's standards.

Back at home, *First Tuesday* covered social issues of children in care and abandoned babies, and included Pauline Duffy's sensitive film about stillborn babies. Peter Gordon's *A Summer Holiday* was a delightful portrait of, in the usage of the day, mentally handicapped children, on a trip to Teignmouth in the face of local hostility. A grim portrait of life in the then unhealthiest community in Britain, Middlesbrough's Wilton, even woke up its irascible MP, Stuart Bell, later exposed as Britain's laziest MP for not holding any constituency surgeries in 14 years.

Perhaps the most harrowing film was John Willis's *The Leftover Children*, featuring severely autistic children in violent distress at Beech Tree School in Preston. We reported on racial attacks in London at a time when they went uncovered by the news. Indeed, in Mark Galloway's *Murder in Glodwick* we deconstructed the senseless fatal stabbing of, in the killer's sister's words, 'a little Paki boy', that rated one short paragraph in the *Daily Telegraph*.

With enormous tenderness, Mark also made *Katie and Eilish*, the heart-breaking story of two beautiful conjoined four-year-old twins from County Kildare. Joined at the pelvis, their life expectancy was so limited that their loving parents decided on an operation to separate them at Great Ormond Street Hospital, in the knowledge that one of them would probably not survive. Only Eilish did. With superb film editing by Barry Spink, the film touched the hearts of 12.5m viewers in a 9.00 p.m. slot, a record number for *First Tuesday*.

Barry, who won the highest awards in his field, was one of a corridor of fine editors who made – and often saved – *First Tuesday*'s films: Graham Shrimpton, Terry Warwick, Clive Trist, David Aspinall, Steve Fairholme, who joined Yorkshire Television on Day One and was there to the end, and more. Equally, it is invidious to select names from the cameramen and sound recordists – yes, all men in those days, I fear – but it was the talent and commitment of Mike Shrimpton, Frank Pocklington and Alan Wilson that most illuminated our films.

Peter A. Gordon was another fine producer/director. His *Under Interrogation* was shot in a Birmingham police station at the invitation of the much-criticized West Midlands Police, who hoped that it would show their treatment of suspects in a better light under the new provisions of the 1984 Police and Criminal Evidence Act. Unfortunately for them, some of their detectives forgot they were being recorded and proceeded to roundly abuse and bully their suspects. When senior officers from the force came to Leeds to see the film before transmission they arrived all smiles and left all scowls. Their attempts to stop the film failed.

Some TV programmes really do make a difference, and Peter's *Cold Blood: the Massacre of East Timor* made a profound difference, both to the country and to the film-makers. In 1991 the West knew little and cared less about the genocidal occupation of East Timor by Indonesia. Six Australian journalists had been killed by the military in previous attempts to cover the story. Travelling undercover as textile buyers and tourism operators, and with amateur video equipment, Peter, cameraman Max Stahl and a Timorese-speaking researcher Kirsty Sword got on to the island and lost the secret police, in order to film the resistance fighters in the mountains. Then, at a protest march in the capital Dilli, the Indonesian Army opened fire, killing 250 people as they fled into a graveyard. The massacre was filmed in all its atrocity by Max, who managed to bury the vital cassette in a grave just before he was arrested.

On his release he returned to the graveyard and recovered the cassette; it was smuggled off the island in the underwear of a brave Dutch woman. The footage was so damning that we immediately released it to TV news companies and it led bulletins around the world. There had been killing on the island before, but never on TV. This swiftly became known as the Dilli Massacre, showing the world the reality of East Timor and leading to weapons embargoes, United Nations condemnation and world political pressure on Indonesia to give East Timor its independence, a movement that grew progressively irresistible.

So, in May 2002 the Democratic Republic of Timor Leste became the first new sovereign state of the twenty-first century. Peter was a guest of honour at the celebrations alongside one of his interviewees, Jose Ramos-Horta, now a Nobel Peace Prize holder and future Prime Minister. The first President was the rebel leader Xanana Gusmao, and alongside him was his wife, our researcher Kirsty. After the film she had devoted herself to activism on behalf of East Timor and had befriended Xanana on illicit visits to the Jakarta prison where he was held as a political prisoner. As for Max Stahl, now a national hero, whose footage had been so influential, he had abandoned England to live in East Timor to set up a national film archive and record the birth of a nation. It was a remarkable story.

In retrospect, it was also a risky, even foolhardy, project to sanction, even if all involved knew the dangers. Back then there were no risk assessments or war zone training, and no cell phones. I remember when we had a crew in Afghanistan making a documentary about land mines for Channel 4 and a message came through that the crew had come under shell and rocket attack while filming with the *mujahideen*. I endured a horrible 24 hours before confirmation arrived that everybody was safe.

Another film to make a difference was *Vicious Circles*, made by Jill Turton (reader, I married her). In the fetid slums of Karachi and elsewhere in Pakistan she found women were mixing infant formula baby milk with polluted water; when their babies got diarrhoea and dysentery they were treating them with Imodium, which was being sold in dosages banned in the West and without Urdu labelling warning of the known side effects. As a result, babies were dying from intestinal paralysis; one such distressing death we filmed with the parents' consent. During the shoot, Johnson & Johnson claimed to have withdrawn the infant formulation of Imodium from Pakistan. But we filmed chemists still selling it and recommending it to mothers. The children were still dying. After transmission we heard – but cannot confirm – that the film was shown in a board meeting of Johnson & Johnson at their New Jersey headquarters. At the end of the screening, the chairman asked if the film was fair and accurate. Nobody denied it. At any rate, Johnson & Johnson promptly ordered a worldwide withdrawal of the infant formulation of Imodium.

Jill Turton. (Grant McKee)

Jill also made *Too Close to Home*, a follow-up to John Willis's ground-breaking *Alice: a Fight for Life*. Within a mile of the studios, in the terraced streets of Armley around an old asbestos factory of Turner & Newall, she unearthed, by trawling through death certificates, a startling cluster of mesothelioma deaths. These were not deaths of factory workers but deaths in the neighbourhood, and it established that there were previously unsuspected environmental hazards from asbestos. Eventually, some 600 local houses were discovered to have traces of asbestos; it cost Leeds City Council about £9m to clean them. In the literally thousands of internal Turner & Newall documents discovered during the research was the surprising snippet that the company had hired private detectives to do surveillance on James Cutler when he worked on the original *Alice: a Fight for Life*.

We were also capable of humour. *Trevor, it's the Bailiffs* followed a team of incorrigible debt collectors. Pirated VHSs of *Paul Sykes: at Large*, Nick Lord and Roger Greenwood's tragicomic portrait of the serial convict heavyweight boxer, became cult viewing on rock groups' tour buses. Roger Finnigan made *Brezhnev's Daughter* with extraordinary access to the scandalous, alcoholic Galina, and had to fight for his honour to avoid being added to her catalogue of lovers, a list that began with a circus acrobat.

One *First Tuesday* that never happened was a live outside broadcast on the day the long and bitter miners' strike ended in 1985. We set up the OB unit at the Miners Welfare Club at Kellingley Colliery, near Castleford, once Britain's biggest pit and ultimately its last. Unfortunately, the local banks had resumed loaning money to the miners that morning, and by mid-afternoon the beer was talking. Abuse of 'the media' grew to the point where some of the crew had to lock themselves in an OB truck as it was rocked from side to side. Eventually, we negotiated safe passage back to Leeds and rushed a stand-by programme on air with seconds to spare. (Thirty years on, I still have a recurrent dream that the programme is about go out and there's nothing to show.)

As well as *First Tuesday*, the department was productive in making programmes elsewhere on ITV, for Channel 4 and even on one occasion for the BBC. *One Day in the Life of Television*, a remarkable collaboration with the British Film Institute, in which every minute broadcast in Britain on all channels one day in 1988, trailers, idents, regional, network, BBC, ITV, Channel 4, the lot, including behind the scenes footage at all the stations, was recorded for posterity as a time capsule of British television and condensed by Peter Kosminsky into a two-hour documentary. We made *The Hunger Machine* and *The Dispossessed* for Channel 4, two series on global challenges that would be a hard sell today. *The World This Week* was a challenging current affairs series that again looked far beyond British parochialism. John Jeremy and Roy Ackerman's *Swing under the Swastika* movingly told the extraordinary story of the jazz musicians who survived Auschwitz by playing jazz for the SS. Roy was another who became a highly successful independent producer.

I have a particularly soft spot for *Fair Game*, an investigative series into the dodgy corners of British sport. Greg Dyke was between jobs and to our delight he agreed to present it. I was never so sure of winning a commission than when we saw all the heads turn as we went into Channel 4 with him. It was also *Fair Game* that brought the phrase 'Fifty-seven Old Farts' into the lexicon of the day. The quote came from Will Carling, the England rugby union captain, describing the blazers who ran the game at Twickenham – and who promptly lived up to their description by sacking him as captain. It was a great story, but I felt awful that our programme was wrecking a sporting career. A weekend of frantic phone calls with his agent, press outrage and some saner heads at Twickenham happily saw him reinstated 72 hours later.

The ending of *First Tuesday* and its partial absorption into ITV's short-lived *Network First* was a blow that the department never fully recovered from. There were no longer any guaranteed network slots. The decline was gradual but inexorable.

Around then I went upstairs as Director of Network Programmes. Chris Bryer took over until he moved to France, and he was followed by Helen Scott, two highly experienced programme makers with solid journalistic expertise.

Yorkshire made the first *Network First* with Nick Finnis' report on sperm donors, and we were the slot's strongest contributors. Of special note were two films on pressing women's issues that played a significant part in law reform: *Women Who Kill* successfully campaigned for provocation through domestic abuse to be taken into account in spouse killings; Glyn Middleton's *I'll Be Watching You* was similarly seminal in the campaign to make stalking a criminal offence. There were exclusive interviews with Christine Keeler, and the first TV interview with Norman Scott in Diana Muir's *When Jeremy Thorpe met Norman Scott*. Thorpe complained to the Broadcasting Complaints Commission, alleging breach of privacy, and turned up in person at the hearing to make his case; it was thrown out.

3-D was a peak-time current affairs show presented by Julia Somerville, with the formula of three sharp reports in 30 minutes. It ran in peak for six series and nearly 100 episodes, maintaining Yorkshire's investigative tradition and concern for social issues, with reports on Nestlé's improper marketing of powdered baby milk in India and doctors practising infant euthanasia in Britain and America.

ITV's drift towards more populist fare saw Yorkshire produce *Holidays from Hell* and its spin-offs, with increasing use of user content and covert filming. There was the consumer strand *We Can Work it Out*, presented by Judy Finnigan and Christine Talbot. Peter A. Gordon created an enduring genre of clip shows with a series of *Hundred Best …* collections, but these will need another memory; I had left by then.

I had been Director of Network Programmes for about two years when it all blew up. The word was out that Ward Thomas was going to bring the maverick Bruce Gyngell out of retirement from Australia. It was obvious that there could be no co-existence between him and John Fairley, and I began ringing round company directors with my view that such a move would obviously cost Yorkshire its greatest asset. To my horror, none seemed too bothered; one even suggested it was deserved, a revenge served five years cold for John's support of *Shoot To Kill* (and the embarrassment the film doubtless caused to said director in his establishment clubs).

John left; Bruce arrived with his pink shirts, yellow sofas and miso soup; and my days were clearly numbered. Not long after, Donald Baverstock died. John and I drove together to his funeral at Bolton Abbey, a small statement of where I stood which I trust would have met with Donald's booming approval.

So my time at Yorkshire came to a sticky end. I had little respect for Ward Thomas and Gyngell, and no doubt vice-versa. Numerous disputes and intrigues rapidly blew up. In particular, Gyngell ordered that all documentary subject matter would have to be cleared by the advertising sales people, which was obviously unacceptable (although I was not around long enough to know whether this was actually implemented). Then he wanted to cancel a £1m plus drama-doc by Peter Kosminsky, *No Child of Mine*, about child sexual abuse and prostitution. I explained that as this was a *Network Centre* commission not only were we throwing away invaluable work and profit at a difficult time, but that it would still be made elsewhere, and that under Yorkshire's contractual obligation to take the network schedule we would have to show it anyway.

While I was on holiday (always a bad mistake to leave the country during a crisis) Gyngell paid off Peter's contract and cancelled the film. Of course it got made, through TVS, and Yorkshire duly showed it, but my position was untenable and I quit.

One small detail epitomized for me the lack of class at the top of the company at the time. An agreed statement on my reasons for resignation cited 'differences over programme-making policy'. Which was true. But by the time it appeared in the press the next day it had been slyly amended to cite 'differences over programme department structure', as if I had quit over some mere administrative detail rather than the undermining of Yorkshire's programme-making culture.

It was a hurtful divorce from a company and staff I felt deeply loyal to, but in retrospect I am glad not to have been party to the subsequent surrender to Granada, the sweeping away of people and programmes and the reduction of a mighty TV production centre to a shell. I was privileged to have been there at the high water mark of ITV and YTV and to have worked alongside great talents. Many of those who were there, at every level of the company, have since said they were the best days of their working lives. Me, too.

Chapter 10

Peter Kosminsky

Peter Kosminsky. (Nick Lord)

In June 1985, as Margaret Thatcher attempted to starve the IRA of the 'oxygen of publicity', the BBC's Paul Hamann was preparing a documentary featuring an interview with Martin McGuinness. While Director General Alasdair Milne was on a cruise in Scandinavia, the BBC Board of Governors responded to pressure from Home Secretary Leon Brittan and pulled the programme. I was an assistant producer in the BBC TV Current Affairs Department at the time and a member of the NUJ. With other officers of the Lime Grove Chapel, I helped organize a strike in protest. On 7 August there was no broadcast news of any

kind in the UK – no TV or radio news on any network, BBC or commercial. Even the World Service news shut down. Nothing like it has ever happened before or since – a united protest by broadcast journalists across the country against an attempt by government to stifle free speech. The strike was successful, and the programme was ultimately transmitted. But it was made clear to me that I had no future in BBC journalism. I left the organization that had trained me and in the autumn of 1985 joined the Documentary Department of Yorkshire Television to work on *First Tuesday*, then under the editorship of John Willis.

One of the joys of that era was the opportunity to work for, and in the process be trained by, a great practitioner in your field. When I arrived in Leeds in 1985, clutching my Producer/Director union card, John Willis was already a great star in our firmament. His 1975 film *Johnny Go Home* had won the Best Factual Programme Bafta and was, at least for me, a template for the kind of documentary I dreamed of making. It used a powerful personal story to introduce an important issue of public policy – in this case the dangers faced by teenagers who flee home for the bright lights of London.

One of the less joyful aspects of that period, within ITV at least, was the rigidity of the trade union shop system. You could only direct a documentary if you had an ACTT union director's ticket. Many of my producer colleagues at YTV, who had been promoted through the researcher route, did not hold one. So, as a new director on the block, I soon learned that one of my responsibilities was to 'carry the card' for others. On one memorable occasion I was flown to Miami simply to sit in the corner and read the newspaper, while an award-winning documentary producer got on with his film – a strange awakening for a naive refugee from the sheltered world of the BBC.

My first major assignment in my own right was what we used to rather quaintly call a foreign tour. This involved being sent overseas for several months, returning with two or if possible three *First Tuesday* stories, for transmission over a number of editions of the programme. My baptism of fire was to be such a trip to the Americas. Nick Lord, a longstanding YTV researcher, was already across the water, digging for likely stories. I was to join him to 'stand them up', and a film crew would follow, alarmingly quickly as it seemed to me at the time. I had a few short weeks to prep three films across an entire continent. Bear in mind that at this point in my career I had barely left the country for work, let alone made a full-length documentary.

Nick Lord met me at the airport in Richmond, Virginia. Two things became apparent to me as we drove south through that forested state. The first was that Nick Lord was very, very angry. He had been a researcher at YTV for nine years and had had every expectation of promotion to producer in his own right. A forthright Yorkshireman,

he made it very clear, as he drove too fast down the snow-lined blacktops, that the very last thing he had wanted or expected was to be required to work for a green, Oxbridge-educated, BBC-rejected nobody who had been parachuted in to steal his job.

The second thing I realized was that, despite being a lifelong non-smoker, I was in the process of contracting lung cancer. Furious, Nick pointedly chain-smoked as we drove south together in that confined space. Any chance he could lay off for a bit? Silence. Any chance we could open the window? If looks could kill …

Nick and I were in Virginia to make a film about Marie Deans, an extraordinary paralegal who was fighting a one-woman war against the death penalty in that state. The film took us inside the Mecklenburgh Correctional Center, then home to Virginia's death row, to meet some of the men working their way through the Federal and State appeals systems with the help of Ms Deans, struggling to avoid humanity's ultimate sanction. Some of the inmates I

Nick Lord in the USA. (Nick Lord)

The YTV crew with the electric chair. (Nick Lord)

met had committed truly appalling crimes, too grisly to describe here. And yet the men we interviewed seemed to bear little resemblance to their rap-sheets. In some strange way, death row was rehabilitating them. Years of preparing their various appeals, studying legal precedents, taking the courses necessary to argue their cases in court, seemed to have returned them to civilisation. Or maybe it was just being away from the drugs?

One of the sequences in the eventual film was shot inside the 'death-house' at the old Virginia State Penitentiary in Richmond. The officers in charge on execution days gave us a graphic tour, ending (just as it did

for the condemned men) in the windowless room housing the electric chair itself. I'm just about the most psychically insensitive person you'll meet, but even I felt a palpable presence in that room where so many men had met their deaths in agony. I can only describe it as a feeling of evil, of utter dread. I felt it the moment I entered the room and it returns to me now as I write this sentence. I doubt I will ever forget it.

Next stop on the tour were the streets of the Bowery, where YTV researcher Roger Finnigan had been preparing a film about homelessness in New York City. *New York: the Quiet Catastrophe* took us to the town's ancient armouries, now converted into dormitories for thousands of the homeless, and to the crumbling welfare hotels of 42nd Street, where families unable to find affordable accommodation were lodged alongside New York's glitterati enjoying a night out on Broadway. Roger had spent weeks getting to know some of the families. The stories they told, of life in a society without a safety net, of children growing up in rat-infested squalor, were heart-breaking. I remember smugly thinking such things could never occur in the UK, where our welfare state would offer protection. Wrong again!

For some time we had been asking the city authorities what happened to homeless people who died on the streets. Finally, they agreed to take us to Hart's Island, a prison colony where such unfortunates were apparently buried in mass graves. The only problem was the weather. It was bitterly cold in New York that winter and the ferries weren't sailing. Finally, at the third attempt, we were accepted on to a small tug heading for Hart's. The wind-chill drove the temperature down to 40 below that day on the Hudson. As we attempted to film the crossing, Andy, our camera assistant, keeled over, the only time I have seen someone pass out from the cold.

The scene we were eventually allowed to film on Hart's Island is probably the most shocking and upsetting I've witnessed in 35 years in television. Prisoners hurried from their barracks in the bitter wind, scrawled the names of the dead, often misspelled, on to the sides of cheap pine coffins in thick, black magic marker, then heaved the pale caskets into an open grave. Some of the coffins were tiny – clearly containing children. As the men hurried back to the warmth of their cell block, a warder scattered lime across the sombre pit. The sound spooked a flock of seabirds, which rose lethargically to circle above us in the gun-grey sky. An American flag hung limp on its flagpole. As we travelled back to our comfortable hotel in Manhattan, no one spoke. Wretched, utterly wretched.

Probably the best-remembered documentary I made while at YTV was *The Falklands War: the Untold Story*. This was a programme conceived by the former *Sunday Times* Insight journalist Michael Bilton, to be transmitted across two hours on ITV on the fifth anniversary of the conflict. John Willis wanted us to track down and interview combatants and families from both sides, and this required a team of researchers with very specific skills. Patrick Buckley, a bilingual producer with considerable reporting experience in South America, came on board, alongside staffers Ros Franey and Jill Turton, who would bring their famously sure

John Willis, producer/director, with colleagues from the YTV Documentaries Department. Mandy Wragg, a production assistant, is on the right, and Grant McKee, producer, is peeping through between them. (Chris Edmondson)

touch to the UK interviews. Clive Gordon joined us as archive researcher. On his way to becoming one of our leading documentary makers, Clive unearthed previously unseen stills and amateur footage of the invasion and occupation which brought those sequences to life.

The Argentine shoot was memorable in a number of ways. Arriving in 1985, less than three years after the conflict, we discovered that we were the first UK TV crew into Argentina since the ceasefire. As we attempted to shoot interviews at Puerto Belgrano, the naval base from which the ill-fated battleship had sailed, hundreds of recruits gathered to hurl abuse and chant patriotic slogans. We were hosted on our visit by Naval Intelligence, charming Anglophiles in gleaming white uniforms who turned out to have had a less than spotless record during the 'Dirty War'. As the hostility increased, we looked round for our jovial minders, but they were nowhere to be seen. We were on our own.

Three years after the collapse of the junta, Buenos Aires was still a very tense city. Grey Ford Falcons, a hated symbol of repression during the reign of the military, still toured the wide boulevards, shotguns poking ostentatiously from their open rear windows. But in other respects, Buenos Aires was a thrilling city to visit in those heady, newly democratic days. I sat in a street café in Recoleta, the most fashionable district of the capital, and watched the glamorous Paris returnees promenade by. I later discovered that Recoleta was built around a notorious graveyard, from which the skeleton hands of Eva Peron had recently been stolen. The city was raising money by public appeal to ransom them back from the kidnappers. I thought this said a lot about that troubled land.

As we approached the end of our Argentine shoot, Patrick Buckley and I discussed our options for the last two days of shooting in the elegant penthouse our hosts had insisted he occupy for the duration of his visit. We had planned an interview with the incumbent Foreign Secretary, Dante Caputo, as a courtesy, but it seemed likely to contribute little to our film. Time was running out, and in those days you couldn't afford to waste expensive film stock on interviews you didn't need. We resolved to cancel it. Later that evening, Patrick and I were invited to dinner by our generous host, a fluent English-speaking Captain and cricket lover from Naval Intelligence. After several delicious courses in one of Buenos Aires' most salubrious restaurants, we reached the brandy stage (yes, I'm afraid so).

Ever so casually, and in tones of the deepest regret, the Captain suggested that, 'Were we to be thinking of cancelling our interview with the Foreign Minister, he would beg us to reconsider.'

Patrick and I exchanged a look. Patrick's room had clearly been bugged, and the Captain's operatives had been listening to everything we said. We went ahead with the interview to avoid a confrontation with our deeply dodgy hosts – but without any film in the camera.

In 1989 I was working on a documentary for YTV about John Stalker's inquiry into an alleged police 'shoot to kill' policy in Armagh, Northern Ireland in 1982. Despite our best efforts, all the people we wanted to interview were either dead, disappeared or firmly refusing to talk. Then we had a breakthrough. John Thorburn, a former Head of the Greater Manchester Murder Squad and the operational head of Stalker's Armagh inquiry, agreed to be interviewed by me – but only off the record. I had spent many months getting to know John, a hammer-headed Glaswegian and winner of the Queen's Police Medal, and knew he had never before spoken to the press. It was too good an opportunity to waste. But how to include his testimony if he wouldn't go on camera?

I'm thinking back to that day. I had more hair then, and what I had was brown not grey. I was a more confident man, given to rash undertakings which I would repent at leisure. I still lived with my wife back then, and our daughters had yet to make an appearance. I was standing in the front room of our home in London E5, talking on the phone to YTV's Director of Programmes John Fairley, trying to persuade him to let a man who had never before shot a frame of drama make a 4-hour serial for primetime TV.

'It's the only way we can tell this story,' I enthused. 'He won't go on the record.'

Let me take a moment to tell you about that time, before ITV was dismantled and sold off by hatchet-faced men in Savile Row suits. It was an alliance of powerful regional companies, each with guaranteed access to the network budget and schedule. Unlike the monolithic, centrally commissioned channels of our current broadcasting landscape, the ITV schedule of 1990 comprised the taste of up to fifteen different Directors of Programmes, giving it its unique character. It also presented an ambitious young man like myself with a real opportunity. I had to persuade just one man (in this case John

Fairley) to back my insanely ambitious scheme and it would happen. No committees, no double or triple ticks – just John backing his hunches. It's no exaggeration to say that I owe my entire subsequent career to the decision John made that day – the only time in my professional life when I can remember putting down the phone, jumping into the air and yelling 'YES!!!' at the top of my voice.

We made it, but only just. In truth, it was borderline insane to allow a man with nothing more than unearned self-confidence to take on a multi-million pound drama with 104 acting roles, thousands of extras and shot in three counties across twelve weeks. The first day of that shoot, surrounded by a crew I didn't know and a cast I had no clue how to direct, was one of the most frightening of my life. I literally had no idea whether I would be able to shoot a scene of drama or not. Nonetheless, the film got made and went on to win its fair share of awards; but, in truth, it was only after *Shoot to Kill* was transmitted that the drama really began.

One scene showed John Stalker and John Thorburn being entertained to lunch at a golf club by the then RUC Chief Constable, Sir John Hermon. In the establishing wide shot, an 'extra' poured cold tea into the actor playing Sir John's glass, standing in for brandy. To be honest, my mind was elsewhere. Our John Stalker, actor Jack Shepherd, was a vastly talented but occasionally difficult individual. As I struggled to frame my notes to him diplomatically, I missed the fact that the extra had filled the Chief Constable's glass with a ridiculous amount of 'brandy'.

Shoot to Kill, written by Mick Eaton and based on the testimony of the stymied Stalker enquiry team, made a number of allegations against Royal Ulster Constabulary officers in connection with the shooting of those unarmed men in Armagh in 1982. But it was Sir John Hermon who sued us for defamation in the Belfast courts, in part at least because of that overfilled brandy glass. Amongst other things, the veteran policeman felt we had intentionally portrayed him as an excessive lunchtime drinker, an 'old soak'. YTV decided to counter-sue Sir John in the London courts, and hired a well known silk to argue our case. I reviewed our research with Brian Hepworth, the chain-smoking solicitor from Mishcon de Reya who had 'legalled' the film for us in the first place. He felt we had a strong case. Then, unexpectedly, producer Nigel Stafford-Clark and I were summoned to a meeting at YTV in Leeds – on a Saturday morning! This was unheard-of. All the execs present were in mufti – sitting round the boardroom table in that all but deserted building. A QC from Belfast was present and in uncompromising mood: given the sectarian make-up of juries in Northern Ireland, we would never get a judgment against Sir John Hermon in that jurisdiction. We were certain to lose. Acting on behalf of our insurers, he strongly advised us to settle.

I still remember the silence which greeted his extraordinary statement. Though John Fairley argued stoutly against, it was clear that the board had already made up its mind. YTV paid unspecified damages to Sir John in an out of court settlement and *Shoot to Kill* has never again been screened, in public or in private.

The ripples of that cataclysmic event continued to affect all those involved in the years which followed. John must speak for himself on this matter, but I believe the board never forgave him for allowing *Shoot to Kill* to be made and broadcast. Eventually he was forced out, and I think it's fair to say that Yorkshire Television never properly recovered from his departure. He was replaced by the late Bruce Gyngell, known primarily for breaking the strike at TV-AM. On his first day at YTV, he hauled me into his office in London and fired me.

I hired a van and drove to Old Street to buy a filing cabinet. Returning to YTV, I began to clear my office of ten years of research files and documentation. None of my colleagues met my gaze as I made the journey to and fro with crate after crate. Those were uncertain days, and no one wanted to be associated with me in case they were next for the chop. When the miserable job was done, I sat in the van in the square below and cried my eyes out. One of the happiest periods of my life had come to an end without warning, and I had no idea what to do next.

But, as I've often observed in our strange and wonderful industry, that setback turned out to be an opportunity in disguise. Bizarrely, there were still people prepared to allow me to write and direct drama and, after a faltering start, I managed to make my way as a freelance programme-maker. But those days at YTV still hold a special place in my heart, even though they ended sadly. And the memory of John Fairley backing a young Turk who wanted to try his hand at drama, and then defending him stoutly when prudence would certainly have urged him to keep his peace, will never leave me. Quite apart from anything else, I owe that man for a lesson in passion and integrity on which I draw every day of my working life.

Chapter 11

David Green

(David Green)

Alan Whicker in Alaska, well above the Arctic Circle, in 1977. He refused to adopt conventional levels of thermal protection against the sub-zero conditions, and retained his natural look as a debonair Englishman abroad. (Valerie Kleeman)

'Alaska runs off the edge of the imagination,' proclaimed the legendary Alan Whicker in that unmistakable voice, with its delicate inflections so easily imitated. It was the opening line of *Whicker's World: Alaska*, and I was recording the first of twenty-nine *Whicker's Worlds* which I went on to produce and direct with the Great Man. Even now,

I can imagine him saying dismissively that twenty-nine is 'a kind of record'.

Still in my twenties, I was green enough to stop my first ever recording session with him, only seconds after he started rehearsing, to suggest a slight change of delivery tone.

'Do you really think so?' came the disdainful reply from the other side of the recording-booth glass.

After a long silence while he considered my temerity, he started again, changing and improving it ever so slightly, but only after severely reprimanding me for stopping him in full rehearsal flow. I got the message – let him get to the end in future – and came to understand it over the years as part of a rigorous and ruthless professional routine which had helped project him to the very top of his profession. But he had obviously remembered the moment because he reminded me of it nearly thirty years later. I belatedly realized I had earned my spurs that day, even though my timing could have been a little better.

In 1968, as I was leaving Bury Grammar School, Whicker left the BBC to join a consortium organized by Telefusion, which won the franchise for Yorkshire Television, where he was said to have become the largest shareholder. At YTV his large and eclectic output and massive viewership were to outshine even his BBC days. He became the major face of an upstart television station which quickly became the trendsetter for the ITV Network with a unique and original programme portfolio that won what Whicker

WHICKER'S WORLD: THE ABSOLUTE MONARCH
Alan Whicker meets The Sultan of Brunei
Wednesday 28th October 1992 at 9.00pm on ITV

Written, Researched and Narrated by Alan Whicker
Produced and Directed by David Green
A SEPTEMBER FILMS PRODUCTION FOR YORKSHIRE TELEVISION

Whicker interviewing the Sultan of Brunei during his silver jubilee celebrations. (Valerie Kleeman)

would have described as 'remarkable ratings, rare reviews and real respect'.

Probing without prying, diffident, puzzled, apparently onside, he tackled amongst others General Stroessner of Paraguay and the brutal 'Papa Doc' Duvalier of Haiti with his Ton Ton Macoute enforcers – 'a little roly-poly man in a homburg', in Whicker's phrase, who toured Port-au-Prince in his Mercedes throwing money out of the window and quoting his poetry. Years later, I filmed a similar big beast with Alan – the Sultan of Brunei in his 1,778-room palace – a task Whicker described as being like 'trying to interview God'.

Many memorable *Whicker's World* series, filmed across five continents, graced the first decade of Yorkshire TV. In the very early days he was spotted occasionally in the YTV buildings, but he appeared there less and less often as the years went by. Rumours built up of a remote man, never saying thank you, never sharing the glory, never buying a few drinks on location. But why should he? It was

Alan Whicker interviewing the dictator of Haiti, 'Papa Doc' Duvalier. (Terry Ricketts)

unnecessary carping. Everyone at Yorkshire benefited from the celebrity upgrade that he brought to the company. He was one of the medium's first great stars, alongside David Attenborough, Richard Dimbleby and even Bruce Forsyth – and this was his way of doing things. If it had been Hollywood, no one would have batted an eyelid. But in Britain we still expected bonhomie and fluffiness from our celebs and we remain, to this day, uncomfortable with success. With Whicker, it was the programmes that counted, and a remarkable bloody-mindedness about everything being geared to his work. He would allow nothing to get in the way.

I couldn't believe my luck when in November 1971, fresh out of Oxford, I was offered my first job in television as a programme researcher for Yorkshire Television, who were already blazing a trail as the brightest star in ITV's tangled firmament. I knew them to be strong in my twin passions of drama and documentary, and naively hoped to land on one of these TV equivalents of Mayfair or Park Lane. It turned out, instead, to be Baker Street, in the guise of Hughie Green and his quiz show, *The Sky's the Limit*, where Peter Holmans press-ganged me into finding contestants and writing questions. My starting salary of thirty pounds a week was not to be sneezed at, however, after endless minimum-wage nightshifts at the Kellogg's factory in Manchester. The kind and generous Richard Whiteley, who left us far too early, teased me mercilessly that Green was secretly my father, and MD and Deputy Chairman Ward Thomas scolded me for interviewing potential contestants in Belfast while representing the company on a day of massive bombings across the city – bizarre, as if I could choose which day the IRA were not going to be active. My mum, however, was proud to see me on air every week, adjudicating the answers.

Fourteen months later, in January 1973, Holmans honoured his promise to extricate me from the Green Machine and appointed me a trainee director on the soap he was taking over, *Emmerdale Farm*. So I tentatively entered the TV drama world at twenty-four and went on to direct two episodes every three weeks for the first two years of a landmark show that became the bedrock of the company and remains so right up to the present day. I was fortunate enough to have more experienced future YTV luminaries like Keith Richardson, David Reynolds and John Kaye Cooper working for me as floor-managers, and the highlight of my tenure was dressing up Toke Townley, an *Emmerdale* elder, in a Manchester City scarf which he bought at the village fete. Yes, I was a real Man City supporter half a lifetime before the glory hunters moved in.

After *Emmerdale*, I directed four episodes of a new children's drama series called *Nobody's House*. But after being blown away by *Whicker's World: Vancouver*, I knew it was time to chance my arm with John Fairley's celebrated YTV documentary department. Not quite sure why that particular episode, but I watched it like a hawk and knew I could contribute to the franchise. Here was showbiz and drama masquerading as documentary, and I've always maintained that *Whicker* was the very first factual entertainment programming, decades before the term was first used for lesser shows in the 1990s. I walked nervously into Fairley's office and

Magnus Pyke in full flow.

About to be placed in a horizontal plane to explain why images in a driving mirror are displaced from left to right, whereas mountains in a still lake appear upside down.

Demonstrating friction to a willing pupil.

plucked up the courage to ask him if I could cross over. Without hesitation he said yes, mumbled something about their loss being our gain, and I had found a mentor. It was to change my life forever.

I was tested by directing just one *Calendar* item before being quickly shunted on to *Don't Ask Me*, one of the first prime-time science shows.

'If you can direct you can produce,' boomed lofty Duncan Dallas, the cerebral Head Honcho.

This was the usual sink-or-swim YTV mentality, which I had down to a T by now. And produce I did, in what I quickly discovered was a highly creative madhouse. Loveable lunatics like Magnus Pyke and David Bellamy were running the asylum, tempered by the worldly wisdom of Miriam Stoppard, whom I developed a crush on – although it was her in-house YTV make-up artist and friend, Carol Cooper, whom I finally married not long after – and then quickly divorced.

Dallas dispatched me to Houston, New York and Scranton, Pennsylvania on my first American tour of duty as the director on a series of three medical documentaries, including the much-celebrated *The Boy in the Bubble*, filmed in Texas. It was midwinter, and Jimmy Carter had declared the State of Pennsylvania a disaster area, as 15ft snowdrifts halted our B.F. Skinner shoot and kept us chained to our Holiday Inn, where Austin Mitchell regaled us for hours with stories about his complex life. New York was little better, as we struggled to film 'Awakenings' man, Oliver Sacks, in the bitter cold. Manhattan warmed up, however, when Mitchell's formidable wife Linda turned up to keep an eye on him.

On returning to the Kirkstall Road Studios, there was barely time to watch Norman Hunter bite someone's legs before being sent to France and Yugoslavia to direct two episodes of Robert Kee's series on European Communism. The vain Kee, a distinguished journalist with an icy determination who preceded each take by combing his hair in the camera lens, viewed me as cannon fodder – but the experience proved invaluable. Indeed, the YTV documentary department had quickly become a blur of great projects, all written and presented by celebrated journalists. And, most tellingly, the clarity and intellectual rigour of the content was always of the highest quality. I felt very privileged to be a small part of it. But I was now a very old twenty-nine and still no sighting of 'The Whicker Man', whose awesome reputation provided the best of the bitchy gossip in the Yorkshire TV bar. Then one day I walked into the company library, empty except for the browsing John Fairley. He casually announced that the director he was about to dispatch to Alaska to join the waiting Whicker team had fallen out minutes ago, and my time had come. Tomorrow.

John Willis, who has remained a good friend over the years, marked my card, having recently returned from grappling with *Whicker Down Under*, and I arrived at the Captain Cook Hotel in Anchorage ready for my date with destiny. That first evening, I had a cordial and jolly first meeting with Mr Whicker. Valerie Kleeman, his partner, whom I came to like and greatly respect over the years as the power behind the throne, was a little more reserved.

'What have we here?' I sensed her saying to herself.

And I knew for sure it would be no easy ride when Frank Pocklington, Whicker's veteran cameraman said, 'Don't worry, David, I'll help you.'

He never did, and it soon became a baptism of fire. As I led my reluctant crew into battle next day, Whicker rigorously tested me:

'What do you want me to do?' … 'Why?' … 'What's the story?' … 'How will it cut together?'

This never happened again, and I quickly understood the significance of these searching Day One questions.

Monty Python and a phalanx of jealous newspaper hacks regularly took Whicker to task for chronicling only the lives of the rich and famous, and for simply choosing warm and cushy locations. There was some truth in this, but it was not always so. He revelled in the cold and snowy Alaskan conditions and didn't baulk when, for the sensational opening shot of the film, I sent him walking hundreds of yards away from the camera and then back again towards it, appearing as a pin-prick over a totally white horizon in an endless freezing and snowy waste. If it made good TV, his instinct told him to do it. We flew to the North Pole to reveal the physical hardships of working on the oil pipeline at one of the coldest locations on the planet; we shot tranquillizer darts from helicopters at angry polar bears, then landed to attach radio-collars to track their breeding grounds for conservation purposes; and we flew up Mt McKinley on a ski-plane in thin air at 10,000ft to interview a famous local explorer. This was not tea at the Waldorf Astoria, or drinks at Harry's Bar.

On the flight back down the mountain, 'Whicker's luck', a phrase he often used to fondly describe his good fortune in life, was very much in evidence. He and Valerie flew down first with the explorer in a tiny plane, which returned to pick up the small crew. On this second flight the plane ran out of fuel, which the young hippy pilot had failed to check properly. When he started tapping casually on the fuel gauge I knew we were in trouble. However, he managed to land it perfectly on the narrowest of winding mountain roads, languidly retrieving a large petrol can from the rear of the plane – all of which we filmed. This had obviously happened before, and soon we were on our way down again with some unique footage. The commentary didn't make it exactly clear who was in which plane. And, on second thoughts, I've totally forgotten anyway.

It wasn't until the end of Day Two that I plucked up the courage to suggest that, rather than a catalogue of carefully-researched travel gobbets about the cold wastelands around us, the building of the great pipeline from Prudhoe Bay to Valdez across this vast sub-continent should be the focal point of the film. It had scale, drama, conservation issues, limitless money, great characters and strong storylines, particularly the dominance of the Teamsters and the abuse of power against migrant labourers. Whicker agreed, and was magnanimous enough to say that these were his instincts too but he was glad I had put it in perspective. I had been accepted – for now. The best story, however, was never filmed. One weekend every month, a jumbo jet was chartered to fly over 300 hookers from Las Vegas to the snowy wastes to amuse the workers along the pipeline. Nigel Turner, Whicker's long-time researcher, was horrified

(L to R) Ron Gunn, sound recordist, Lee Corbett, assistant sound, Dick Dodd, cameraman, Dave Dillon, sparks, Mel Bradley, grip. (Charlie Flynn)

that I should even bring this up – 'we are not that sort of show'.

However, I could see that I had tickled Whicker's populist instincts. With a little more confidence and experience, I'd have had my way. My time was to come.

Most of the YTV crews were tough, talented, hard-bitten professionals – Dick Dodd, Peter Jackson and Alan Pyrah are particularly worthy of mention – and, on *Whicker's World*, long trips abroad were the norm. On this challenging first shoot I fondly remember the day in June 1977 which we all took off with the rest of the UK to celebrate the Queen's Silver Jubilee. Don Atkinson, a cheerleader of a sound recordist, went to great trouble to respect this occasion – Union Jacks, a loyal toast and a proper celebration – so that even the most republican of us shed a nostalgic tear for Blighty and an ordered world on the other side of the globe. Our intrepid leader, ever the English gent, was also very much part of this memorable day.

Don Atkinson, Sound Recordist. (Charlie Flynn)

Whicker with a group of dancers in Kerala in 1978. (Valerie Kleeman)

For a northern lad from a humble background whose parents managed to fly him to Europe just once on a school charter, my subsequent travels with Alan were to become mind-boggling: Singapore, Bangkok, Jakarta, Surabaya, Nias, Kashmir, Rajasthan, Kerala, Northern Travancore, Delhi, Agra, Los Angeles, San Francisco, Chicago, Houston, New York, Venice, Egypt, Beijing, Xian, Australia, New Zealand, Tahiti, Easter Island, Iguazu, Rio, Sun City, Cape Town, Kuala Lumpur, Pangkor Laut, Brunei – not to mention the regular commuter flight from Leeds to Jersey, where Whicker lived in isolated splendour with the devoted Valerie, whom he affectionately called his constant companion. I suspect she disliked the phrase as she was much, much more – totally involving herself behind the scenes for over

forty years as dedicated researcher, underrated location photographer and *confidante extraordinaire*.

What I will always remember most is Whicker's unerring instinct for knowing when to listen. He left his subjects to reveal themselves unhindered, with the dying art of the prolonged silence.

'You can ask the rudest, most personal questions if you smile,' he said, and, 'You should never patronise your subject.'

He knew how to pose the questions others would be too embarrassed to ask but to which they would love to know the answers. I was producer on the second of two memorable films which Alan made in the seventies with the superstar plastic surgeon Kurt Wagner, who operated in a cap with Mickey Mouse emblazoned on it, and Kathy his glamorous and buxom Beverly Hills wife. Kurt said he never needed to divorce her because he could always change her – and, to keep the marriage fresh, he did so every year. Only Whicker could ask a woman with new, silicone-implanted breasts what they weighed, then silently wait an eternity for the answer, finally teasing her to break the silence by getting her to balance them to camera.

Her hands jiggling her boobs, she declared, 'A few pounds each I think, Alan, and don't you think they look wonderful!'

From behind the camera, I watched him perform this magic in film after film – with everyone from kings and famous film stars to the most buttoned-up of ordinary folk. Without exception, he eventually got them to reveal their very innermost thoughts, leaving them unaware of their new mental nakedness: Liza Minelli on the Orient Express; the richest man in the world, the Sultan of Brunei, in his opulent palace; the last of the British tea planters in India; the first women cops and first gay cops in San Francisco; and, most memorably, the great Peter Sellers in Beverly Hills.

We spent a long day filming the last ever interview with Sellers in his grotesque Hollywood villa adorned by trophy wife, Lynn Fredericks. She later married and quickly divorced another YTV icon, David Frost, with whom, two years later, I made a YTV Elvis documentary in Memphis, where we were unceremoniously ejected from Graceland for unauthorized filming. Sellers was obviously not well, slipping and having to be supported by Alan as they descended the steps to the garden together. He was quiet and reserved at first, continuing to be a little unsteady on his feet. But as the day wore on, Whicker got under the skin of his interviewee, who started to reveal his deepest and darkest secrets to Whicker's cattle-prod of silence.

'I hate this town … people cross the road when they see me coming to avoid talking about yet another one [of my films] that has just bombed … I get very depressed on a daily basis out here … it's a cultural desert … I feel trapped in paradise … and need to get home before my mind dies completely … no friends … no future … for a fading funny man.'

It was sad and painful to watch, and even more poignant to edit, when he died overnight a few weeks later in London. By

Whicker, with Peter Sellers in Hollywood, in 1980. (Valerie Kleeman)

7.00 a.m. the next morning, Paul Fox, YTVs Director of Programmes, who famously called *Whicker's World* the jewel in the crown of YTV when he arrived from the BBC in 1975, had cleared an ITV network slot that night, and our remarkable footage was transmitted as Peter Sellers' obituary programme. I supervised a troupe of editors who were already assembling the best of the LA interviews even as Whicker was boarding a plane from Jersey to Leeds to link it all together live from the YTV studio. It was a joy that day to be part of the awesome YTV factual machine in full flow – and on home territory. The old ExTel journalist was at his best, drafting and re-drafting all day to a strict deadline. Above all, he could write. With his golden pen, he could link commentary to pictures like nobody else. His was elegant, sparing prose, every word, every pause, every syllable crafted to enhance the story he was telling. Nothing superfluous, every word counting. He was truly a master of his craft.

The Peter Sellers interview, like Kurt and Kathy Wagner, came out of the *Whicker's World: California* series that I produced and directed for YTV in 1979/80. All six films achieved stellar midweek ratings in the competitive 9.00 p.m. slot and stirred up many controversies, particularly *Plato's Retreat*, on a swinger's club in Los Angeles, and *Staying Alive*, a film about regular people with an everyday dread of casual violence learning to shoot to kill to protect themselves in this new Wild West. The series also featured a film about Hollywood Brits, and our feisty researcher, Barbara Twigg, succeeded in persuading a plethora of transplanted UK movie and TV stars, including Sellers, Joan Collins, Christopher Lee, Britt Ekland and

Alan Whicker's interviewing style was greatly enhanced because he always met his interviewees on their own territory. Although his real-life world scarcely touched sports arenas, he was happy to talk to Christopher Lee on a golf buggy. (Valerie Kleeman)

Patrick Macnee, to subject themselves to Alan's charms. She tried hard but had no success, however, with Jane Seymour – then Tinseltown's hottest TV star, who had moved to LA in 1976 after her Bond girl success in *Live and Let Die*. Jane is now my partner and we live together in Malibu. Sliding doors.

Plato's Retreat would be edgy primetime TV material in the twenty-first century. In 1979 it was a scandalous TV first. Valerie was reluctant when I first mentioned it, thinking it would sully Alan's reputation. But I sold him the obvious: here was a damned good story about LA decadence, littered with lively and eccentric characters, including an 83-year-old granny in a threesome with two twentysomethings, a plain suburban couple who arrived together and made out with several other couples that very night, and a colourful group getting closely acquainted in a jacuzzi.

Famous for his meticulous note-keeping, Whicker jots down an aide-memoire at the start of another journey. (Terry Ricketts)

Whicker, charming and deferential in his blazer and socks (no shoes allowed on the mattresses) was at his best. His dapper appearance, with signature moustache and slicked hair, juxtaposed magnificently with the seedy surroundings. He was by turns politely interested, innocently perplexed and finally suitably shocked, while Valerie constantly averted her eyes and looked awkwardly to the ceiling, in a similar yet different way to the participants. His questions were, as always, what the Great British Public wanted to hear: Don't you get just a little jealous? How can you do this and still go home together? How do you know it's safe? How would you feel if your daughter were here? He then asked the owner, Larry, why he called it Plato's Retreat. Larry said he just liked the name and only afterwards found out that Plato was gay, but it was too late – it was a defining moment, surrounded as we were by the madness of La-La-Land and its ludicrous characters. Needless to say, my world-weary YTV crew were not in the least bit shocked and got a little tetchy with me when I failed to get them permission to stay for a drink or two after filming. Paul Fox was irate when he saw my edit a few days before transmission. He instructed me to tone it down, which I did, although it still rated its socks off. It was history repeating itself, as only weeks previously Fox and I had played out a similar exchange over Kathy's breasts.

Whicker's reputation for an obsession with the lives of the rich and famous, exacerbated by the famous Monty Python *Whicker's Island* sketch, was partially laid to rest in this California series. Three of the six films focused on Alan's keen journalistic nose for strong policing, drugs, violence, gun control and extremists masquerading as good citizens, particularly in America. The two films that I set up for Whicker with the San Francisco police were tough and challenging assignments for him and the team. Mostly filmed during the course of very long nights on patrol, there were live bullets flying over our heads on two separate occasions as we tried to avoid unofficial no-go areas in the black-and-whites. All credit to our steadfast YTV crew, who supported Whicker magnificently out on those mean streets. He was unmoved by the danger around him, and we caught a tiny glimpse of the Second World War journalist who had been in the front line of the 666-day Italian campaign.

The third film, *Staying Alive*, created quite a stir, as Whicker bonded with the potential victims and prey of gun-toting petty criminals and junkies all over California. Carol and Russell O'Rea ran a drab liquor store on one of the meaner streets of San Francisco. Both in their sixties, he was heavy and sweaty, she a smiling, bespectacled little old granny. They turned out to be TV gold, more experienced in gun culture than they looked. One night, when Carol was working alone, a large, nervy guy had entered and asked for a pack of Camels. A little jittery, she suspected the worst and, as she bent down to pick up the cigarettes, she saw he had a 9mm Luger automatic and froze. He told her to empty the till and then lie on the floor. She counted out a meagre $39 and, as she got down, put her finger on the trigger of a 38/40, a large, old-fashioned gun that she kept behind the counter, and shot him straight between the eyes. He was in his death throes, twitching, when she then casually walked around the counter and put a second bullet into his neck.

When the police arrived, she said, 'Listen, take that money out of his pocket, he's got my 39 dollars.' And then, she told us, 'Even though it was all bloody, I put it in the cash register and they took him away. I had dum-dum bullets, ya know, they enter the skull and fly into hundreds of pieces, just pulverise the brain.'

Whicker skilfully waited and waited, and then picked his words carefully: 'So you didn't really need that second shot?'

'No, I didn't, I just wanted to see how it feels!'

Then he went for broke: 'Was it the first time you'd killed anybody?'

'There's been a few more – about four – but I shoot twice, that's all I shoot. If I can't get them in those two, I quit.'

Any glimpse of a private life was put on hold during these lengthy three- to four-month filming trips (Whicker expected no less), although I did meet my second wife, Jane Emerson, while working on the gun film – a blessed coincidence that led to twenty-five years of happy marriage and three children, now successful adults. Thank you, Alan. During this time, I occasionally returned specifically to the YTV fold to make specials with Whicker under my September Films banner – it was not in my DNA to produce under the umbrella of any other ITV company. My favourite moments in the nineties block of *Whicker's Worlds*, which included *Sun City*, *The Eastern and Oriental Express*, *Miss World* and *Pavarotti*, belonged to Dante Barbareschi, an amusing and outrageous tour guide on *The Ultimate Package*, a four-part, round-the-world luxury tour for the well-heeled, on a private jet. Whicker was always at his best trading humour with his most extrovert characters

'What about the poor, put-upon rich husbands?' asked Alan rather slyly

'We had a lot of husbands who kicked the bucket – husbands always kick the bucket, and wives never do, do you notice that, Mr Whicker?'

'Really?' came the curt and clever reply, encouraging Dante to open up even more.

'Women are always the survivors. We had a long cruise of three months and quite a few husbands died. I remember we used to go up on the top deck and kick the bodies into the water.'

Now an unusually long Whicker silence.

'You couldn't put them in the refrigerator with the caviar and lobsters, could you? Not in First Class anyway.'

More classic Whicker silence

'The wives were left as widows, but most of them got a lot of money, which made things easier.'

'Yes, they often go blonde from grief, don't they?' mused Alan

'We are a bit cynical, aren't we, Mr Whicker?'

'A bit,' said the Master.

Personal memories abound: the warm and genuine thumbs-up across the stalls as the lights came up after the premiere of my feature film, *Buster*, at the Odeon, Leicester Square in 1988 (Whicker was proud that so many of his young directors, like Jack Gold, Mike Tuchner and Fred Burnley, went on to make movies); the occasional recognition in his commentary of my dreadful puns such as the 'jumbos on the runway' description of a formal procession of brightly-decorated, ceremonial elephants crossing the tarmac at Kerala airport in India in 1978; and the sharp, brief and pointed hand-written note I received from him after the Sultan of Brunei invited me back to Brunei, alone, after the film transmitted, to commission me to make a presentation package of highlights from his Silver Jubilee celebrations and his royal state visit to Britain, to be gifted to a select few like the Queen and President Clinton – 'at least somebody's hit the jackpot!'

He was always affable and friendly towards me, but never a friend – and I regretted that after so many years on the road together. Maybe the generation gap was too wide. Maybe. But I hugely respected him for the consummate professional that he was – a brilliant, popular journalist and observer of the human state who achieved legendary status among his peers and was loved by the great British public. And behind the *Whicker's World* YTV documentaries were an army of television professionals who learnt at his feet. I was lucky enough to be one of them and, like many others at Yorkshire Television during those halcyon years, I carried the spirit of his command of the profession into every moment of my subsequent career. We will never see his like again.

David Green, originally a YTV trainee, now directs feature films in Hollywood, and lives in Malibu with his partner, Jane Seymour.

Chapter 12

Nick Gray

Nick Gray, producer/director and Geoff Druett, interviewer and presenter. (Nick Gray)

Thirty years ago, the world of television was a very different place. Back then, no one had heard of reality television, so when the idea was mooted for a series called *Jimmy's*, going behind the scenes of a Leeds hospital and to be transmitted in the daytime schedule, there were some who were understandably nervous.

The title was the local nickname for St James's. In the first episode, medical students were introduced to the hospital, a nurse in intensive care talked to her latest patient, a man was prepared for an operation to remove a cancer from his throat and a mother gave birth by Caesarean section.

The man who made the decision to let the cameras in was the hospital's chief executive, Ian Donnachie. His ambitions for the series were that it should be positive, that there should be instructive health messages and that it should – in a way that does not happen in real life – introduce members of the hospital staff to each other. To this end, we could film

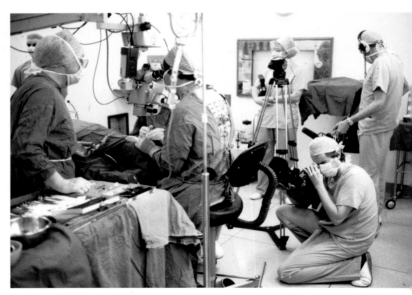

Filming an operation at St James's Hospital in Leeds. (Nick Gray)

everywhere, making the hospital the star of the series. The audience eagerly followed the stories of ordinary people. They liked not being told what to think by a 'voice of God' commentary. Viewers could quote back to me whole scenes of dialogue as though it was classic text. Without quite realizing it, we had invented a new television genre now called the 'docu-soap'.

Twenty years on, it is difficult to believe how revolutionary *Jimmy's* was. It was a serial, constructed like a soap opera (I had previously worked on *Emmerdale*) in that it had four or five storylines running at any one time. There were no interviews and except for a brief 'Previously on ...' at the beginning of each programme, there was no commentary. We knew we were inventing a new form – threading several narratives together in a single programme – and we knew the risks.

The success of *Jimmy's* truly surprised us, the producers. There was a report from Bedford of a man involved in a road accident asking the ambulance driver to take him to Leeds so that his favourite doctors in *Jimmy's* could treat him. Another time, a researcher came in one Monday morning having spent his Saturday afternoon at Elland Road, where he claimed to have joined in with the crowd as they sang the theme tune. Some viewers thought the programme might not be documentary but drama: a letter praised the dialogue, claiming to detect the hand of Leeds playwright Alan Bennett.

There were occasional disasters. After all, people can die in hospital. One case we were following ended in tragedy when the patient suddenly died of an illness unrelated to his treatment. After a few weeks we approached his widow to ask her permission to show the film that ended his story. She assented, on the grounds that she and her family wanted to see him again as he had been in life.

For several weeks we followed the hospital's treatment of an old man in intensive care. It became obvious that he was not going to recover, so we asked his wife, who was always at his bedside, if we could continue filming. She was a kind, thoughtful lady who lived not far from the hospital. In time, the old man expired, and we duly asked his wife if we could use the film to show the work of the Intensive Care Department. She looked confused, but we persisted:

'We need his nearest dependant's consent for the film to be shown.'

'Oh,' she said. 'You need to speak to his wife. She lives in Leicester. I'm no relation at all.'

The daytime ratings were so startling that Yorkshire Television's programme controller John Fairley scheduled a Thursday night hour-long repeat of the week's two programmes back-to-back after *News At Ten*. When he showed the figures to his opposite number at Thames TV, together they convinced ITV to run the second series twice a week at 7.00 p.m. peak time.

Over ten years *Jimmy's* ran for 160 episodes. The highest rating was of 10m viewers. It was sold to many parts of the Commonwealth. We were told that *Jimmy's* would be sold to South Africa if we cut out all black contributors, which of course we did not do. The format was copied in similar hospital serials in France, Eire and Australia. The Hollywood producer Steven Bochco asked for tapes while developing his hit hospital drama series *ER*.

Chapter 13

Marylyn Webb

Of all the major news events in Yorkshire TV's life, none was more testing or more stressful than the murderous reign of Peter William Sutcliffe, a lorry driver from Bradford, now and forever known as 'The Yorkshire Ripper'. It affected the whole team, but none more so than Marylyn Webb, who found herself Calendar's *leading reporter on the long saga of the hunt for the Ripper. Marylyn died tragically in 2014. But she had given us her own account of those days.*

Marylyn Webb. (Terry Ricketts)

30 October 1975. A cold, foggy, miserable morning, and the body of a woman is discovered on playing fields beside the busy Scott Hall Road in North Leeds. Wilma McCann had been murdered within yards of her home. It could not have been a more sinister start to Peter Sutcliffe's cruel catalogue of butchery that was to overshadow so many people's lives, including mine, for the next five years.

That morning, however, the event was, sadly, just another day at the office. Having delivered the film and reported back to base, my diary shows that in the afternoon I was reporting on the discovery of another body (completely unrelated) in Sheffield.

As the attacks and killings in the North of England began to show the signature of a single individual, an atmosphere of menace grew. The then male-dominated media assumed the killer had a grudge against prostitutes – but women realized that if they were in the wrong place at the wrong time, and alone, they were all potential victims. The killing of sixteen-year-old shop assistant Jane McDonald reinforced this fear.

I was acutely aware of this as I covered all the Ripper attacks in the YTV area and spoke regularly to the detectives in charge of the investigation. I was also the only female reporting regularly on television about the killings. For all I knew, the Ripper was watching every bulletin. Did he revel in the publicity or did he resent it? No one knew. As a result, I never went anywhere on my own in the evenings. I wouldn't accept any speaking or other engagements. I suspected everyone – even neighbours! A family friend was a local policeman, firearms and Task Force officer. Whenever he visited, if he knew I was at home alone, he would make sure I could see it was him before I answered the door. He knew I would not answer if I didn't know who it was.

I had asked the detectives in charge of the case whether I might be a target. They said it was a possibility and that if I felt it necessary I could have police protection. But having to cope with other people living in the house at all times was, to me, intolerable. I chose to be vigilant instead. Election night was an assignment I dreaded. I would make sure I was accompanied to the count or at least dropped off and picked up again at the door.

In the *Calendar* newsroom the realization that every woman in the region felt in danger came when Meryl, the wife of our head of local programmes, John Wilford, told him of her fears and those of her friends. She explained how women were afraid to go out alone and made sure they always went to evening events in a group. The next morning in the office, he called me over to ask if I was of the same opinion. I told him in no uncertain terms that I was, and that the police also believed by that time that the next victim could be anyone's wife, mother, sister or daughter.

To give John his credit, he immediately set about making a documentary, *Who is the Ripper?* It highlighted the fear and risk to all women and the fact that prostitutes had probably been targeted because they worked alone in lonely places. Their deaths had been no less traumatic to their families.

Subsequent killings upheld these fears as the Ripper grew bolder and more callous. A teenager, Josephine Whittaker, had been walking, literally round the corner, through the suburban Savile Park area of Halifax, to visit her grandmother. At his trial Peter Sutcliffe admitted he had walked with her, engaging her in conversation about her visit. He then dropped back behind her, asking her to tell him the time by the nearby hospital clock, before hitting her over the head and savagely stabbing her.

University student Barbara Leach's accommodation was in a Bradford terrace with a dark back alley. Tragically, Peter Sutcliffe just happened to be there as she arrived home. Jacqueline Hill, another university student, had been to buy food at the Arndale Centre in Headingley before walking back to her student flat. As on other occasions, Sutcliffe was disturbed or distracted in his attack on her by a passer-by. He halted his assault on her body but then resumed it when he thought the coast was clear. He was not in a mad frenzy. He knew exactly what he was doing.

In retrospect, I don't think he would have had the courage to kill anyone he knew. He could only take out all the pent-up anger and frustration (of his life with his wife Sonia) on strangers. If it is any consolation to the families of the women and girls murdered, Sutcliffe's trademark blow to the head killed them outright. They would have known nothing of the attack. I met most of the families of the Yorkshire victims, which is why I have never written about the Ripper years for financial gain and never will. The agony of loss for all of them was too great to ever be exploited.

For the women he attacked and failed to kill, the horror and damage will live with them forever. I will never forget meeting Ilkley journalist Yvonne Mysliviec the day she returned to work after recovering from what was most likely an attack by Sutcliffe in 1979. She had been walking over the railway footbridge at Ilkley station when she was aware of being followed and glanced round to see a man she described to me as 'Italian looking, swarthy with curly black hair and a beard'. Moments later, she was hit on the back of her head and left for dead. She invited me to feel the dent in her skull. It was a miracle she survived. When Sutcliffe was caught he fitted her description exactly.

On the day he was arrested there was a great feeling of euphoria and relief. It was a big night for *Calendar* as we gathered reaction to the news from throughout the region.

After the programme, as we were preparing to go home, producer Paul Dunstan said to me, 'Do you want to come up with me and the crew to talk to the McCann family?'

My instinctive reaction to the prospect of going up to Scott Hall Road in the dark was to hesitate. An instant later, I realized there was now no reason to refuse. Firstly, I would be with the crew, and of course, to the best of our knowledge, the Ripper had been caught. It just shows how deeply entrenched in the psyche the fear and caution had become.

It was not surprising that the police never suspected Peter Sutcliffe of being the Yorkshire Ripper on the occasions they had questioned him. He was such an insignificant little man. Even his best friend said he would not have suspected him of such evil. After five years of living with the results of his deeds I had butterflies in my stomach the morning I arrived at Dewsbury magistrates court for Peter Sutcliffe's first court appearance. I knew what he looked like from the photograph of him in his lorry, but what would this 'monster' be like in the flesh? I am sure everyone in the court was as astounded as I was when this meek little man stood in the dock, answering the magistrate's questions in a polite, soft, light voice. Could this really be the butcher who had terrorized the North of England for five years? It was.

Having given the police such a long and detailed description of his murderous campaign it was assumed that Sutcliffe would plead guilty. So the film crew and I were dispatched to London – the trial had been moved there – for what we thought would be just a couple of days. I had always avoided London as much as possible. I can't bear being surrounded by concrete and clay and millions of people. In 1972 I had turned down the offer of a job with LWT when it was first formed, simply because I knew I would hate living in the city and commuting on the underground. To be more than a few minutes from open countryside would, for me, have been thoroughly depressing.

However, much to everyone's surprise, Sutcliffe pleaded not guilty, and so the trial at the Old Bailey lasted not two days but a month. What he had realized very quickly was that if he pleaded guilty he would end up in a nasty, violent high security prison, where he would probably be bullied. Whereas if he could persuade the doctors and jury that he was mentally ill he would go to a nice, comfortable secure unit, where he would be looked after well.

Cunning, calculating and very much in control, the seemingly quiet, nervous little man set out quite deliberately to convince the psychiatrists that he was mad. What they didn't know was that he had all the answers.

His wife Sonia, whom he'd known and loved since they were both sixteen, had suffered from schizophrenia. He knew all the signs and symptoms. The doctors believed everything he told them and took it at face value. The story that convinced them he suffered psychotic delusions was a lie based on a childhood game. He told the psychiatrists that when he worked as a gravedigger an angel on one of the gravestones told him to kill prostitutes.

One of my colleagues, who was a childhood friend of Sutcliffe, told me that when they were children a group of them played in the cemetery. One of the graves had a carved angel on top of it. It was on a slope and a drainage pipe ran just beside it. When one of the children called through the top of the pipe it sounded as if the angel was speaking! Sutcliffe convinced the doctors with this tale, and they only conceded that they might be wrong under intense questioning from the prosecution. It's just as well the jury was more grounded!

So, a five-year nightmare was over and the right verdict had been reached. A great shadow had been lifted from my life. I had to admit, though, much as I had not relished the prospect of my prolonged stay in London, I had thoroughly enjoyed it as a working experience. Listening to and assimilating each day's evidence and then condensing it into ten-minute live reports for that night's *Calendar* programme was both challenging and thrilling. I knew the region was on tenterhooks for each day's revelations in the lunchtime and evening bulletins. We had to chase across London to and from the Old Bailey and the studios in Soho to meet deadlines and programme times. The task was made so much easier by being able to take taxis everywhere and staying in a very comfortable hotel.

I have just been reading, for the first time since 1981, letters sent to me from viewers complimenting me on my reports, and from my then boss, Graham Ironside, who wrote:

In view of the public comment – and that of the Director of Programmes, no less – it may seem superfluous for me to add my congratulations to you for work of consistent excellence throughout the long and difficult trial of Peter Sutcliffe. However, I want to do so because, in all sincerity, it represented a memorable chapter in the distinguished history of *Calendar*. I was acutely aware of the problems and the pressures which would – and did – pile up, but can honestly say I never felt a moment's doubt that we would emerge at the end of the day with the best coverage. We did, and I thank you.

It was the pinnacle of my journalistic career!

Chapter 14

Vernon Lawrence

Vernon Lawrence

Les Dawson became a leading comedian after winning *Opportunity Knocks* in 1967, and was given his big break by Yorkshire Television in the 1970s, in a series called Sez Les. Seen here in a sketch with Cleo Laine and Johnny Dankworth, he is remembered best for his off-key piano playing and, with his long-established colleague, Roy Barraclough, as one half of 'Cissie and Ada', a drag couple with pretensions but with a predilection for naughty gossip. The programme ran to 68 episodes from 1969 to 1976; John Cleese, who had just left the *Monty Python* team, appeared in two complete series in an inspired casting with Les. The scripts were written by a team, mainly Barry Cryer and David Nobbs, but Les insisted in writing his own monologues and liked to remind people he was also 'a proper writer', the author of sixteen books. (Gus Lupton)

Paul Fox moved to Yorkshire and deemed Entertainment to be the weak link in the programme department. He cancelled *Sir Yellow* in mid-production and immediately sent for Duncan Wood from the BBC. Duncan had produced *Steptoe and Son* and *Hancock's Half Hour* for the BBC. I was at the BBC at the time, and over a long and alcoholic lunch he suggested I come to Leeds as his Number Two.

When I arrived, Les Dawson was the jewel in the YTV crown, and I went straight into a series of hour-long specials with guests like John Cleese and Olivia Newton John. Our writers, David Nobbs and Barry Cryer, created loads of characters for Les, including the Despond family and Cissie and Ada.

The next pearl to emerge from the oyster at YTV was *Rising Damp* with Leonard Rossiter. Duncan Wood's predecessor, John

The holiday affair which never quite happened. Linda Cochran (Joanna van Gyseghem) and David Pearce (Keith Barron) in *Duty Free*, trying to disguise a moment of lust and steal a kiss under the mistletoe during their holiday in Marbella. The Cochrans and the Pearces were creations of Eric Chappell and Jean Warr in the YTV series which ran from 1984 to 1986. (Shutterstock)

Rising Damp was a regular winner with ITV viewers from 1974 to 1978. Written by Eric Chappell and based on his original stage play, *The Banana Boat*, it featured the intertwined lives of Rigsby, a miserly Leeds landlord (Leonard Rossiter) and three of the lodgers in his rundown Victorian house. Rigsby longed for social status – and for the affections of Ruth Jones (Frances de la Tour), his only female lodger – but in spite of his best efforts he consistently failed. Even when he finally persuaded Ruth to the altar, predictably the day went disastrously wrong. (Shutterstock)

Duncan, had seen a play by a tyro writer from Grantham, Eric Chappell, and recognized a potential comic genius. Eric was to write *Rising Damp* for four record-breaking years, and then deliver two more No.1 hits, *Only When I Laugh* with James Bolam and *Duty Free*, the package holiday comedy with Keith Barron and Gwen Taylor.

During my radio days, I had worked on *The Goon Show*. Harry Secombe had become a beloved friend, and I persuaded him to come

John Thaw, long established as a star of television police dramas, took on his first comedy role for Yorkshire Television's *Home To Roost* from 1985 to 1990. As Henry Willows, he was a middle-aged divorcé living happily on his own in London, his life only disturbed when his cleaner arrived to tidy up. It was something of a shock when his oldest son Matthew turned up on his doorstep, having been thrown out by his mother. (L to R) Reece Dinsdale (Matthew Willows), John Thaw's real-life wife Sheila Hancock (who appeared as 'Sue' in only 1 episode), John Thaw. (Shutterstock)

to Leeds to make a series of specials for us. A cocktail of popular music, opera and fun ensured a regular place in the top ten.

Duncan Wood retired in 1985 and I inherited his position. I had always admired comedy drama – the likes of *Minder* and *Shine on Harvey Moon* – so when John Fairley asked me to read *A Bit of a Do* by David Nobbs, I was fascinated. With my new deputy David Reynolds in place, we felt we could do it. Off we went, David Jason was enticed away from the BBC, and immediately the show captured 15m viewers.

Then came Rik Mayall playing Alan B'stard, the loathsome MP created by Laurence Marks and Maurice Gran, in *The New Statesman*. Inevitably, the series produced some collisions with taste and decency. An inflatable doll, best imagined rather than described, appeared in one episode, with Alan

Only When I Laugh ran on ITV for four seasons from 1979 to 1982. Here the world's most complaining patient, Roy Figgis (James Bolam), tries the patience of Staff Nurse Gupte (Derrick Branche) and his consultant, Mr Gordon Thorpe (Richard Wilson). (Shutterstock)

Yorkshire TV's comedy-drama *A Bit of a Do* was the hit of the entertainment programmes of 1989. Based on the David Nobbs books, it followed the Simcock and Rodenhurst families as they careered from social clash to social clash, starting from the wedding day of the Simcocks' son Paul to the Roderhursts' daughter Jenny. Here Ted Simcock, (David Jason) a self-made Yorkshireman and proud of it, entertains Neville Badger (Michael Jayston) a family friend, Nicola Pagett, the mother of the bride, Gwen Taylor (Rita Simcock) and David Yelland (Gerry Lansdowne, another guest). (Shutterstock)

B'stard doing the inflating. I believe I saved us another visit to the Independent Broadcasting Authority by demanding that the inflation was done behind a sofa. But the rubber lady still managed to tickle the fancy of our studio audience. And *The New Statesman* went on to be presented with an Emmy in New York by the delectable Florence Griffith Joyner.

Every year, TV executives gather in Cannes to trade programmes. There I met Richard Bates, who was punting a treatment for a TV version of his father H.E. Bates' book *The Darling Buds of May*. I phoned John Fairley in Leeds, got his support, shook hands with Richard – and the rest is history.

Richard wanted Bob Hoskins to play Pa. But we Yorkshire Television folk already had the 'perfick' card in our pack – David Jason. Then we needed to find our Mariette – sweet seventeen and probably never been kissed. The YTV casting directors spread their net far and wide, with a seemingly never-ending stream of young hopefuls coming in to read for the part. After innumerable

A 'laugh out loud' moment for David Jason as the roguish farmer/wheeler-dealer Pa Larkin in *Darling Buds of May*. (Shutterstock)

Mariette Larkin (Catherine Zeta-Jones) clearly inherited the Larkin family's fertile genes. The oldest of seven herself, she quickly had a baby after enslaving the heart of the tax inspector sent to carry out searching inquiries into Pa Larkin's tax affairs. The baby, the first grandchild of Ma and Pa, in real life is Daisy Bates, great-granddaughter of H.E. Bates, whose five Larkin novels inspired the series *Darling Buds of May*, and granddaughter of Richard Bates of Excelsior Productions, co-producer of the series. (Shutterstock)

Pam Ferris and David Jason on location in rural Kent in *Darling Buds of May*. With their six children (soon to be seven) they lived in a bubble of happiness, an abundance of food and drink, and an ability to soar above little difficulties with the tax authorities, social convention and, fairly frequently, the law. As the Larkins, they became the best known couple on television – Ma and Pa to the viewers – although few knew their Christian names. Pa Larkin was Sidney and Ma was Florence. (Shutterstock)

David Jason created yet another memorable role in the Yorkshire TV series *A Touch of Frost* as the old fashioned, ill organised but very effective and streetwise copper, Detective Inspector Frost, seen here with Detective Sergeant Maureen Lawson played by Sally Dexter. With little respect for convention or bureaucracy, Frost was endlessly in hot water with his superiors and lived a fairly chaotic life, but never failed to nail his quarry. Yorkshire Television produced 42 episodes between December 1992 and 2010. (Darren C. Miller)

disappointments, a girl from Wales came through the door, and in a matter of minutes our long travail was over. We had Catherine Zeta-Jones – unknown to any of us that day, and today, of course, a queen of Hollywood.

Filmed in a blissful summer in the hop gardens of Kent, *Darling Buds of May* went straight into the hearts of our audience and achieved the unthinkable – reaching No.1 in the audience ratings with its very first episode.

Even while we were making *Buds*, we were thinking about how to tempt David Jason to go on working with us. We floated various projects and books at him, then suddenly he got excited by an old fashioned detective story, *A Touch of Frost*. David had always been seen in comedy or light drama, but we in Yorkshire had seen enough to know he could do straight drama. Thus was born one of the great and long lasting TV series of our time.

Chapter 15

Robert Charles

(Robert Charles)

There's a unique Yorkshire philosophy as far as sport (and most other things) are concerned – you don't have to win to be the best. Any number of years without a cricket county championship didn't lessen the unwritten truth that the county boasts the best cricket team that you could wish to play for or follow. Although the Premier League trophy resided on the other side of the Pennines for decades, this wouldn't allow a Yorkshireman to contemplate any reasonable suggestion that it might be worth following Manchester United or Liverpool. No, the very fact that you were born in the Broad Acres allows you membership of a group of people who have the inbred certainty of knowing they are the best. After all, the land slopes away from Yorkshire, doesn't it?

Looking after television sport in this region is therefore not to be taken lightly. There are certain assumptions that should not be overlooked – 'don't prat around with it', 'show it some respect' and, whatever you do, 'make sure you don't apologise for defeat'. You see, defeat in Yorkshire doesn't mean what it does elsewhere; it's just something that has inexplicably happened, so best ignore it and move on.

I joined Yorkshire TV in 1977 to become editorial assistant on a new weekly sports show called *Calendar Sport*. It came from the local news stable and that was an exciting place to be. Things happened in Yorkshire, not all of them good, but when the region's viewers wanted to know about it, they tuned in to *Calendar*. Joining it was an introduction to people who possessed unerring courage,

Presenters on Yorkshire TV frequently volunteered to assist with fund-raising efforts in local communities. Here Roger Greenwood, sports reporter, Ashley Jackson, the water colourist and the unmistakeable F.S. Trueman prepare to auction a bat autographed by the Yorkshire County Cricket team at an event in Wakefield. (Paul White Photography)

bravado and the drive to make programmes the way they wanted to and, in true Yorkshire fashion, with huge helpings of self-belief.

John Wilford, who had hired me, typified that. He was the man who had produced a most riveting piece of sports television in 1974, when Brian Clough's 44-day reign at Elland Road ended. On the day Clough was sacked, Wilford commandeered a 10.30 p.m. slot after *News at Ten*, found Don Revie, Leeds United's former supremo, eating a meal in a casino in a suburb of Leeds and brought him to the studios to join Clough in what would be confrontational TV at its best. Austin Mitchell was the interviewer who had to simply light the blue touch paper, sit back and watch as two giants of the game launched into verbal hand-to-hand combat. So defining was it that it was even dramatized in *The Damned United* feature film. In so many ways it was what was expected of the output of the station: 'must-watch television'.

This philosophy began in week one of the channel's life in July 1968 when, ridiculous as it may seem now, YTV broadcast live coverage of an England/Australia test match from Headingley. It didn't make a huge impression. But there it was sitting proudly in the schedule as a marker for what the station aspired to.

In 1972, by contrast, what was to be an iconic series began – *Indoor League*. Former Yorkshire and England fast bowler Fred Trueman presented a pub games competition that captured the imagination of the viewing public. Darts, arm wrestling, bar billiards, shove ha'penny and skittles were among the events that attracted pub devotees from around the country. It was the brainchild of Sid Waddell, the Cambridge-educated man of the people, whose association with darts would continue for the rest of his career. His casting of Trueman as host was a masterstroke; the cricketer's no-nonsense style and acerbic wit ('This arm wrestler makes Charles Atlas look like a pocket map'), and his regular sign off ('Ah'll si'thee') gave the show its northern ring. *Indoor League* ran for five years and was instrumental in the rise of darts as a television sport.

The early years of YTV weren't the easiest to make programmes in; strong unions like the ACTT and the ETU often made it difficult to produce shows economically, and outside broadcasts were no exception, as they were heavily manned. I remember a referee at a snow-covered Hillsborough football ground, who had been brought in to do a pitch inspection on the Friday morning for a Saturday game, being asked by one of the electricians to delay his decision to call the game off until after midday, as this would mean the crew could claim an overnight allowance.

Nevertheless, with just one commercial channel in existence, ITV was a money-making machine and, to their credit, programme production was a priority. In the '60s and '70s, Sunday afternoon regional football highlights were the cornerstone of every region. At YTV, under Head of Sport Lawrie Higgins, there were plenty of teams to choose from: Leeds United, Sheffield United and Wednesday, Middlesbrough, Bradford City, Huddersfield Town and Hull City were among the seventeen Football League clubs in our region. The BBC and ITV cartel, who successfully negotiated with football's authorities, secured both League and FA Cup matches which were shown in the ITV regions, providing a real service to the viewers. But this was an era when, unlike today, there had been next to no live football on TV; the FA Cup Final, World Cups every four years and England internationals were the only significant live games at that time.

Every region had its own commentator, and for YTV Keith Macklin was behind the microphone for much of the '70s, followed by Martin Tyler and then John Helm. Being a regional commentator meant you had every chance of going to World Cups and European Championships and broadcasting to the nation. In those days, the professionalism of the commentator didn't always coincide with that of the director. During one game at Rotherham a relatively inexperienced Tyler repeatedly called for a close-up of a particular player so that he could make reference to him.

After the last request he heard the director in his headphones say to his production assistant, 'If Tyler doesn't shut up I'm going to go up on the gantry and smash this bottle of Whyte & Mackay's right over his head.'

The close-up never came. That same director was seen one evening in the car park at YTV trying to get into his car but failing abysmally because he was attempting to unlock the rear passenger door rather than the driver's.

A helpful colleague suggested that he was in no fit state to drive home, to which he slurred, 'I'm not going home, I'm off to direct *Pro-Celebrity Darts.*'

Football didn't totally dominate the schedule; live Roses cricket, highlights of show jumping from the Great Yorkshire Show and the Yorksport Sportsman of the Year Dinner were all regular fare. Interest in sport was unswerving. In 1977 when the Queen came to Yorkshire as part of her Silver Jubilee celebrations, her visit coincided with the resignation of Don Revie as England manager to go to the Middle East to coach the United Arab Emirates; that edition of *Calendar* recorded its highest rating ever with a TVR of 50 – unheard of in regional TV and testimony to the trust and affection those viewers had in their local news provider.

In the mid-eighties, sport at YTV moved under the umbrella of local programmes completely, and one of its first responsibilities was to reflect the climax of the 1985 Football League season. The most successful team in the region at the time was Bradford City, who were the only club in a position to gain promotion or win honours. At the time the televised fixtures had to be chosen, City looked as though they might secure the 3rd Division title on the last day of the season,

Peter Jones joined the company from LWT's World of Sport. He trained a fresh generation of young directors, recruited from a wide variety of programme departments. (Danuta Skarszewska)

John Helm was the company's football commentator and sports contributor for 30 years. Over the years, he has commentated on 25 different sports in 80 countries. (John Helm)

so the match against Lincoln City, another side from the region, at Bradford's Valley Parade was selected as YTV's fixture for a local highlights programme. As it happened, Bradford had already secured the title by 11 May, but it was still to be a day of celebration.

It started like most others: the production team had a meeting to discuss how the programme would look and what would go in it, the running order was done, interviews were arranged and the pre-match events were discussed. The crew went for lunch, and we relaxed, knowing everything was under control from our point of view.

Peter Jones was the director; he had covered many football matches and was an outstanding live outside broadcast director. Not only that, he had made network television documentaries in every continent of the world. He was a colossus in the industry, but you wouldn't know it – he was just a humble Welshman, who shunned the limelight and just got on with being the best at what he did. Commentator John Helm did his final research, spoke to players and staff of the teams as they arrived to find out what the line-ups were and gathered any last-minute news. John was synonymous with Yorkshire sport; everyone knew him and loved him, his contacts were unparalleled and he was the ultimate professional. Helmy was the man you would most want to go for a pint with to talk about sport. He struggled to walk around the Headingley boundary during a Test Match without being stopped every few yards by someone who knew him or someone who wanted to know him; there was nobody with greater respect as a sports broadcaster in the region.

Graham Ironside, the Head of local programmes was there that day; sport had become part of his stable, and this hugely experienced journalist, who had been the engine in the news room under John Wilford's leadership for many years, now had a much wider brief. The atmosphere was calm; it was a warm May afternoon as we prepared to start recording events, ready to edit them later that evening into a one-hour programme to be transmitted on Sunday afternoon.

The Bradford City players came out of the dressing rooms slightly early to a wonderful welcome from over 11,000 fans, and Peter Jackson, the club captain, was presented with the 3rd Division trophy. Great excitement and joy flowed around the stadium; Bradford were the champions and would play in Division II the following season with the likes of Leeds United, Sheffield United and Middlesbrough – the club was on the up.

The game kicked off at 3.00 p.m., and it was clear that this wasn't going to be a classic, as the first half was devoid of incident. There had been very little of note to force its way into the highlights programme as the half drew toward its conclusion.

This was the first time the new sports department had visited Valley Parade to cover a game, and so a couple of weeks earlier Peter Jones and the Outside Broadcast supervisor had visited the ground to check where the camera positions should be. The ground was unusual because it was built on the side of a hill, as its name suggests, which meant that the ideal side to cover the match from was opposite the main stand looking back into it. This required building a scaffolding platform above the tiny Midland Road stand and parking the OB vehicles behind it in the road. Two cameras were to be positioned on the scaffold gantry to provide the main coverage of the match, with one in front of them at ground level to pick up close-ups of the players. In addition to these three, there was a second camera scaffold tower behind the right hand goal and another camera at ground level behind the left hand goal. This was all far from the current level of coverage, where twenty-five cameras for a live Premier League game would be a minimum. Had someone told Peter Jones on that day of the survey that he was to cover the tragic events that were to come, he would have put his cameras in exactly the places he had planned to cover the football from.

At this time football was trying to embrace a new era of commercialism, and after much wrangling, sponsorship had become accepted on players' shirts by the TV companies in 1983, after denying them exposure up until then. However, the agreement with the clubs was that the 32-square-inch shirt logos had to be reduced by half for all televised games. Bradford City's shirts complied, but Lincoln City's didn't. So, a few minutes into the game, noticing their oversized sponsorship, I left the OB truck to walk around the outside of the ground into the main stand to speak to the Chairman of Lincoln City and ask why they weren't wearing the appropriate kit. It soon became apparent that there was very little hope of solving the problem. Did they have their television kit with them? No. Did they actually have one? No. Would they change to a kit without advertising on it at half-time? No.

'Now would you leave me alone, because I'm trying to watch a football match?'

So here was a dilemma. Lincoln City were breaking the rules which had been the subject

Probably the worst disaster ever covered by the *Calendar* team: the Bradford City stadium fire. Fifty-six people died and more than 250 were seriously injured.

of much heated debate over the previous five years, with some clubs being boycotted by the TV companies for refusing to stick to the agreement. I needed some advice. In the days before mobiles, the only quick way of having a conversation was to go to the secretary's office and use his phone. His office was situated in the corner of the main stand, and he could see the pitch and much of the stadium from a large window. He was sitting watching the game. Having explained to him what the problem was, I rang Jeff Foulser at LWT, who was editor of *The Big Match*, and explained my predicament.

'Not much you can do,' was the answer.

Just as I finished the phone call and looked out of the window, the Bradford secretary turned to me and said, 'I think I can see some smoke coming from the other end of the stand.'

We both looked, and agreed – something wasn't right. My first thought was to return to the scanner and tell Peter Jones about it, so I headed out of the office on to the road running along the back of the stand behind the goal and along the Midland Road to where the OB trucks were parked. Breathless, I reached the steps and pulled open the heavy door into the production area of the vehicle. As I looked in, ready to tell my news, I saw the transmission monitor had a wide shot of the stand engulfed in flames. I just couldn't believe it; after such a short time the whole of the side was alight. They said it took three minutes, less than the time it takes to boil an egg, for all of it to catch fire. And there was Peter directing coverage of a major tragedy, when a few minutes earlier he had been directing a football match. John Helm, who had been commentating on a match, was now the voice who had to speak over those harrowing pictures.

It would have been so easy for a broadcaster to find himself lost for words, out of his depth and falling into the trap of saying something inappropriate. John, with his sensitivity and journalistic ability, provided a moving, emotional soundtrack to the pictures that none of us believed we were watching. Bradford was John's home town, making his task even harder; he realized there would be people he knew trapped in the blazing inferno as he described what unfolded in front of him.

Not everyone knew what John was doing as he sat on his gantry and tried to describe what was happening before him. As spectators flooded on to the pitch, some of them could see him speaking into his microphone and thought it was wrong. He began to be stoned from the pitch by some young men who just didn't understand what was going on.

As we know, it all happened so quickly, and there came a point when we had to decide

how this news and the pictures of the horror that had unfolded were to reach the general public. The events were being recorded on videotape in the OB truck; it was not live transmission, so the pictures weren't going anywhere and could not be sent via any link either. A tape had to be taken to YTV studios in Leeds to be played out on the ITV network.

Bill, the videotape engineer, had come to the game on his motorbike and volunteered to race back to Kirkstall Road studios. From there the pictures were played out to LWT and transmitted on the live Saturday afternoon sports show, *World of Sport*. I don't think the editor of the programme, Andrew Franklin, quite believed what was unfolding as he got Dickie Davies to link into the harrowing footage.

Now all the news agencies were alerted, the pictures were being used by all the news bulletins across the country and the world and Valley Parade was a picture of devastation. The dead and injured were being taken away to the mortuaries and hospitals, and we left the scene at about 6.30 p.m. in stunned silence. We didn't know what the casualties were; the police weren't releasing any numbers at all.

On my return, when I walked through the front doors of YTV, the phone was ringing on the reception desk. The security man answered it and handed it to me, saying, 'It's for you.'

It was an officer from the West Yorkshire Fire Brigade who said, 'Whatever you do, don't wipe the videotapes of that fire. You don't realize how unique and valuable they will be.'

That was the beginning of days of emotion and anguish in Bradford, the region and the world. Everyone seemed to know someone or be related to someone or just know someone else who knew someone who had died. The grief was palpable. We had been going about our jobs, they had been going to enjoy a football match, and it ended in tragedy.

Peter Jones and John Helm won awards for their work from the Royal Television Society. Over £3.5m was raised through the appeal fund to help the families and survivors, but nothing could bring back the fifty-six who lost their lives that day. I hope it still applies at YTV today, but we immediately stopped using the word 'tragedy' to describe someone scoring an own goal or some other sporting mishap, or that awful expression 'he's on fire' for a particularly good streak of performances. We had found some perspective in our coverage of sport, through the most hideous of lessons.

It took a long time for the shadow of the fire to leave us, and we were the lucky ones. We mercifully didn't lose loved ones, but there was still the reminder of that terrible day as the enquiry progressed, stories emerged about the survivors fighting to rebuild their lives and the pointing of the finger of blame continued.

Slowly, for us, things returned to some sense of normality, and sport, like life, continued. The Sports department expanded, and we were joined by Brendan Foley and Nick Collins, while Dawn Carrington looked after us all like a mother. Life was beginning to become fun as we produced more and more programming. Nick Powell joined the group as part of a new rugby league series called *Scrumdown*. Rather like a *Match of the Day*-style programme, we sent an OB unit

to a game on a Sunday and at 11.30 p.m. that evening showed the highlights.

Never had a sport been so welcoming. We were able to enjoy unprecedented access and treated the game with the respect it deserved, rather than the 'music hall' badge that the BBC's treatment wore. John Helm was the commentator, and his co-commentator was the former Welsh rugby union star David Watkins, who had changed codes to join Salford. Some way into the series, we made our first visit to Post Office Road to cover a Featherstone Rovers home game; we had our production meeting and then went across to the Railway Tavern, which was rocking, where they had laid on pie and peas for us. Watkins was not himself, he was anxious. Asked why he looked so concerned, he said he hadn't been back to Featherstone since the first time he played here for Salford after his big money transfer north. He recalled that early in the game he was unceremoniously dumped to the floor by three very large Rovers forwards.

As he came round, semi-conscious, he looked up at the three of them gazing down at him, and one of them helpfully suggested, 'Twinkle, twinkle, little star'.

He just could not get that anxiety about returning out of his system. He was right. On cue, an enormous punch-up started in the pub between a husband and wife, who were dragged into a back room amidst shouting, screaming and flying beer. All his worst fears were confirmed.

Even though the programmes were only shown in Yorkshire, we even crossed the Pennines to feature Yorkshire sides on their travels or to show big games like St Helens v Wigan. When we ran a competition we always got entries from Lancashire, as stories abounded of rugby league fans there retuning their aerials to get YTV. On one such trip to Oldham the delights of the social club almost put a spanner in the works of the coverage. With five minutes to kick-off, Peter Jones was heard on talk back imploring his Camera 2 cameraman to talk to him; another voice piped up suggesting he was still in the club helping the stripper rub baby oil into her chest! Oldham was an interesting place for pre-match pies too; the choices were beef, steak & kidney and meat. Most people steered clear of 'meat'.

In 1989 the programme won the Royal Television Society award for Best Outside Broadcast. Years before the introduction of dedicated sports awards, it had to fight off competition from the BBC's *Trooping the Colour* and an underwater OB from Eilat. The show featured highlights of the Yorkshire Cup Final between Leeds and Castleford, which had contained some fantastic tries and given us the chance to produce an award-winning programme. Then, as we headed successfully into the 1990s, the rug was pulled from under our feet as the rugby league did a deal with Sky, and *Scrumdown* was no more.

However, we did break new ground with a football show called *Goals on Sunday* (thanks to Richard Whiteley for that title). With so many teams in our region, it seemed like a good idea to put a compilation of Saturday's matches together on a Sunday just before lunchtime. It featured some extended highlights of one game followed by the goals from all the rest. The trick was going to be getting the clubs to agree to it. Putting a two-camera OB into a ground could have led to demands for a fee that would make the half-hour programme too expensive. The man who made it happen was Don Robinson, at the time Chairman of Hull City.

He said, 'Tell everyone that you already have agreement from me and that will give them the chance to follow' – which of course they did.

So it was to Boothferry Park for the first programme and the beginning of a very successful run. On 11 February 1990, as the whole of the ITV network waited on a wide shot of a door for the appearance of Nelson Mandela leaving prison, YTV were playing *Goals on Sunday*. Of course, Mandela kindly waited for the programme to finish before he appeared.

With Sky threatening to take most football away from ITV and the BBC, we began to diversify internationally. We made the *Energiser World Cup Power Play* football series for distribution around the globe to preview Italia 90, and covered the Hampton Classic Horse Show on Long Island and the Bermuda Classic Rugby Tournament regularly during the nineties. Our cricket coverage of the Scarborough Festival grew, and with what now seems great prescience, we ran a series of *City Centre Cycling*, closing down city centres in Sheffield, Leeds, York, Bradford, and Lincoln on a Friday night.

By the mid-nineties the domination of pay TV was apparent, football's Premier League had been formed and so had rugby league's Super League. Those two sports would no longer provide a full offering to the ITV regions, and although there were still some Football League Cup opportunities for a while, and the award winning *Rugby League Raw* programme came to YTV and went to the BBC in the early 2000s, regional sport coverage was to be a thing of the past. It was no longer financially viable to send out big OB units to cover expensive sports; the pay TV broadcasters had found the goose to lay the golden eggs, which they continue to exploit to this day.

No region in the country likes to celebrate its own like this one, but sadly the opportunities to do so no longer exist. The erosion of sport on ITV can clearly be traced back to the days when they turned their backs on their regions and decided that a one-size-fits-all policy would work.

How wrong could they be, as viewers turned their backs on the homogenised offerings, and in the words of Fred Trueman, said, 'Ah'll si'thee.'

Chapter 16

Talking of Sid Waddell

(Sid Waddell)

Back in the *Calendar* office, in spite of the demands of the daily transmission of news, ideas continued to bubble out in a steady flow, writes Graham Ironside. The source, more often than not, was the Geordie, Sid Waddell. Yes, that Sid Waddell, the 'Voice of Darts' on the BBC and Sky TV.

Between producing features for the nightly programme and scribbling scripts for drama ideas, he constantly lobbied to make a series based on the pub games of his far-from-misspent youth. In spite of his outstanding academic achievements, including a degree from Cambridge, Sid clung grimly to his working class roots, his North-East heritage, his telly-for-the-people beliefs. He foresaw a great future for a programme based on the pastimes of the people with whom he had spent his formative years. His persistence paid off then; and indeed, as viewers of Sky Sports well know, it continues to pay off to this day, in the form of the Ladbrokes.com World Darts Championships, among others. *The Times*, no less, in a fine tribute article to Sid after he died, memorably called it 'inadvertently ground-breaking'.

As always, it grew from the informal, innovative, intuitive atmosphere in which the youthful YTV producers worked in the early days. Sid made his big bid at a meeting in the office of Donald Baverstock. Today it would be termed 'a brainstorming session', but in 1973 it was a casual meeting which just happened over a few cans of Double Diamond at the end of the working day.

One of Sid's pastimes from his days in the Miners' Welfare, as he described it to Donald, was shove ha'penny, a game based on the delicate skill of 'skipping' coins over a tabulated scoreboard; slightly like one-dimensional bowls, it was always played in the back room

Sid Waddell (right) with Terry Ricketts, sound recordist. (Terry Ricketts)

of the pub. His bid sparked something in Donald's mind, and his imaginative vision swiftly drew a bigger picture. From his young days in the Rhondda Valley, Donald knew of the enthusiasm for shove ha'penny in working men's clubs. He'd seen the enthusiasm for darts when a tournament organized by the *News of the World* was shown on ITV's *World of Sport*. But he needed more ideas ... and so, researchers were dispatched.

Back they came with more ideas and suggestions – pool, bar billiards, skittles, table-football, women's darts, arm-wrestling – all vigorously pursued in small pockets all over Yorkshire and, indeed, Britain and, significantly, usually vigorously accompanied by competition-level beer drinking.

Thus the basic elements were put in place, but how to present them to the public? Sid was not one to entertain self-doubt for long and set out the scenario: a lively (meaning 'boozy') venue; a host of personalities; a lot of action; a crowd of excitable fans; and commentators capable of creating a frenzy of enthusiasm. And he hit the jackpot.

First, the venue – the recently-opened Irish Centre in the York Road in Leeds. A popular gathering place for the socially-minded, and thirsty, inhabitants of that part of Leeds, it already staged numerous entertainments every week and thus had experience of coping with crowds and dealing with those who occasionally became over-excited in the later hours of the evening. It was particularly popular with members of the construction industry when rain stopped play for the day. There they could re-plan their work schedules, or plan a punt at the bookies, over a pie and a pint, without the restrictions of the licensing hours which limited drinking in pubs in those days.

In fact, the bar did close for an hour between 5.00 and 6.00 in the afternoon, to allow the cleaners time to carry out their duties, but clients with sufficient foresight were able to order enough in advance to see them through the one-hour period of drought. Sid swore he once heard a customer in the crush ahead of him at the crowded bar at about 10 minutes to 5.00, ordering 81 pints.

When Sid raised a quizzical eyebrow, it brought the unapologetic explanation: 'Well, there's nine of us.'

The personality all but fell into his lap. Fred Trueman, Yorkshire's legendary fast bowler, had recently retired but was making heavy weather of his attempt at a new career as a stand-up comedian. He was signed up as the presenter, armed with no more than a pint glass, the pipe which seldom left his hand, a cardigan and a craggy smile. His scripts were written by Sid and his fellow commentator, Dave Lanning, at the time the highly skilled *TV Times* writer and commentator on a wide variety of sports. The amalgamation of the volatile talents of the two wordsmiths sparked off a reaction akin to phosphorus hitting water, as admiringly noted in the aforesaid *Times* article.

Fred was given a sign-off for the end of each programme which became a catch-phrase (Sid later called it Yorkshire gobbledy-gook) – 'Ah'll si'thee.'

In one introduction, Sid colourfully promised the viewers, 'We've got potters and slotters, twiddlers and nudgers.'

One arm-wrestler with an inclination to trendiness – bleached hair and wearing tailored denim in the Irish Centre! – was described as 'the Narcissus of the knotted knuckles'.

Alas, Fred never fully mastered the skill of reading the auto-cue and introduced him as 'the nancy boy with the knotted knuckles'. To the end, he insisted that misreading was entirely accidental.

The series was entitled *The Indoor League* and it ran, first in the YTV region only and then on the whole ITV network, from 1973 until 1978, attracting audiences of 5.5m.

Marcus Berkmann's tribute to Sid in *The Spectator*

Was there life before darts? I am old enough, just about, to remember such a time. One minute, in or around 1978, there was no darts on TV. Next minute, there was nothing else, and Eric Bristow, if he had felt inclined to stand, would have been elected prime minister by a landslide. As with snooker, the glory years of mass popularity were but brief, but once established as the chosen sporting endeavour of people who don't like moving too quickly, darts retained a substantial fan base, and continues to thrive even in these slimmer and more austere times. There really is something to be said for a sport whose greatest exponent, Phil 'The Power' Taylor, looks like a man who has sat on the same bar stool every night for 35 years, eating pork scratchings and sounding off about *Top Gear*.

And the man primarily responsible for all this wasn't a player or an administrator. It was the commentator Sid Waddell, an excitable Geordie whose nuclear-powered enthusiasm and surreal turn of phrase placed him at the peak of his profession in the 1980s and '90s. It is no exaggeration to say that many of us watched the darts mainly to hear what Sid would say next. Most commentators these days, on every sport, are former practitioners, and while their expertise is undoubtedly greater than the journalist-fan types who used to get these jobs, they tend to lack their flair and, crucially, that tinge of madness that separates the great from the merely good. Waddell had more than a tinge. He died in 2012, a day after his 72nd birthday. Darts has never been the same since.

Dan Waddell, son of Sid, has written a memoir of his father, full of humour and life and wonderful stories. Sid, he says, was:

> a self-confessed bighead and the source of his cockiness was his upbringing. Though he was born into spit and coal dust, he was lavished with the sort of attention earls and barons would die for.

Of that lucky postwar generation for whom social mobility was not just possible but actively encouraged, he went to Cambridge, where he was patronised more by the college servants than by his contemporaries.

Graduating with no strong idea of what he wanted to do, he drifted into television, as was actually possible in the early 1960s, and made quirky documentary films before inventing *The Indoor League*, in which overweight, slightly polluted middle-aged men played pub games such as table football and cheese skittles under the watchful eye of Fred Trueman.

'Ay up,' said Trueman, holding a pint of bitter, and 'I'll si'thee.'
It was one of the strangest programmes ever conceived, and Sid wrote the script.
'I don't talk like this,' said Trueman, when the first episode was being recorded.
'You do now,' said the executive producer.

The Indoor League showcased the distinctive Waddell prose style for the first time. A crack shove ha'penny player was 'the Spassky of the sliding small change'. When Sid started commentating on darts in 1978, riding shotgun to Dave Lanning, he was more tentative, but the classical allusions and wild metaphors could not be suppressed forever. Eric Bristow against Bobby George in the 1980 final was 'like having a ringside seat at the Colosseum'. Of Keith Deller in 1983, 'he's not the underdog, he's the underpuppy.' When Bristow met Dave Whitcombe in the 1985 semi-final, silence reigned. 'You could hear the drip off a chip,' said Sid.

Drink features prominently in this tale. Although Sid was always scrupulously sober behind a microphone, the participants weren't. Jocky Wilson was so drunk after a heavy defeat that he got Sid in a headlock while repeatedly telling him that he loved him.
'I love you too, Jocky,' said Sid, while being strangled. But he could never say over the air that players had had a few. Only that they were 'overpsyched' or, best of all, 'guilty of over-preparation'.

Sid's fans were legion, and sometimes unexpected. On one occasion Stephen Fry shared the commentary box. Phil 'The Power' Taylor was playing and, as usual, winning.
'Once upon a time he was breaking all records,' said Sid. 'Now he's only breaking all hearts. Nothing you can do, total eclipse of the dart.'
'Ah, Bonnie Taylor,' sighed Fry.
There were, says Dan, a few things Sid was unable to walk past: a pub, someone seeking an autograph, a shop selling Cornish pasties. He baulked at any hint of pretension. 'I've never eaten yoghurt in me life,' he once told his son with great pride. His favourite novel was Saul Bellow's *Henderson the Rain King*. Like many performers he was insecure and paranoid, and like many writers he never learned to drive. He was extraordinarily gifted and much loved. Dan's book is hootingly funny, deftly structured, a joy to read and highly recommended.

Chapter 17

Meet the Stars

With Graham Ironside

The staff at YTV understandably grew somewhat blasé about the presence of some of the greatest names in entertainment as they appeared regularly in and around the studios. It wouldn't be out of the ordinary to queue up in the canteen behind Dame Vera Lynn, Patricia Hodge or Barbara Dickson. Indeed, the semi-permanent staff of *Emmerdale* became another gang of mates and colleagues. Jean Rogers, Frazer Hines, 'Amos & Mr Wilkes', all became a familiar presence. Leonard Rossiter, Frances de la Tour, Richard Beckinsale, Don Warrington, Gwen Taylor, Keith Barron, James Bolam, Peter Bowles, Richard Wilson, Nanette Newman – a veritable *Who's Who* of television all came to Leeds.

Some superstars, however, just brought the whole building to a standstill. David Essex, at his peak, had that effect when he appeared on *Calendar* one night. By the afternoon the studio and reception area were uncommonly busy with young female staff, and by the time he tried to get into his limo to leave, the main drive and part of Kirkstall Road was choked with excited fans fighting for autographs.

When Dame Shirley Bassey and Elaine Page arrived in the studios to rehearse,

A personal souvenir photograph from Nanette Newman for Rod Lofthouse, the sound recordist on the series, at the end of shooting *Stay with Me Till Morning* for Yorkshire TV in 1981. The message reads: 'To Rod. Aren't YTV sound men wonderful? Much Love, Nanette.' The feelings were mutual, to say the least, since she was one of the most popular stars with YTV production teams. Having appeared in her first film at the age of eleven, she starred in more than twenty big-screen productions, many of them directed by her husband, Bryan Forbes, whom she met on a film set when she was seventeen. They were married for 58 years. *Stay with Me Till Morning*, based on the novel by John Braine and adapted for television by him, was transmitted in three 1-hour episodes in 1981. (Rod Lofthouse)

Shirley Bassey. (Shutterstock)

Catherine Zeta-Jones in a thoughtful moment on Folkestone beach, studying her part as Mariette in *The Darling Buds of May*. (Darren C. Miller)

all work stopped. Every office with a TV monitor was switched to the studio output and everyone watched.

However, one of the biggest show-stopper occasions took place not in a studio, but in a brand-new hi-tech sound-dubbing theatre, the company's biggest investment for years. Brilliant as the new facility might have been, it was far from being the main attraction.

That came in the form of a certain comely young actress appearing in a new series which had just started production, *The Darling Buds of May*. The downing of tools that day had nothing to do with union disputes – and it was remarkable how many males found a desperate need to become thoroughly acquainted with the working of a sound dubbing suite.

Big stars seemed to love being out of London and, more often than not, became enamoured of the atmosphere in the studios and of the county in which they were based.

Gerald Harper was a self-confessed example. He was cast in Yorkshire's first attempt at a soap opera, as the owner of a local newspaper called *Gazette*. The initial approach from Yorkshire was rather tentative:

'It would mean coming to Yorkshire … probably having to live in Yorkshire for a time.'

Replied Harper, 'I accept NOW!'

When he arrived and was shown to 'his' dressing room he found there was, in the entire building, but one such facility, which he had to share with, on his left, a newscaster being made up for that night's *Calendar* and, on his right, a clown preparing for a children's programme in a neighbouring studio.

Although *Gazette* never became the success YTV anticipated, he nevertheless was Actor of the Year in 1969 and moved seamlessly into a new series, revamped and re-titled *Hadleigh*. It then ran for another seven years, pulling audiences of 17m at its peak.

Looking back, Gerald Harper still warms to the memories of working at Yorkshire TV: 'I loved it. Nice place, nice people. Magical.'

Dame Thora Hird all but needed a season ticket for the train from London to Leeds.

Nor did she limit her comedy lines to the studio production. One night, as she prepared to record an episode of *In Loving Memory*, she was casually chatting to the audience during a break when she spotted her press officer, a quiet, self-effacing young man, sliding discreetly into a seat in the bleachers.

'Ooh, look everybody,' she said. 'There's Neil, my boyfriend in Leeds. Yoo hoo, Neil, love, have you fixed up everything for our dirty weekend in Blackpool?'

Some of the stars could be temperamental under pressure. Leonard Rossiter did not just rehearse until he got it right – he rehearsed until he couldn't get it wrong. But occasionally his steam valve blew. Rehearsing a *Rising Damp* sequence in the studio, Ronnie Baxter, the director, asked him to move his position slightly.

'Why? What's my motivation?'

Ronnie gently explained that he would be able to get a better picture.

LR erupted: 'Oh, it's all about pretty pictures, is it? Right, I won't get in your way.'

He then marched up to the back of the seating in the studios and there he sat seething, with arms folded until such time as he could be soothed and coaxed back on the set.

Chapter 18

David Taylor

(David Taylor)

Jimmy Young had seized his moment. Paul Fox was relaxing in the Radio 2 studio at Broadcasting House, having seen off a BBC bigwig in a live debate about television.

'I've always wanted to do TV,' said the veteran DJ.

Fox suggested they give it a try, and thus, from the womb of his successful and long-running morning radio show, was born *The Jimmy Young Television Programme*.

It was a difficult birth. Yorkshire's former newsroom supremo, John Wilford, was to head the project. A series of six one-hour programmes would replace *The South Bank Show* during its 1984 winter break. And what a slot – Sunday night immediately following the late ITN news. But would it work? Could the 1950s crooner handle TV?

Between music, Jimmy Young had made his name doing so-called 'soft' radio interviews with politicians of the day, Margaret Thatcher included. Reputedly, he was her favourite interviewer. His philosophy was that just as much could be elicited quietly as confrontationally. He had a loyal audience. In Kirkstall Road the hope was that those mid-morning listeners would become late night viewers.

The Jimmy Young Television Programme was part chat show, part current affairs. Each week, a major political figure, together with other specially selected guests, would face a studio audience. Jimmy would quiz the politician and chair the subsequent free-for-all. He glowed as he imagined the press coverage if someone spilled the beans. Would he get more space than David Frost on TV-AM or Brian Walden on LWT?

Little did Jimmy know of the coverage in store. The first intimation of trouble came with a telephone call from programme controller John Fairley. Apparently, the tetchy DJ had taken exception to John Wilford on a visit to Broadcasting House when Wilford put his feet on Jimmy's desk as they discussed the upcoming series. Shock horror! Fairley's solution was that I'd become Jimmy's producer in London, with Wilford editor of the core production team in Leeds.

I'd asked for one condition – that David Poyser, a colleague from YTV's science department, be his London-based researcher. Intelligent, hard-working, funny and charming, Poyser would be ideal with Jimmy.

Working lunches were fixed near Broadcasting House. Jimmy had two specific restaurants, no others. He dictated tables and seating and insisted his agent and minder, the long-suffering Jacquie Evans, be present. For meetings at YTV's London office, Jimmy ordered sandwiches of tinned salmon only. Private and ultra-conservative, he eschewed society yet craved exposure. In many ways, his foibles were endearing.

Jimmy rang me at home to thank me for 'rescuing' his TV debut. Having gained Jimmy's confidence, I found the confidence to broach the idea of a makeover. A new suit? A freshly woven toupée? After all, image was so important – and YTV would pay. A reluctant visit to Armani proved embarrassing. Whatever he tried on, poor Jimmy looked like a circus clown. Wardrobe relented and ordered yet another boxy suit from Jimmy's long-standing tailor.

The toupée was easier – commissioned from Simon Wigs of Bond Street. Jimmy was measured up. Hair-for-hair, the new toupée would match the old one. Alas, the hairpiece didn't make the first show because the man who was weaving it was ill and couldn't do the final cut.

Nevertheless, *The Jimmy Young Television Programme* launched with a scoop. Neil Kinnock, elected a few weeks earlier to lead the Labour Party, agreed to do his first major TV studio interview. A trailer was shot in London. Jimmy was seen slipping from 10 Downing Street, his beloved Margaret in residence. A sequence at Camden Market went less well, as stall holders heckled, 'Look, there's Jimmy Young and his wig!' Jim may have believed otherwise, but his crowning glory was so obviously false – and the nation knew it.

Winding up at Piccadilly Circus for a drink, Jimmy moved to my side at the bar and said, 'Let me stand close, you make me feel safe.'

A day or so later, the *Daily Star* ran the headline 'Keep Your Hair On, Jimmy!' Stafford Hildred, the *Star*'s TV 'insider', claimed a YTV technician had told him that high winds had whipped off Jimmy's toupée during the shoot. Complete fantasy. But the puns and hilarity began to build. Hildred appealed for witnesses to the 'hair-raising mystery' ('If you saw Jimmy lift his lid, do drop me a line'). The toupée threatened to become bigger than the man.

Next, Saatchi and Saatchi blasted ITV's winter line-up as mediocre. The agency said Jimmy would deter an upmarket audience because of his Radio 2 image. The production team closed ranks. Who cared about Saatchi? Jimmy was YTV's 'man of the people'.

The Saturday recording went smoothly enough. Kinnock, the man of the moment, delivered a polished performance – 'the envy of the Saatchi brothers themselves', wrote *The Times*. But somehow the show was too pat, over-prepared, sedentary. From the managing director's office Paul Fox ordained, 'Get him out of his chair, on to his feet.' Footwork and follow-up had been absent. Even Kinnock's 'revelation' that he still bought his suits at M&S was cued from an idiot board held up in the host's eyeline, Jimmy refusing point-blank to wear an earpiece.

Programme one rated well, and quotes from Kinnock made the headlines. 'You'll never keep it up,' chided a sceptic. The producers thought otherwise, while at TV-AM someone let slip to myself and Poyser that Frost was lining up Sinn Fein president Gerry Adams for an interview, his first in the wake of an IRA bombing at Harrods. Poyser hot-footed it to Northern Ireland and, picking his way through a minefield of security, secured Adams for Jimmy's second show. Adams would fly to Leeds to face the outrage of an English audience. Scoop!

For balance, two other politicians were booked – Conor Cruise O'Brien, the Irish minister responsible for banning Sinn Fein from the Republic's airwaves, and John Hume, founder of Northern Ireland's Social Democrat and Labour Party. Imagine the ratings!

But Jimmy would have none of it. Journalistic coup or no, he was not prepared to give Adams exposure on British TV. Jaws dropped. In a welter of meetings and phone calls Taylor and Poyser did everything they could to change Jimmy's mind. Up north, Wilford prepared a stand-by programme on the Pill. Appeals were made to programme boss Fairley, but he was powerless. After all, it was *The Jimmy Young Television Programme*. His name was up there, and Jimmy had the final say-so.

A last-ditch meeting was fruitless. Over his tinned salmon, Jimmy sat firm. The London producers conceded, privately accepting that JY wasn't really up to the relentlessly hard-line Adams. The team discussed a programme on contraception and checked Jimmy was going for his final toupée trim in Mayfair with the now recovered wig-weaver. So much for cutting edge current affairs. The TV series seemed set to be as bland and formulaic as the JY radio show. Forget ratings and press coverage.

Meanwhile, however, still smarting at his refusal to be interviewed, the *Daily Mirror* set their stalkers on Jimmy. As he emerged from Simon Wigs with his freshly cut toupée – snap! The picture and story filled the whole of page three on the Friday before the second show. 'Oh, Jim!' ran the headline, 'What Will Wogan Say When He Sees It?'

Terry Wogan was on holiday. Lucky Jim, because in the handover banter between their Radio 2 shows, Wogan invariably took a rise out of him. That morning JY was spared. But Wogan would be back on Monday!

An avalanche of tabloid coverage ensued, much of it fiction. Jim's wig was everywhere. Even the *Sunday Times* ran a couple of columns: 'The trouble with Young's toupée', ran the story, 'was that it was just too old.' YTV's make-up department had apparently thrown their hands up in horror when they saw it, uttering phrases like 'falling apart at the seams'. Again, nonsense. But the nation was agog – what would the new wig look like?

The man himself was not amused. 'I've never been stitched up like this in my life', Jimmy told me. Relations cooled. The

Pill programme passed virtually without comment, but the toupée story grew and grew. Said the *Daily Star*, 'It doesn't look very lifelike. Now the joke in the Leeds studios is that they're sprinkling Jim's shoulders with artificial dandruff to make it look real.' An entire wall of the London production office was filled with cuttings.

Come Monday morning and the radio handover with Wogan, Jimmy's tension was palpable. He jabbered twenty-to-the-dozen to smother the Irishman. Of course, the wig was never mentioned.

'How could he?' said Jimmy. 'He has one too.'

Amid the toupée turmoil, a *Sunday Times* report went unnoticed: David Frost had booked Gerry Adams for his Sunday show. But it was Jim who got the headlines!

Chapter 19

Simon Welfare

(Simon Welfare)

Two chance encounters changed my life. Actually three if we include, as of course we should, meeting the lovely young woman who became my wife. But since that is not a story for these pages, I'll go, as I so often had to when I was a *Calendar* reporter, struggling autocueless to deliver a piece to camera on some street corner, for another take (my record was 24).

Two chance encounters changed my *working* life. The first took place at a party in South London in 1967. I knew only one of the guests, a fellow student from university. We fell into conversation.

I asked her, 'What are you going to do when you leave?'

'Come on, Simon. You know I'm a medic, so you won't be surprised to hear that I'm going to be a doctor. What about you?'

'Not sure, but I rather fancy a job in the telly.'

'Well, Daddy's starting a TV station. You could try writing to the Programme Controller, Donald Baverstock. They're looking for a few people who'd be new to television.'

A few weeks later, I found myself sitting across the desk from Donald in an office in Portland Place, cunningly chosen, I assumed, so that BBC employees could sneak across incognito from Broadcasting House directly opposite.

Donald was not in a good mood. The pressures of ensuring that a brand new ITV station would be on the air in only a few months' time were clearly affecting him. I sat nervously on the edge of my chair waiting for the dark cloud to blow over so that the job interview could begin. Suddenly a career in television didn't seem such a good idea.

At last he looked up from his script-covered desk and, waving my curriculum vitae impatiently, threw me a question: 'It says here that you worked on your school magazine, a *weekly* magazine. What was that like?'

I took a deep breath, relieved that I had been given an easy start by the man who had famously invented the dark art of TV interviewing. But I never got the chance to answer. Instead, I had to duck as a huge ring binder, bursting with paper, whizzed past my ear.

'Sorry, boy,' Donald muttered, as it exploded on to the floor. 'They *will* keep sending me the corporate plan, and I can't abide it. Don't think it's got much to do with programme making. Anyway, I suppose you can have the job. Get a good degree and I'll see you after your finals.'

And that was it. It was not until I had gone down the stairs, past the symbolic but clearly unread copies of the *Yorkshire Post* in reception and out into the spring sunshine, that I wondered what I was actually going to do. And I realize now with gratitude that in my eleven years at Yorkshire Television I never really found the answer to that question. From the start, life in the Kirkstall Road, especially for me, *Calendar*'s most lowly reporter and later ITV's least qualified science producer, was intoxicatingly unpredictable.

And so I should not have been surprised when, one morning in late 1969, John Fairley stopped me in the wide corridor outside the *Calendar* newsroom, asked me what I was doing at lunchtime, announced that we were going to make the science documentary series promised in the company's franchise

Arthur C. Clarke, the prolific science fiction writer (extreme left), stands by as a Yorkshire Television crew prepare to shoot another episode in the series based on his novels. The British-born author, based in Sri Lanka, presented three series of 52 episodes between 1980 and 1994. Simon Welfare, the producer, lines up a shot, watched by, on the right, producer John Fairley and cameraman Peter Jackson. (Charlie Flynn)

application and whisked me off to York in his yellow Triumph Spitfire to meet a lecturer at the university who had some ideas for us.

Dr Deryck Goodwin was a man who suffered fools gladly, to my great relief. Only now, more than forty years on, will I confess that I did hardly any science at school and that I emerged from my one bamboozling year of physics having scored not a single mark. John cannily never volunteered his own science credentials, and in any case, after eighteen rather shaky months in television, I had at least acquired one vital skill: the ability to disguise my ignorance.

And so *The Scientists* was born. Desperately clutching Goodwin's 'science-for-dummies' crib sheets, I found myself discussing reinforced plastics with the inventors of carbon fibre, being mesmerised with disgust at a squirming colony of rats revealed beneath a sheet of corrugated iron on a Manchester building site, missing every ferry on the west coast of Scotland as we investigated the then new science of fish farming and, for *The Science of Sport,* a rather desperate bid to appeal to an ITV audience, asking a bemused football legend, the Manchester United midfielder and hero of England's 1966 World Cup-winning team Nobby Stiles, to explain exactly what made him such a terrifying player (the unscientific reason was thought to be his tendency not to wear his false teeth on the pitch).

Somehow, fuelled by adrenalin usually generated by panic, and juggling our time between our day-to-day duties on *Calendar,* we delivered each programme just in time for

Duncan Dallas, an Oxford chemistry graduate, joined Yorkshire at the start of transmission in 1968 from the BBC, where he had trained as a producer. After producing several documentaries he began to specialise in Science Features and created a new department. He recruited a highly innovative team of researchers and directors, with the aim of creating a high level of public interest in scientific topics, succeeding with series like *Don't Ask Me, Don't Just Sit There* and *Just Amazing.* His team of resident experts, Rob Buckman, Miriam Stoppard, Magnus Pyke and David Bellamy, became popular and influential presenters. (Adam Hart-Davis)

transmission in a slot all too clearly reserved for 'franchise fodder', opposite *Match of the Day* late on a Saturday night. The critics were respectful and even enthusiastic about our efforts, but audiences were small. Not even my own nearest and dearest watched, as I discovered to my chagrin. One night they dutifully settled down to view a programme that I was rather proud of: it was about lasers, then cutting-edge technology, and featured the amusing Nobel prize winner Arthur Schawlow demonstrating his invention's weird ability to pierce one balloon inside another while leaving the outer one intact. When the final credits rolled, no one moved. The silence of my home-grown audience, I realized, was not a sign of rapt attention; they had been asleep from the off. Somehow, at the very moment that the end-caption hit the screen they awoke, dutifully muttered 'Well done' and headed off to bed.

The following year, 1971, we hit our stride, thanks in no small measure to the emergence from the smoke in Tony Essex's documentaries office of Duncan Dallas. Duncan actually knew some science. In fact, he knew an awful lot of science and had a top-class degree from Oxford to prove it. He brought a unique blend of knowledge, intellectual rigour and lightness of touch to the series. And he had a secret weapon: he could talk to scientists in their own language, and this made him fearless in running the gauntlet of secretaries and lab assistants to reach the most venerable researchers and thinkers on the planet.

One afternoon, I watched open-mouthed as he rang the double Nobel Prize winner Linus Pauling. Barely five minutes elapsed before the great physicist invited us to film him in California, and a week or two later off we went. The shoot, like so many in those joyful days when we thought a production manager was someone who worked in the clothing factory down the road and a budget something the Chancellor smuggled into the House of Commons in his battered red box, was quite an adventure.

Between interviews about the scramble for the 'double helix', in which Linus had played a key role, and his controversial belief that vitamin C taken in large doses would cure almost all the ills that flesh is heir to, we drove the spectacular Highway 1 between Los Angeles and San Francisco. But it was not all fun: at the Pauling ranch at Big Sur, I trod in a cowpat in a field after a family barbecue, slipped as I climbed over a stile and broke all the fingers of my right hand. I didn't dare tell Linus that the extra-large dose of vitamin C that he prescribed did absolutely nothing to ease the pain.

Duncan was an opportunist of the best possible kind. One afternoon, while we were passing the office of the legendary theoretical physicist, star lecturer and bongo drum player Richard Feynman at Caltech, Duncan decided on the spur of the moment to pop in and invite him to take part in a future programme. Feynman was nowhere to be seen, and we assumed that he had gone out to buy the groceries on the shopping list scribbled in the corner of an equation-covered blackboard. We left a message. Feynman called us back: he would meet us at his club the next day. This turned out to be a darkened room in downtown Pasadena, where we found the eminent physicist sitting on a stool drawn up to a stage on which a naked young woman was doing extraordinary things with a twenty-dollar bill. Apparently oblivious to this disconcerting backdrop, the great man listened to our stammered pitch and agreed to film with us when he visited his Yorkshire mother-in-law in Ripponden that Christmas. He kept his word, but I am afraid to say that I have clearer memories of the genesis of *Take the World from Another Point of View* than of the programme itself.

Other programme makers joined us. *Calendar*'s Rochdale alchemist Barry Cockcroft, never keen to stray far from his northern patch (though he graciously made an exception when offered a trip to Venice to make *The Heirs of King Canute*, a programme about flood control), turned the unpromising story of Lancashire County Council's 'greening' of old coal slag heaps into precious metal: a Silver Ear at the Berlin Agricultural Film Festival. And he only had to travel a few miles in a different direction to Wrightington to film a pioneering and rather gory hip transplant operation for the unimaginatively-titled *Rheumatism and Arthritis*. Those of us who had to watch the rushes understood all too well what Barry meant when he described the sequence as 'carpentry on humans'.[1] Bizarrely, although by then I should not have been surprised, Barry even contrived to film the master interview for another programme with a doctor who had achieved the unheard-of feat of curing an American boy of rabies, in the heart of the Yorkshire Dales, thousands of

---

1. The great unsung hero of our production team was our press officer Michael Crossley. Though famously squeamish, he volunteered to sit through the rough-cuts of our medical programmes. Whenever he announced he was feeling faint, the editor's scissors came out to adjust the sequence.

miles away from Willshire, Ohio, where the drama had unfolded.

From Education came the laid-back brainbox Hugh Pain, a man who never failed to complete *The Times* crossword in less than ten minutes over breakfast, to reveal, in *Urban Pests,* how scientists were facing the challenge of controlling the rats and pigeons that were colonizing and fouling Britain's cities. To my intense relief, since my command of numeracy is almost as non-existent as my talent for physics, Austin Mitchell, who along with Paul Dunstan had joined our ad hoc team, copped for Hugh's more cerebral offering, *For Amazement Only*, a show devised, according to its slightly desperate *TV Times* billing, to prove that 'mathematics is fun'. Flying serenely across France and Germany in a blimp for *The Return of the Airship*, also directed by the busy Hugh, was much more my line.

David Taylor brought a whirlwind of cheerful energy from the north; a good thing,

since, to begin with, he had to combine working for Yorkshire with another job, producing the weekly farming programme at Tyne-Tees. David's first contributions – *The Flesh Harvesters* and *Magnus and the Beansteak* – were born out of his deep knowledge of agriculture and food production, but soon he had imbibed enough of whatever it was in the canteen tea to embark upon more eccentric enterprises. *In a Monastery Garden*, which chronicled the work of an elderly monk who was attempting to breed the perfect honey bee, was perhaps more picturesque than informative, since Brother Adam, who was born in Germany, spoke little English. Even more bizarre was *An Experiment in Time*, in which we spent a week crouched over a specially adapted microscope to film Dr Janet Harker of Cambridge University painstakingly dissecting the sub-oesophageal ganglion of a rather large American cockroach. This was the site of the creature's biological clock – Janet was the first scientist to find one. I have no idea whether this game-changing work earned her any awards, but this unlikely film brought us one from the British Association for the Advancement of Science. As so often happened, the shoot was far less solemn than the programme: between takes Janet busied herself with snaffling the cockroaches that had escaped into her assistant's voluminous beard, and I contrived to ask a question 150 words long, which sent David rushing out into the corridor howling with laughter.

Not all the programmes were shot on location. Peter Jones, *Calendar*'s stalwart and unflappable director, presided benignly over studio shows such as *Mars – Now that the Dust Has Settled*. A TV version of a scientific slide

Cameraman Charlie Flynn puzzles out how to shoot a difficult operation while avoiding making it too grisly for viewers of *The Flesh Harvesters*. (Charlie Flynn)

show, this drew upon the extraordinary and revelatory 'album' of more than 7,000 close-up pictures of Mars being sent back at the time by NASA's Mariner 9 spacecraft. The pictures were shown to a group of experts, who included one of the twentieth century's great popularizers of science, Carl Sagan, on a giant eidophor screen; we thought that very smart, since NASA used one at mission control.

Here Comes the Sun, one of our more prophetic programmes, predicted the rise of renewable energy. Once again, the greatest dramas took place off-screen. The researcher who had landed the best trip – to a solar energy 'power station' in the French Pyrenees – crashed his car en route and fled home immediately without ever visiting the place. John Willis and I and our crew were entrusted with the trip: to the Marémotrice de la Rance, a tidal power station in France. Because we were in a hurry – we had, as usual, settled on the subject for the programme only a few weeks before transmission – we flew to Dinard in two small planes. The pilots left us to our filming and returned home in one, leaving the other behind. A few days later, we arrived at the airport to find them back but frantically turning out their pockets: they had left the key to the parked plane in Yorkshire. The local *serrurier* was summoned, and we flew off into the night. When we landed at Leeds/Bradford, John was greeted by his wife Janet. She looked rather pale. No wonder; she had taken a wrong turning in the dark and had found herself heading on to the runway.

By 1973, our science documentaries – *The Scientists* at some point had morphed into the slightly more enticing-sounding *Discovery* –

were an established and, we were told, valued part of the ITV schedule. In the autumn of that year, we set off to the United States for a shoot that sowed the seeds for the *annus mirabilis* that followed.

Yet again, we settled on our programme subjects very late in the day. David Taylor had spotted a curious story in the *New Yorker* about a young woman called Robin Bielski who, with the help of one of the pioneers of biofeedback, Dr Neal E. Miller, had learned how to control her blood pressure by thought alone. I, too, had been reading magazines and guessed (accurately) that a vivid account of a day in the life of the emergency room at Parkland Hospital, Dallas, the hospital to which President Kennedy was rushed after being shot, might make a dramatic film. Both turned out to be decent, even powerful documentaries, but in my mind they were eclipsed by the third one we shot during our month-long trip.

Duncan had been sent an advance copy of a book by a British neurologist living in New York, and no sooner had he read the blurb on its dust jacket than he was on the phone to its author. It's no exaggeration to say that in *Awakenings* Dr Oliver Sacks told a story that was stranger than fiction, odder and more disturbing even than one of the dark Grimms' fairy tales that it resembled. At Beth Abram Hospital, in New York, Sacks had come across a group of elderly patients who had been cared for there since contracting encephalitis lethargica, 'sleepy sickness', a mysterious illness apparently related to the flu epidemic that swept the planet at the end of the First World War. These now elderly men and women had lived out the decades mostly in a deep sleep, catatonic, barely waking, cut off in every sense from the outside world. In 1967 Sacks, fascinated and moved by their plight, decided to try to treat them with L-Dopa, then a new drug that had been developed to treat sufferers from Parkinson's disease. The results were astonishing: most of the patients awoke; they could move around; they remembered the songs popular when they were young.

But the 'resurrections' and the euphoria were brief, and Sacks could only watch as they sank back into their weird sleep. And that was how we found them when we walked into the ward. Duncan realized at once that we could not stick to the usual conventions of documentary making. Since we were allowed no lights, filming, he decided, would be in black and white. There would be no set-ups: we would simply shoot anything that happened and supplement what useable footage we managed to get, with a long interview with Sacks and his arresting home movies of the 'awakenings'.

And that is what we did. Every morning we turned up at Beth Abram and watched and waited. This was a place where even routine happenings seemed surreal. When a therapist threw a ball into the middle of the ward, some of the most 'frozen' patients sprang suddenly into action, rushing forward to catch it, before relapsing into their familiar catatonic stupor. Another sang me a verse of a Victorian parlour favourite, 'Love's Sweet Song', its words yearning for a lost past suddenly ineffably poignant:

Once in the dear dead days beyond recall,
When on the world the mists began to fall,
Out of the dreams that rose in happy
    throng

Low to our hearts love sang an old sweet
    song
And in the dusk where fell the firelight
    gleam
Softly it wove itself into our dream ...

Emotions felt on location do not always survive in the cutting room, but when we watched the finished film we knew we had made something special. Yet after its Saturday night transmission, silence fell. Only seventeen years later, when we saw the *Awakenings* movie, starring Robin Williams and Robert De Niro, did we discover that our documentary had not, after all, been forgotten. The director, Penny Marshall, had restaged scenes from it, meticulously, frame by frame.

'Flattering', was Duncan's verdict. 'And of course better lit.'

But in retrospect, it was the last week of this American shoot that had the most far-reaching consequences. There had long been vague talk of a science magazine programme, and we spent a dispiriting few days gathering short reports for a pilot. I only remember one: an interview with an ex-NASA employee called Abe Karen who had invented an 'instant' filler for potholes. A few weeks after our return, an editor called me into the cutting room to show me the very surprising result. I asked a question, Abe began his spiel, and then suddenly across the street behind him ran a man wildly brandishing a gun, followed by two of New York's finest. We had filmed this Keystone Cops moment on the last day of the shoot and had been too tired to notice the drama unfolding in the background.

That clip, to my great regret, was never shown, but neither was the magazine programme. We abandoned the idea after long discussions at the Monday morning talking-shops that Duncan ran in a genial but intellectually rigorous collegiate style. That was easy; far more difficult was to find something to replace it. But time was short; Paul Fox had already secured a slot. We cast around. One Saturday afternoon, I caught the last minutes of a phone-in on BBC Radio 4. The format was simple: children put their science questions – such as 'Why is the sky blue?' – to a group of scientists. To my surprise, I found it gripping: the experts were using the fundamental principles of science to explain the world around us and doing so in an entertaining way. Perhaps, I wondered aloud at our next meeting, we could somehow translate this simple idea into television. When someone suggested that we should take inspiration from popular Victorian science lectures and their spectacular demonstrations – Professor C.V. Boys FRS's extravaganza on soap bubbles, Henry Dircks' hair-raising Pepper's Ghost illusion and the great Michael Faraday's *The Chemical History of a Candle* – we breathed a sigh of relief. But not for long; we knew that hitting the right note in the Wednesday night slot that Paul had annexed for us – 'hammocked' between ITV's top-rated soaps *Crossroads* and *Coronation Street* – would prove a challenge.

Choosing a title for the show took another long meeting. Duncan, after rejecting all the producers' ideas, turned to our office secretary Sally Binks.

'Your idea, Sally?' he barked.

Sally thought for a moment, looked her boss straight in the eye and shrugged: 'Don't ask me, Duncan.'

David Bellamy with production assistant Angie Lavelle in Greenland, en route to film a programme entitled *Bellamy on Top of the World*, a study of icebergs in the Arctic. (Charlie Flynn)

And so it was that *Don't Ask Me* went into production. We raided the music library for a theme tune (*House of the King* by the Dutch band Focus), issued an appeal for questions and recruited a trio of experts: Dr David Bellamy of Durham University, Dr Miriam Stoppard, then research director of Syntex, makers of 'the Pill', and Dr Magnus Pyke, a retired food scientist and Secretary of the 'British Ass.', aka the British Association for the Advancement of Science. We recruited a talented and lively team of researchers: Gwen Singleton, Pauline Pogorelski and Val Zabels.

We cast actor Derek Griffiths as the presenter and he brought in Johnny Ball, who later did for children's maths with *Think of a Number* what *Don't Ask Me* did for general science, to contribute a few jokes. Duncan allocated the jobs: David Taylor would produce David Bellamy's answers, Kevin Sim took on Miriam's and I was assigned to Magnus. All we had to do then was to produce a hit show.

That summer, and in the four that followed, we lived on coffee, our wits and adrenalin as never before or, certainly in my case, since. The production schedule was punishing. On Wednesdays, tired out after recording the programme the previous day, David, Kevin and I leafed through the latest batch of questions sent in by the public and made a shortlist of those we thought we could answer. Not until we had faced a series of interrogations by Duncan that started on Thursday and invariably continued until late on Friday afternoon, could we finally settle on the items for the next programme to be recorded the following Tuesday and order the show's trademark larger-than-life props from designer Richard Jarvis and the ingenious and astonishingly long-suffering Alf and Ian Rowley. Their eyelids were definitely not for batting, even when I asked them to build, amongst other things, a giant zip, a model of the city of Königsberg, an Ames Room that played fascinating tricks with perspective or huge vats filled with custard for volunteers to run across, so that the show could, as one critic put it, go 'the extra mile with wild demonstrations of the scientific facts'.

Tuesdays, when the show was recorded, were an odd mixture of nightmare and exhilaration for all of us. First stop for me was the studio to check whether the props I had ordered would actually work, then off to the canteen to brief Magnus. He sat hunched over a scrap of paper on which, after a barrage of questions patiently answered by our endlessly cheerful and (thank goodness) knowledgeable researcher Val Zabels, he would map out his demonstrations on more tiny scraps of paper. The afternoon was spent wrestling with words and apparatus. The recording, presided over by the chirpy and resourceful David Millard, began at seven sharp, and as the minutes flew by, tension rose in the gallery; everything had to be in the can before, precisely at nine, the electricians pulled the plugs. Magnus, by contrast, grew more relaxed as the evening wore on, nodding off, between appearances, on the chair he always made sure was ready for him behind the set.

Don't Ask Me was a huge and instant hit. The presenters became overnight celebrities, Magnus, with his 'windmill arms', especially so. We knew he had 'arrived' when *New Scientist* asked its readers to name the best known and most characteristic scientist of all time and Magnus emerged top of the list of the living, trailing only Newton and Einstein in the overall table. But so relentless was the schedule that I remember little of those hectic summers beyond a few scattered moments: the gallery erupting when two sopranos managed to break a glass by singing a piercing note; Magnus yelling as he demonstrated inertia by breaking a broomstick with a poker and sent his false teeth flying across the set; a baby alligator biting a chunk out of David Bellamy's arm; a bemused visiting Australian tycoon, whose interest in some joint venture with Yorkshire Television may or may not have been bolstered by the sight of a studio

Magnus Pyke and his autobiography.

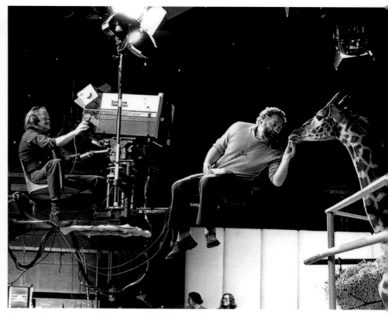

David Bellamy needed a special hoist to lift him high enough to make the acquaintance of this giraffe for *Don't Ask Me*. (Shutterstock)

containing, in one corner, half a dozen disconsolate penguins marooned on a block of ice, a giraffe in another and the aforesaid custard 'running track' in the middle. As *Don't Ask Me* soared higher in the ratings than any science programme on British TV before or since, the readers of *TV Times* voted it their favourite TV show, and Magnus – no ageism in broadcasting in those days – carried off another award for being the most promising newcomer to television.

Looking back, those long summer days seem surreal, but at the time we had no time to see ourselves as others saw us. Gwen picked up a call to the office from security saying quite calmly that 'there is a giraffe at Gate 2'; and Val remembers how Pauline was told to send a taxi all the way to Cambridge University to collect a 'Siamese' double banana.

In the winter months, after a break to recover, we continued to make documentaries, among them an appropriately strange and wonderful film about Tourette's syndrome and an equally curious profile of the American behavioural psychologist B.F. Skinner, who, it was said (unfairly), had brought up his children in a 'box'. Both were produced by Duncan, while Paul Dunstan somehow even managed to make a programme about concrete entertaining and contributed a riveting account of a woman who underwent a brain operation while still conscious. Kevin Sim, David Green and I found another extraordinarily affecting medical tale: *The Boy in the Bubble* told the poignant stories of parents and doctors who had to resort to extreme measures to keep alive children with little or no immunity to infection. Its 'stars' were a small boy from Texas called David Vetter, who had spent most of his life confined to a sterile plastic tent, and a British toddler, Anthony Nolan. Today, Anthony is the better known of the two, thanks to the charity founded in his name by his remarkable mother Shirley, but in 1975 David was the story. The PR operation at the hospital in Houston that cared for him was slick, and its response when I called them to ask if we could film their 'bubble boy' was uncompromising: virtually every journalist and TV network in the world had been chasing the story, and every request had been turned down, even, I was told, 'your BBC's'. But Duncan had taught us well: rebuffs from PRs should themselves be rebuffed. So I rang up David's doctor and, when he made mildly encouraging sounds, muttered something about happening to pass through Houston in the next few days. Wangling a ticket to Texas on a flimsy promise turned out to be the easy part, and so it was that the next day I found myself on a plane to Houston heading for my one and only world-wide scoop ...

We could, I imagine, have carried on making *Don't Ask Me* for years; by the beginning of 1979 there were still hundreds of questions left unanswered in the files that now threatened to overwhelm the office and our valiant secretaries. But after more than 60 episodes, we had had enough. He would, Duncan confidently assured an alarmed Paul Fox, find another hit.

'You must', Paul said. And Duncan did. Several more, in fact, including *Don't Just Sit There* and *Where There's Life*. But I played no part in them because I was researching an idea for a curious offspring

of *The Scientists* and *Discovery*. I had been struck by the number of times that, while the crew was wrapping after an interview, a scientist would produce a file from a drawer in their desk and rather sheepishly confess that they had been researching a mystery such as Stonehenge, UFO sightings or some example of unusually advanced technology from the ancient world. John Fairley was enthusiastic, which was why, while the others toiled in Studio 3, I was ensconced in the British Library at Boston Spa ordering up such yellowing rarities as *Ein galvanisches Element aus der Partherzeit?* (the definitive work on the 'Baghdad battery'), *Rains of Fishes* by E.W. Gudger, Samuel Lothrop's list of the Giant Balls of Costa Rica, and – this caused a *frisson* at the front desk – an article about UFOs by Timothy Ferris published in *Playboy* (the BL had duly wrapped it in brown paper). Meanwhile, Julie O'Hare stoically telephoned people who claimed to have seen 'phantom cottages', falls of frogs and other weird manifestations, to ask them about their experiences.

'But who,' John asked in yet another encounter in the corridor, 'is going to present these programmes? I'm seeing Paul tomorrow and must have something to tell him.'

I hadn't a clue, but later that evening as I sat scratching my head at the kitchen table, I thought back to a conversation several years earlier on a beach in Sri Lanka. Michael Deakin, acting on the principle, quickly established in the office, that if you had enjoyed visiting a place on your holidays you should find a reason to return there on expenses, had met the science writer Arthur C. Clarke in Colombo. On his return, Michael wasted no time in persuading

Arthur C. Clarke at home in Sri Lanka. (Charlie Flynn)

Arthur C. Clarke at work. He made 52 mystery programmes for YTV. (Charlie Flynn)

Tony Essex to commission the rather cumbersomely named *Arthur C. Clarke – the 2001 Ideas of the Prophet of the Space Age*, and recruited me to do the interviews.

One morning as we sat between takes on the rocks on the stunningly beautiful beach at Unawatuna in the south of the island, Arthur looked out to the Indian Ocean and began to tell me a story. It was every bit as gripping as his books and short stories, but this tale, he claimed, was true: it had, after all, been published in *The Times*. In 1874, somewhere off that very shore, a schooner, the *Pearl*, had been enveloped in the tentacles of a gigantic squid and dragged beneath the waves. That horrific image of a monster dragging a ship and all hands down to Davy Jones's locker came back to me as I sat at the kitchen table trying to cast a presenter for the mystery series. I realized that Arthur, with his vast knowledge of even the most arcane areas of scientific research, would be the perfect choice.

And so he proved to be. He was sceptical ('The only things I'm reasonably sure about UFOs is that they're *not* spaceships') but prepared to believe that sea monsters could exist ('No man in his right senses could have imagined the sperm whale, or the giant squid – or the hideous little dragons of the abyss. Compared to them, there is nothing particularly remarkable about the "great Sea Serpent" – except for its success in eluding us'). Yet in the face of credulousness Arthur was the master of the witty put-down ('Only one thing can be stated with certainty about such structures as Stonehenge: the people who built them were much more intelligent than many who have written books about them'). And he shared our feeling that 'whether they are important or not, easily seen through or impossible of solution – mysteries are *fun*. Even if they are only nature's practical jokes, they add to our enjoyment of the marvellous universe around us.'

Producing *Arthur C. Clarke's Mysterious World* wasn't all laughs of course. Perhaps the most heart-stopping moment for me was when the pilot flying us on a yeti hunt in Nepal turned round to answer a foolishly-timed question, completely ignoring the fact that we were flying straight towards a Himalayan peak. And John Fanshawe suffered a painful and embarrassing accident while producing the segment about the Giant Balls of Costa Rica, snapping an Achilles tendon while indulging a little too enthusiastically in a dance at a jungle disco. But having cunningly chosen to include the word 'world' in the series title, we set about travelling the planet with gusto: to a total eclipse of the sun in India; to the secret inner sanctum of the Soviet Academy of Sciences in Moscow and its experts on the Great Siberian Explosion of 1908; to Tübingen in Germany, where Dr Arne Eggebrecht produced electricity from the ancient 'Baghdad Battery'; to Stonehenge, where an American teacher demonstrated his theories by walking on the lintels of the circle; and to Death Valley, home of the moving stones, from where researcher Adam Hart-Davis tried and failed to ring in from Grapevine 1, its lone public telephone.

Back in Leeds, in the freezing portakabin behind the bowling alley to which John Fairley had been exiled for daring to bid for a different ITV franchise, we tried to make sense of our Nennius's heap of stories. Everyone – John, directors Charlie Flynn and Michael Weigall, researcher Nick Lord, even our secretary Penny Tankard – lost sleep, except for me; pills to dull the pain of a back injured while dancing a Scottish reel sent me into blissful oblivion each night. The publishers of the tie-in book panicked and refused to bind most of the copies; pulping would be easier that way. We cut and re-cut and wrote and re-wrote until the exasperated film editors picked the programmes up from their steenbecks and marched them off to neg-cutting. As transmission approached, we worried that the curse of the crystal 'Skull of Doom' had got us: after all, the director had repositioned it to improve the shot, ignoring dire warnings from its owner that a dreadful fate awaited anyone who dared to touch it.

Perhaps the skull had lost its power, or never had any (our expert had pronounced it a fake), because we found ourselves riding high in the ratings and topping a viewers' poll in the *Sun*. But it was not until Terry Wogan started cracking jokes about the programmes on his daily radio show and comedians

Family time for Duncan Dallas, Head of Science Programmes at Yorkshire Television for nearly 30 years, shown here with his wife, Liz Bryce, whom he met in the Science Department, and their sons Charlie and George. After he left television, Duncan created a Café Scientific based in a wine bar near his home in the Leeds suburb of Chapel Allerton, with the aim of creating easy access for ordinary members of the public to science and scientific experts. The idea caught on: after securing backing from the Wellcome Trust and other bodies, Cafés Scientific sprang up all over the country and, sponsored by the British Council, in many countries abroad. (Adam Hart-Davis)

lampooned us, that we knew for certain we had a hit on our hands.

Years later, when I asked Arthur to name his favourite show (we had made 52 by then), he replied, 'No question. The one in which the Goodies sent us up rotten.'

Mysterious World was my swansong at Yorkshire, but the bonds of friendship forged in the science office, on location, and on those tense Tuesdays in Studio 4 stayed strong. One day, almost exactly 40 years on from the first *Don't Ask Me* programmes and shortly before he died, I rang Duncan and found him in a rare nostalgic mood, his thoughts returning to our salad days.

'It was hard,' I ventured when it was time to go, 'but goodness we had fun. And it was far, far better than work.'

There was a silence so characteristic of the thoughtful Duncan that I was at once transported back to those *Don't Ask Me* interrogations.

At last he said, 'Yes. You could say that.'

Chapter 20

David Taylor

I came to the YTV Science department straight from doing farming programmes for Tyne-Tees. They must have thought I had something to give because they plunged me straight into a film which was to be called *The Flesh Harvesters*. Aware of the grisly scenes ahead, I was happy that the cameraman was Charlie Flynn, a seasoned countryman and former gamekeeper from Aberdeenshire. Flynn soon proved he had the stomach for the task.

We were shooting at an artificial insemination centre where semen was collected from prime bulls. To gather semen, technicians used a tease like a pantomime cow on wheels – a driver at the front, back to back with a colleague who collected the genetically valuable sperm.

To the bull, the tease looked like the hindquarters of an attractive heifer. To the man in the rear, it was a clever way to hijack semen. As the bull mounted the tease and thrust through a larger-than-life vagina, the man directed the bovine penis into a cylinder and collected the ejaculate. With a tonne or more of passionate bull on top, it took guts. Nevertheless, cool as a cucumber, Flynn and camera replaced man and cylinder.

'Action!', shouted director Harris Watts.

A fresh bull was released. Quick as a flash the randy beast mounted the tease and

The YTV crew for *The Flesh Harvesters*. (Rod Lofthouse)

ejaculated all over rubber-clad Flynn and his camera. Stoicism!

From the wild white cattle of Northumberland to calves incarcerated in plastic bubbles at the Royal Veterinary College, the locations kept coming. *Beecham's* revealed piglets reared in cages like battery hens. At Cherry Valley, Lincolnshire, in vast darkened sheds, ducks mushroomed from egg to table in six and a half weeks. As the crew lit one shed, the lights went up too fast and thousands of ducklings stampeded. So soft were these unnatural birds that dozens broke legs and wings and had to be destroyed.

To illustrate a new rearing technique, I bought a sow about to farrow. A vet was hired to perform a hysterectomy. The idea was to remove her uterus with the unborn litter still intact. The piglets would be delivered into a germ-free chamber before moving to a minimal disease rearing unit where they'd grow 15 per cent faster than those born and reared traditionally. It was new and fashionable in the hard-pressed bacon and pork industry.

The Flesh Harvesters was shaping up. Emotive sequences illustrated the relentless march of science and profit from pastoral to factory farming. But it needed a final twist. That came in the shape of synthetic food – steaks, sausages and burgers spun from soya beans. It was the sci-fi future. Meat would be out and vegetable protein in. Farm animals would become mere curiosities. We learnt from Peter Williams, a farmer friend, of a likely evangelist for artificial food – a scientist who worked for Distillers Whisky.

A call was placed and, yes, the whisky wizard would rendezvous with us in Perth, where the crew was filming the famous Aberdeen Angus bull sales. His name was Magnus Pyke. Arms whirling over a filmed lunch, Dr Pyke delivered a scintillating case for bean steak. Peppered with comic anecdotes and analogies, his science was irresistible. Why push feed through animals when it could be spun directly into perfectly palatable protein? To make the point, he extruded mock meat through a tableside processor. Pyke was priceless.

'Who is this man?' enthused John Fairley back in Leeds. 'He's the Groucho Marx of science! He must have done TV?'

'No', I reported, 'just the occasional talk on food technology in concert intervals on Radio 3.'

Fairley made a snap decision. With more than enough blood and gore to bulk up *The Flesh Harvesters*, I was despatched again to Scotland. The brief was to sign up Pyke for a *Scientists* episode of his own: *Magnus and the Beansteak*.

A few feverish weeks later, as *The Scientists* went to air, those not watching *Match of the Day* were predictably shocked by *The Flesh Harvesters*. The film prompted questions in the House of Commons. But when *Magnus and the Beansteak* aired, a phenomenon was unleashed.

Pyke was to become to general science what Patrick Moore was to astronomy, everyone's idea of a mad boffin. In fact, his remarkable talent for popularization disguised a serious scientist with a distinguished career. During the Second World War it was Pyke at the Ministry of Food who designed the nation's diet on which rationing was based. Then came *Don't Ask Me*. As it launched, so too did Pyke. In series after series he whirled and beguiled. Summer after summer, in the seven o'clock slot between *Crossroads* and *Coronation Street*, *Don't Ask Me* rarely slipped from the Top Ten. Pyke became a national treasure and much parodied. He did commercials for Hoover and was appointed general secretary of the National Association for the Advancement of Science – all thanks to a talent-spotting farmer friend of mine in the Dales.

Chapter 21

Miriam Stoppard

Dr Miriam Stoppard, on location with a Yorkshire TV crew.
(Charlie Flynn)

I strayed into television. No desire to be in front of the camera; no inclination to do other than pursue my medical career. I'd got a kind of toehold in radio, though. I was working as research director of the pharmaceutical company that pioneered the Pill. At the time, the Pill was controversial and beset by critics and doubters. Being the only female voice in the industry, the media pounced on me to defend the Pill whenever it came under attack, and my voice became known. Eventually, I found myself as BBC Radio London's resident doctor, and I guess that's how the Science Office at YTV got

wind of me. They approached me crabwise and asked if I had any female colleagues (they wanted a female voice) who could present medicine on TV.

I suggested two or three names and thought no more of it, but a month later they came back and asked if I'd like to try it myself. Always game, I said yes, and found myself trying to describe a DNA molecule on camera. I was shockingly bad. The executive producer, Duncan Dallas, someone I was to know well and work with for 18 years, gave me a few notes and we tried again.

Years later, when I asked him why he'd taken a chance on me he said, 'You took direction.'

So I fell into the hands of the producers in the YTV Science Office, the team conjuring up *Don't Ask Me*, among whom there was a clear pecking order: David Taylor, who'd bagged David Bellamy, a biologist who looked and sounded like a cockney pugilist; Simon Welfare, who'd claimed Magnus Pyke, the epitome of the dotty professor who nonetheless believed himself to be the arbiter of scientific truth (and we often butted heads); and lastly, the lowest of the low, Kevin Sim.

Kevin came to see me in my Maidenhead office and made his disenchantment with the idea of being in charge of me very plain.

His opening words on meeting me were, 'I have to be honest, I have no appetite for working with you. David Taylor has bagged Bellamy, Simon Welfare, Magnus Pyke, and I'm left with you.'

I remember thinking (and smiling), we're going to get on just fine. I'll show the bugger. I cautioned him that I was five months pregnant; was he sure he wanted a gravid woman on the show?

His rejoinder was, 'We're game if you are.'

There then began a three-year apprenticeship in studio presentation of *Don't Ask Me*, every time tongue-tied, panic-stricken and clumsy. I felt sure the cameramen could see the whites of my eyes. I've seen myself in those early shows and I was terrible. Two of my early medical items involved babies, the first being to demo the primitive palmar reflex in a newborn baby (it's a vestigial reflex from the time we were tree-dwelling apes and babies had to hang on to their mother's fur as they swung from branch to branch). I did it by showing said newborn baby could grasp a clothesline so tightly it could take its own weight. With terrified mum just out of shot, baby and I managed it for a few seconds, amidst gasps from the studio audience. The second item served to demonstrate that babies under a year old will hold their breath (and not drown) if they find themselves underwater. I demoed this in a public swimming pool, into which I gently dropped a baby from the side; she was filmed underwater with her mouth tightly shut, and emerged, none the worse for wear, a couple of minutes later. I became known as the woman who threw babies into swimming pools.

Things took a turn for the better when, deep into Series III, I was doing an item on knobbly knees, which are the province of men, in fact a male sexual characteristic. I had

a man with his trousers rolled up pointing out the excrescences round his knee joint, and for the first time I felt I was enjoying myself. I can do this, I thought, and in an unguarded moment I lifted the hem of my dress to show how the female knee is smooth and round. It brought the house down. The next morning there was a message from Paul Fox, MD of YTV, to lift my dress more often.

Kevin decided that I was strong enough to carry a show on my own without my two co-conspirators, and ever with an eye on the main chance, he chose what was then a controversial no-go subject – when to turn off life support on a comatose patient. During a production meeting I happened to let slip that as a junior doctor I had turned off a patient's life support. Kevin jumped. Would I open the show with this confession? Knowing that I had been only the instrument who did the turning off, and not the decision maker to do so (in fact the decision was taken by a consensus of very senior doctors), I agreed.

The following morning, the press fell on me and I was hounded from pillar to post. I couldn't move without a camera in my face. Who was I to decide if someone was to live or die? What right had I to end a life? Was I senior enough to make a decision of such gravity? I thought my medical career was over and I'd be struck off the medical register. To my surprise and relief, those senior doctors who had given me my fateful command came to my rescue and co-authored a letter to the press exonerating me from any blame. But it was a close shave and a seminal moment.

A short while after, with his tail in the air, Kevin decided we'd do a 'special' on AIDS. He'd fly in an AIDS patient from the US and we'd do a whole show on HIV/AIDS. I was an eager conscript to the cause. It's hard to believe now, but at the time the country was riven by AIDS hysteria, and I felt I had a role as the calm voice of reason.

There were obstacles, however. No studio crew would do a show alongside someone with AIDS – the air would be contaminated! Determined to find a way, Kevin and I decided to do the show in a working men's club and found a scratch crew who would work with me. We did the show, and Kevin, eager for publicity, had called a press conference.

I was tired, so was my AIDS sufferer, a woman who'd contracted HIV from a contaminated blood transfusion, and I said to the gathered members of the press corps, 'Look the message is simple. A picture says more than a thousand words. If you print anything print this picture.'

Then I kissed the woman on the lips.

The next day was a slow news day. The picture went round the world: *Newsweek*, the *Washington Post*, the *LA Times*, the *China Times*, the *Malaysian Times*.

Kevin and I had got the message out.

Towards the end of Series IV I was pregnant with my second son, and for the final show I was coming up to my delivery date. During rehearsals and then when recording the show, I was having Braxton Hicks contractions. The make-up girls were pale and anxious lest my waters would break.

I happened to mention it to Kevin and, as we went into the close, Duncan Dallas came on to the floor and said in an aside, 'If you get a contraction while you're on camera, refer to it.'

'Goodnight and see you next time. Ow, ow, ow …' And I raised myself off the stool

The *Where There's Life* team taking a break from filming in the Philippines in 1983. (L to R) Miriam Stoppard, Rob Buckman, Rod Lofthouse, Don Atkinson. (Rod Lofthouse)

I was sitting on with the pain. 'It's OK. I'm just having a contraction!'

Duncan got his way. Kevin didn't. As I sped off to London and the Westminster Hospital for the birth, he shouted, 'If you'd had a baby here he could have played cricket for Yorkshire!'

The structure of *Where There's Life* … (Paul Fox's inspired title) gradually emerged. I (and sometimes Rob Buckman) would undertake four- to six-week filming trips abroad to gather short films that we'd bring home and use as jumping off points for a discussion with a studio audience. Those filming trips were one of the high points of my working career. With a crew (up to ten in those days) we'd sally forth to Japan, Israel, France, the Philippines, Honduras, Australia, to pick up interesting medical stories to bring back home. A surefire destination was the US – East or West Coast. We knew if we went to those locations we could pick up stories on the street, especially on Hollywood and Vine, the Golden Gate Bridge and the Bronx. We were a family. We moved together as one and supported one another through thick and thin. The crew and I did this for seven or eight years on the trot. I only realized how tightly knit a group we'd become when I overheard the assistant cameraman say in the cafeteria one day, 'Hey, lads, Miriam has signed for another year!' and be greeted with cheers.

We were more than a family, though, we were an edifice. Researchers in the Science Office would begin rooting out 'stories' in the spring. Then a pair of them would travel to the chosen country, acting as scouts to build our stories brick by brick from scientists, patients, families, doctors, interesting technology or fascinating locations. One of them would phone me in the UK to brief me, and we'd chat around the subject. This careful dialogue allowed me to hit the ground running in a foreign location. Often we'd scamper, the producers (ace John Fanshawe, prodigious Gwyneth Hughes) and I, from the airport to the lab or bedside, and I'd do my first introductory piece to camera an hour or so after landing, the crew having arrived and set up before me. Truth be told, I was only ever as good as my researchers and producers. I was a front man, no more.

Many of the films we made were on cutting edge science, and I found myself a student of new ideas, new technologies and new medical practice. One such was a visit to Michel Odent in Pithiviers, France, to study his birthing techniques and imbibe his philosophy of childbirth. He knocked me sideways with his startling new approach to delivering babies. He practised obstetrics but he'd started out as a surgeon and brought a surgeon's precision to the inexact science of childbirth. First, why would a woman lie on her back to give birth when this means she's pushing her baby out uphill? Why not encourage her to stand up and use the force of gravity to help the baby out? A no-brainer. In traditional UK labour wards anxiety and stress went hand in hand with childbirth, and they slow delivery down. Why not let a woman do her own thing, go down on all fours if she wants to, sit in a pool if it's comforting, cling to her partner's neck standing upright to share the strain of a contraction? All no-brainers.

The proof of the pudding was that Odent had the best obstetric results on the planet: shortest labours, fewest interventions, fewest C-sections, fewest complications, healthier babies. I was totally won over. For my impassioned outro the producer suggested I come out of Odent's hospital and, standing on the steps, just say what I felt in my heart. And I did. All women should know about Odent. All obstetricians should follow his lead. All women should have an Odent birth. Why hadn't I had one? (Both of mine were flat on my back.) How soon could we adopt Odent's methods in the UK? I became an Odent proselyte. I incorporated his theory and practices in my next pregnancy book. I launched Odent in the UK.

Where There's Life … took up a chunk of my time, but over 18 years I did several more series and specials for YTV: *Baby and Co*, with a soft set and babies crawling everywhere and poking me in the eye with a huge toy spider; *Dear Miriam*, a show about warring families and resolving conflict (with a family therapist in the background); specials like *Christmas is Coming … This is a Government Health Warning!*, with lovely James Bolam and Richard Wilson, Alun Armstrong and Gwen

Taylor, me playing a doctor, the butt of their jokes and dressed in a red sequinned number bought on Rodeo Drive at the behest of the LE director to 'look as much like Joan Collins as you can'. I guess I could in those days. Another special was about reuniting twins separated at birth, presaging *Long Lost Family* by three decades.

We tilted at windmills and did a show on 'QUALYS' – basing allocation of treatment on how much it would improve the quality of life. In the studio we had a young single mum of three who needed a kidney transplant or she would die and a 60-year-old who needed a hip replacement. Which of the two should get NHS funding? Their cases were argued by their doctor, their family and themselves, then the audience was asked to vote for who would be treated, as the NHS could only afford one of them. To my utter astonishment, they voted for the hip replacement and, using the audience vote as real, I was left to say to the single mum, 'I'm so terribly sorry but I'm afraid you're going to die.' A blistering indictment of crowd psychology.

Duncan Dallas thought up a series for me entitled *Woman to Woman*, in which I interviewed eminent women about their professional lives, how they'd managed to succeed in a man's world and how they'd achieved some kind of balance between work and life. High on our list of candidates was Margaret Thatcher. Duncan and I talked for hours how best to approach our subject. I had met Mrs Thatcher several times and chatted to her, because my then husband, Tom Stoppard, was a favourite of hers, and I used to tag along. We decided that I should approach her personally, which I did, and

to our glee she agreed to be interviewed. I sent along a list of questions I wished to ask her, but she brushed it aside and said, let's just chat. As the date for the interview approached, Duncan and I would tick over the exact wording of my questions, how I could approach difficult topics, how I could couch sensitive issues in non-confrontational language. In a flight of fancy Duncan fantasized about what would happen if I could persuade Mrs Thatcher to drop her guard. A confession? A revealing anecdote? A tear? No, we couldn't imagine she'd ever show her vulnerability.

On the appointed day Mrs Thatcher greeted me affably and asked my advice about what she should wear on camera. We went up to her dressing room and chose a skirt and blouse, the blouse with a bow at the neckline ('I like bows, they're softening'). I suggested that her lipstick was too dark a red and that she should try a pinker shade, which she did. I also suggested that we soften her hairline, and she agreed. In her sitting room at Number Ten we then embarked on the two-hour-long interview. About 20 minutes in she touched on her early life and the influence of her father, whom she adored. As she spoke, I was so intent on following the plan Duncan and I had hatched that my eyes were down and fixed on my clipboard of questions. I decided on the next one and, taking a breath, looked up. To my utter astonishment I saw there were tears in her eyes. In the eyes of the Iron Lady! The burgeoning question stuck in my throat, and I held my breath as a tear rolled down her cheek. I became known as the woman who made Mrs Thatcher cry.

What do I remember most clearly? Two studio discussion programmes, one emanating

Dr Miriam Stoppard in Sydney, Australia, for Yorkshire Television's popular science series, *Don't Ask Me*. (Rod Lofthouse)

from Australia and the other from Israel. The crew and I covered the Sydney Gay Mardi Gras and we used it to ask the question: how old do you have to be to know you're gay? In our film we followed a 13-year-old boy (and his wonderful mum) through his joining a gay group participating in the parade. Then, back home, we filled the studio with young gay people and asked the same question: the

Aussie boy knew at thirteen, how old were you when you knew? I became a fag hag overnight.

The second moved me to tears. On an Israeli trip we filmed young Down's Syndrome people who, in a research project run by a professor of Psychiatry and a professor of Plastic Surgery in Tel Aviv, had their facial features made 'normal' to assess the effect it had on their lives and happiness. In Israel everyone who'd had the surgery was glad they'd had it done and felt their lives were immeasurably better because people didn't prejudge them on their appearance. When I showed this film to a studio audience of Down's Syndrome people in the UK and asked if they would have liked the operation to change their facial appearance, not one person demurred. The studio was redolent of lost time, lost opportunities, lost lives.

We were trailblazers all right. Our motto was, there's no subject we can't tackle, we just have to find a way, be it incest, eating placentas or …

Chapter 22

Chris Jelley

Chris Jelley, Head of Educational and Religious Programmes (1979–1990).

It was 14 August 1979 and, as I drove up to the Yorkshire Television entrance in Leeds, my car was stopped by a rather large group of people.

I opened the window to be met with a menacing 'Who are you?'

'I'm Peter Scroggs's successor.'

'Umph … management … well you had better go in.'

It was the first day of what was to become a seven-week strike at ITV, and my first day of 23 years employment at Yorkshire Television. It had all been something of a dream, starting with a phone call in my office at BBC Television's Continuing Education department.

'Are you alone?' the voice had said. 'Well, I have something to say which may be to your advantage. When would be a good time to talk?'

Later that evening at home, I took another call: would I like to meet Paul Fox, Yorkshire television's managing director? He was looking for someone to run the education department … could I meet him? … tomorrow at the London Office would be convenient.

It turned out that not only education but children's programmes, and even religion, were to become my bag.

I was soon in the new world of Outside Advisors. YTV had an Education Committee under the benign chairmanship of Prof William Walsh, and Religious Advisors in the form of Revd Margaret Cundiff, Revd David Calvert and the charismatic Monsignor Michael Buckley. These clerics were a great deal more demanding. Expecting a serious discussion about our religious programming, I called my first meeting of the Religious Advisors.

The production team of *All Stitched Up* preparing a new episode of a series on knitting and sewing for Channel 4 in 1985. (Standing L to R): Tiggy Trethowan (floor manager), Sue Hamelman (PA), Penny Rea (stage manager), Fiona Greig (programme director), Val Zabels (producer), Gwen Singleton (researcher). Seated: presenter Les Gammon

Jess Yates. (Shutterstock)

Yorkshire TV production staff welcome Archbishop Chrystomos of Cyprus as a special guest on one of the religious programmes the company produced. (L to R): Mary Watts (producer), Chris Jelley (Head of Department), Archbishop Chrysostomos, David Calvert (religious advisor) and Margaret Cundiff (religious advisor).

I had barely begun when Michael Buckley intervened: 'The purpose of this meeting is to agree how many church services we [Catholics] get and how many the others get … and of course, how many hymns we get in this new Sunday evening religious show that Yorkshire is to do.'

Stars on Sunday with Jess Yates had recently come to a colourful end, with Frank Kilbride of the YTV education department smuggling Jess out of YTV in the boot of his car before the press could besiege him over his relationship with a rather lovely actress.

Instead, we were now to do *Your 100 Best Hymns* presented by Derek Batey, famous for presenting the Border Television quiz show *Mr and Mrs*.

Luckily, Mary Watts had briefed me, and agreement was reached. And on six Sundays of the year YTV's outside broadcast crew would thenceforth be mustered for a weekend of 'sin and sanctity': after covering a local race meeting on the Saturday, they would reassemble in more solemn mode to transmit a live service from a church in our region.

For many years we filled the God slot on early Sunday evenings with choral hymns. Sometimes we would mount something larger such as *Christmas Carols from Ripon Cathedral*, with Huddersfield-born James Mason doing the readings.

A distinctive feature of Yorkshire's educational programmes was what you might call their freshness and spontaneity. In other words, they featured real people who made

James Mason. (Shutterstock)

mistakes, just like everyone else, and viewers loved them. Coming from the BBC, I was used to programmes often being heavily scripted; if a presenter made a mistake, no one thought twice about redoing the action, or even a single sentence, and then going through the process of editing the 'corrected' version into the take. Then, within a few days of arriving at YTV, I was sitting in on a recording of *Farmhouse Kitchen*.

Dorothy Sleightholme was demonstrating one of her homely traditional dishes, creaming the sugar and marge, adding the flour, a drop of water and so on.

'Now, having mixed it all together, into the oven with it, don't forget, gas mark 7' … pause … realization … 'Oh dear, I've forgotten the salt and pepper … Oh well, better late than never' … throws them in and pops it into the oven.

'Excellent,' says Graham Watts, director, 'now let's move on to the guest.'

Farmhouse Kitchen ran for 17 years, and guests included a host of, at the time, young unknowns: Mary Berry, Delia Smith, Rick Stein and others.

Later, I was to offer Graham a larger film budget for a series he was working on. He politely declined.

'Oh no thank you, Chris, it would take up so much more time … and I would have to spend longer in the cutting room!'

We followed some brilliant teachers. Fanny Waterman, founder of the Leeds International Piano competition, did six programmes for us, produced by Terry Henebery. Her drawing room would be full of film crew, parents and hangers-on like me … and woe betide any parent who didn't turn up for their child's lesson; they were required to

A high point in the historical series *How We Used To Live*. The sailing ship *Zebu* returns to port at the end of many years transporting slaves from the West Indies. (Chris Jelley)

take notes of what had to be practised the next week. I remember a lesson with the young Ben Frith, later to win first prize in the Arthur Rubinstein International Piano Masters Competition; Fanny was laughing and joking with Ben, singing her own childish ditties and rhymes, oblivious to all those around her. Her pupils loved her.

How We Used to Live was one of ITV Schools' flagship programmes, and in 1980 Richard Handford's Victorian Series won a BAFTA award for its heartrending portrayal of child poverty and deprivation in Victorian Britain. Written by former teacher Freda Kelsall, this dramatized series focused on showing what it was like, as a child, to live in different eras of British history. Subsequent series were produced by David Wilson and Ian Fell, and such was its popularity that Lord Thomson, Chairman of the Independent Broadcasting Authority, could report in a 1987 speech that, 'The current series of *How We Used to Live* was used by 25,640 classes in its first year of transmission.'

The series was broadcast every year for 40 years. It proved to be a greenhouse for bringing on talented young actors. Peter Firth was an 'urchin' in 1969; Joanne Whalley found stardom after the Second World War series; Peter Howitt graduated to *Bread* and was later creator of *Sliding Doors*; and Lena Headey has found much fame in *Game of Thrones*.

Actress Jane Hazlegrove demonstrates a low-tech wash day aid – the mangle – in an episode of *How We Used to Live*, made by Yorkshire TV's Education Department for the ITV Network.

A scene depicting the results of Second World War bombing from *How We Used to Live*. (Shutterstock)

The programmes were made on location in Yorkshire, and authenticity was all. So much so that, for a Tudor interlude about Shakespearian England, props were asked to source an ancient rare breed of duck to be filmed on the lake at Markenfield Hall. The day came, the ducks arrived, the crew set up, and the ducks were put in the water … where they promptly sank. They had never been asked to swim before!

For the next series, on Stuart England, Swinsty Hall near Fewston was found – a

David Bellamy, with producer, Adam Hart-Davis. Adam later presented two regionally-based science series, *On the Edge* (in which he cycled around the North of England in pink and fluorescent green lycra) and *Local Heroes* (featuring scientific achievers from history), which later moved with him to BBC2. He found the corridors in the Yorkshire Television studio building so long that he frequently jumped on his bike to visit other departments. (Adam Hart-Davis)

magnificent seventeenth-century manor house with an original earth and stone driveway, the perfect setting for the opening coach drive up to the house. The day before the shoot, the kind owners tarmacked over the drive – 'We thought it would make your access easier' – thus destroying our opening.

One notable spin-off from the series was its use in what is known as 'reminiscence therapy'. Michael Scarborough, YTV's Education Officer, would take the series into an old people's home, show an episode or clips and then chat with the elderly about some of the daily activities dramatized in the piece. Once Michael was doing just that, talking about washing day, with its carbolic soap, corrugated washboard, finger-licking mangle, dolly tub and the 'posser', a sort of inverted sieve-shaped half-dome mounted on the end of a long pole. Michael asked

the old ladies what they would do with the washboard, in what way would they use the posser in the dolly tub.

'Eeh, mister,' said one the ladies, 'Tha would howd on to t'posser and pummel yon up and down and up and down among t'cloathes until t'soap gets into t'muck and t'muck gets into t'watter, ond efter a good rinse and some mangling, t'washing can go out in t'back alley as long as it's a Monday.'

His session ended, Michael packed up his dolly tub and washboard, and as he left the old people's home, he heard one elderly lady turn to her companion:

'Eeh, Norma. Calls himself a television producer, and he doesn't know how to poss.'

I was keen to contribute science programming to ITV's schools output and so was delighted when Adam Hart Davis, gathering breath on the squash court over lunch, told me about the book of science experiments for children that he had recently written. *Scientific Eye* proved to be a defining series for Schools TV, designed for viewing in recorded form and in short sequences, showing experiments that teachers found difficult to conduct in class. It proved an invaluable resource for teachers and led on to *Mathematical Eye* (also produced by Adam) and later *Geographical Eye*, co-funded with Dutch and French stations.

YTV alone would never have been able to shoot the *Geographical Eye* series – they were not cheap. Once Deborah Isaacs returned claiming £36,000 of cash expenses from an eight-week shoot in Nigeria, and with scarcely a receipt. The cost accountant lifted an eyebrow as she presented her lack of paperwork, but she pointed out that if she had brought neat and tidy receipts he would have been very suspicious, as they could be manufactured so easily. A year later, when she presented expenses with immaculate receipts from China, he raised another eyebrow. He pointed out that he could not read any of them, so how could he know what she had been spending money on.

In 1999 China was changing very fast. Their mobile phones were still brick-like, but their mobile reception network was extraordinary – far better than in the Dales. Two weeks into a shoot, Viviana Fain-Binda, the associate producer, was in a remote village 200 miles north of Beijing. The surrounding plains were flat, the light grey-blue and the telephone signal clear as a bell. She was in a midden – quite literally – shooting an item on 'night soil'. When standing underneath two latrines, in a wide pit surrounded by pigs, her phone rang.

'Vivi darling,' her husband said, from the comfort of their terraced house in London, 'does Carlos have a piano lesson this afternoon?'

I had made a point of attending the EBU annual meetings of heads of television education departments, and it was in Finland in 1981, on one of these, that I met Channel 4's first commissioning editor for Education, Naomi Sargant. I got to know her when sharing the flight back from Helsinki, and she became a lifelong friend. The BBC had launched a very successful Literacy Campaign and she wanted to do the same for Numeracy. David Wilson had already made *Make It Count* for YTV, which had been well received. Naomi promptly commissioned us to make *Numbers at Work* and *Counting On*. David continued with two Anton Mosimann cookery series, and within three years YTV was Channel 4's largest supplier of educational programming.

One of our producers, Ian Rosenbloom, who had made two series of *Be Your Own Boss*, fronted by Henry Cooper, and two more on *The Marketing Mix*, then ventured into what was at the time uncharted territory, with his *Sex Matters* series. Carol Haslam, C4 commissioning editor, wanted a hit and encouraged Ian to open the boundaries. So Gwen Singleton advertised for a transvestite who would talk about the hows and why and would appear both as female and male in the programme. Later, the crew, lights, camera and sound, plus PA, researcher and Ian, stood in a dark and dingy corridor outside a Liverpool flat. Ian knocked, the door opened and there was a young woman. Taken aback at the sight of all these men, she quickly recovered herself.

'If only I'd known you lovely men were coming', she growled in a husky voice, 'I'd have worn a bigger bosom.'

Channel 4 became a valued outlet for YTV's religious output. Michael Buckley came to me with an idea for a current affairs programme which would focus on the week's issues from a religious perspective. I challenged him to come back in four weeks' time with a synopsis of what he would have chosen to feature each week. To my surprise and his considerable credit, four weeks later he presented me with a detailed synopsis, which we then worked up. I took it to John Ranelagh at Channel 4, and he commissioned what was to become the first of many series of *7 Days*, presented first by Michael Charlton and later by Robert Kee, and throughout lovingly cared for and edited by Barbara Twigg.

The cast of *Runaway Bay* in Martinique.

For YTV, Joy Whitby's *Book Tower* with Tom Baker, later Dr Who, was a prized fixture of the children's schedule; so when she retired from YTV in the mid-eighties, I asked Richard Callahan to join YTV and continue it. Patrick Titley came too, and very soon YTV was producing some of ITV's most successful series. *The Raggy Dolls* featured a motley collection of 'rejects' from a toy factory who climbed out of the Reject Bin and into the Real World. Their adventures showed how disabilities can be overcome by working together with kindness, tolerance and humility towards others. With its catchy theme tune, jokes and music written by Neil Innes, Sad Sack, Hi-Fi, Lucy, Dotty, Back-to-Front, Princess and Claude delighted audiences from 1986 till 1994 and even today attract a loyal following on YouTube.

Puddle Lane had been Neil Innes's first YTV children's programme. He had been at art school with Sally Wells, and she realized that he was the perfect choice to play the Magician who would tell illustrated stories. These were written by Rick Vanes, whose previous credits included *Get Up and Go* and *Mooncat*, featuring Beryl Reid.

Puddle Lane was followed by *The Riddlers*. Produced by Ian Fell and directed by Ann Ayoub, *The Riddlers* became, for almost a decade, a fixture in the ITV children's schedules.

Patrick Titleys's *Bad Influence* picked up on the growth and popularity of computer games. The series ran long enough to feature the launch of the Nintendo 64 console, and for three of the four series it had the highest ratings of any children's ITV programme at the time, with hugely popular presenters, the boyish Violet Berlin, BBC defector Andy Crane and the gorgeous Sonya Saul.

Later, Robert Page from Lifetime Productions was to offer me *Runaway Bay*, a children's adventure series set in the West Indies. It would be expensive, but he had interest from Elipse, a French production company, who would co-produce. I liked it, and ITV commissioned a run of six. However, Elipse's approval of the scripts was required, and this was not always easily acquired. In one memorable disagreement, our synopsis called for the children to solve the mystery of who had scaled the outside of their hotel to steal some jewellery. The children followed an old bent woman, their suspect, to the airport, where they saw her enter the toilets and emerge as a man – mystery solved!

'Non, non, non. C'est impossible,' exclaimed Robert, Elipse's producer.

'What is wrong?' we asked.

'Ah … this is disgraceful and immoral … and we French will not accept it.'

'But why not?'

'Because you are encouraging our children to become transvestites.'

In the end we persuaded him that this was just a case of 'dressing up' – something that surely even French children did.

The next episode was in Martinique, with a cast that included a bewitching eleven-year-old Naomi Harris (later, Moneypenny in the Bond films *Skyfall* and *Spectre*). It was often a logistical nightmare – close-ups had to be shot in both French and English, so that the French could get a more realistic dub, and the five child actors' availability was constrained by very tight regulations. But thanks to Anne Gibbons, the six episodes were finished on time, and we went on to make a further two series.

Shortly after *Runaway Bay*, Amanda Sylvester brought me a script, *Just Us*, by the then almost unknown Kay Mellor, about the family lives of teenagers. It ran from 1992 to 1994, winning the BAFTA award for best children's drama.

A year later, YTV acquired Newcastle-based CD Rom production company, Interactive Learning Productions, and YTV's Schools programmes were subsumed into Yorkshire International Multimedia Ltd, a joint venture with the publisher Nelson. It was to adapt our schools programmes for CD Roms and the international market … but that's another story.

Chapter 23

Some YTV People

John Baxter and Marylyn Webb with Geoffrey Hughes, who played the part of Vernon Scripps in Heartbeat from 2001 to 2007. (John Baxter))

John Baxter
Graham Ironside recalls:

I stumbled across John Baxter after buying a puppy for my daughter and taking it to the vet for jabs. Baxter's surgery was a babel of activity, with the vet himself shooting in and out and talking cheerfully to everyone.

At the time, *Calendar* had taken responsibility for a half-hour slot on a Tuesday afternoon and used it to try out new ideas or run interviews with people in the news or personalities of special interest to the YTV audience. One particular Tuesday, a couple of hours before the show, the interviewee booked for that afternoon rang very apologetically to say he was unable to get to the studios. With the presence of mind which can only be induced by panic, need overcame nerves; I lifted the phone and called John Baxter.

Was there the slightest chance that John might be free … to fill a half-hour programme? Yes, today, 'live', in about an hour and a half from now?

'Graham', he said. 'I've been waiting for your call. I've been dying to have a go at television. I'll be with you in an hour.'

Not only was he there within the hour, but he arrived with a collection of 'props' which he thought he might find useful – including the trusty Gladstone bag, which accompanied him on most occasions. From it he produced a series of weird and wonderful implements which he had used in his profession over the years, including a ruff-style collar he had designed to prevent animals from licking wounds, all with a funny story attached from his life as a vet. But the least visually impressive prop turned out to be the most astonishing: a cheap plastic open-sided salt jar. It was, he explained, an essential piece of equipment he used when operating on

John Baxter, with Roger Meek, an expert on reptiles. (John Baxter)

budgerigars suffering from deviated beaks or ingrown toenails. Such were the problem cases which regularly arrive in the surgery, he explained – and how do you anaesthetize a budgie which might otherwise just expire in your hands?

He proceeded to demonstrate, and his flow of hilarious anecdotes enthralled not only Richard Whiteley, the interviewer, but the studio crew and the production crew too. The reaction from the audience was instant.

So was born *It's a Vet's Life,* which John Baxter and Marylyn Webb presented. It became a highlight of the schedule at 6.30 on a Monday evening and ran for fifteen seasons.

Alan Mason

A later addition to the Calendar stable more or less created his own series. Alan Mason, then head gardener at Harewood House, the stately home just north of Leeds, spotted the fact that nowhere in the schedule was there a slot for gardening enthusiasts, so he wrote in

to say he was prepared to do one . . . and he did.

With a YTV Outside Broadcast unit which was temporarily available, and supported by Marylyn Webb, herself a keen gardener, he proved to be a knowledgeable and passionate expert, and a hard-working one. In a walled garden at Harewood he created a small flower and vegetable garden over the course of a year in a series entitled *Calendar Goes Gardening*, to the delight of viewers and visitors alike.

Ashley Jackson

Ashley Jackson, today a leading English watercolourist, had been an apprentice sign writer in Barnsley in the late 1960s but bravely set out to become a full-time artist, specializing in painting the brooding landscapes all over Yorkshire for which he is now internationally famous. Producers at Yorkshire Television spotted him demonstrating on television in the Midlands and approached him to present a series for the region. So began a relationship with Yorkshire Television which lasted throughout its entire existence. *A Brush with*

Ashley Jackson at work on the Yorkshire Moors. (Shutterstock)

Ashley featured regularly in the local schedules and inspired scores of aspiring amateurs to take up brush and paints.

Michael Clegg

Calendar Editor John Wilford 'discovered' Michael Clegg when they bumped into each other during a filming trip to the remote wildlife haven of Spurn Point. Michael, loud and outgoing, for 20 years delighted Yorkshire viewers with his knowledge, insight and humour. Marylyn Webb, the presenter who worked alongside Michael for many years, wrote:

He had the sort of face that people talk to – and they did, wherever he went. Mind you, they usually ended up listening to him! He only had to sit down for two minutes and a little knot of people would gather round as he told them about the 'old Norse' name of their village or which bird was chirruping hidden in the leaves above their heads.

One of my favourite memories was when he stood in thigh waders in the middle of the River Derwent and, in one take, retold the entire story of the Battle of Stamford Bridge in all its glorious and gory detail. If he'd moved he probably would have fallen in, as he frequently did!

Another time, when we were searching for evidence of otters, he spotted otter 'spraint' [droppings] on a log. As only Michael could, he bent down, dipped his finger in it, put it to his nose and with an ecstatic, toothy grin sighed, 'Ah, the smell of Devon violets, marvellous!'

Michael Clegg, a naturalist and historian whose programmes became an established and highly respected feature of Yorkshire Television's regional programmes. A big man with a big appetite, he kept audiences enraptured with his unrivalled knowledge of his home county's flora and fauna. With a deep, resonant voice, he became known as 'The Barnsley Boomer' – something of a concern for his sound recordists with sensitive equipment. And with his penchant for slipping down muddy slopes and falling into rivers and ponds he became a constant concern to all his colleagues. (Charlie Flynn)

David Lowen joined Yorkshire TV from Westward Television as a producer. After a spell as Editor of *Calendar*, he undertook responsibility for the many regional series which ran alongside the nightly news programme, including *Calendar Kids* the *TSB Rock School* and *Enterprize 80-85*, a series in which young entrepreneurs were given professional help with fledgling businesses.

David Lowen

David Lowen, Producer then Editor of *Calendar*, then Head of Features. On his watch, the *Calendar* family of programmes expanded rapidly and successfully to encompass *Calendar Kids*, *Calendar Plays Pop*, *Enterprize* and sundry others. He moved on to become Secretary of the Royal Television Society.

Richard Gregory

Richard Gregory was News Editor, then Producer, then Editor of *Calendar*. Finally, he became Managing Director of Yorkshire TV, until all the regional companies merged into a single broadcasting company, ITV plc.

He then moved into business circles to become deputy chairman of Yorkshire Forward, the regional development agency, chairman of Sheffield Hallam University and, with an OBE, Chairman of the Yorkshire Bank.

Studio 2 in the Yorkshire TV buildings in Kirkstall Road, Leeds was the main production centre for the nightly news programme *Calendar* and many other programmes produced in the region for the region. Here the Editor of *Calendar*, Richard Gregory, supervises the transmission of his programme. (YTV Archive)

Alan Hardwick

In 1972 I was working as a sub editor on the *Scarborough Evening News* and one of my perks was a day off during the week if I covered Scarborough rugby on a Saturday morning. One of the players was a little chap called John Meade. I never saw much of him on the field because he was always at the bottom of a scrum. I knew John worked for YTV, but we never discussed his job. We were just two hacks with a shared interest in rugby.

One day I was doing the sports editor's job, arranging page changes for the different editions, when John (JB to his many mates) phoned to ask if I knew of a reporter who'd like to earn a bob or two by going to Butlins in Filey to interview some Protestant and Catholic families who were on holiday together from Northern Ireland.

It was a good story because at the time, as younger people will know if they read their history books, there was bloodshed between the two religious communities. The problem was that a film crew had arrived at Butlins, but the helicopter carrying the reporter (oh

(L to R) Ronnie Magill ('Amos' in *Emmerdale Farm*) with Bobby Moore (captain of West Ham and England 1966) and Alan Hardwick at a charity event in Hull in 1980.

yes, those really were the days) couldn't land due to a sea fret.

I promised JB I'd fix a reporter, then realized we had no spare staff. I couldn't go because there was no one else to take over the sports pages. I was about to call JB back when the only other person who could possibly do the job walked in. Barry Hampshire was taking the day off and I asked if he'd go to Filey.

His reply changed my life: 'No chance, mate. I'll do the pages and you head off.'

About an hour later I arrived at Butlins to find three men setting up what I supposed was TV-type gear, looking at their watches and muttering about 'the bloody news desk' and 'bloody reporters'.

Yes, I'd stumbled upon the Hull crew of Richard Gutteridge, Tony Poulton and Jim Spence. I managed a feeble 'Hello, I'm Alan Hardwick.'

No one smiled, and Jim said, 'Well, bloody hurry up will you.'

The interviewees appeared as if by magic, and suddenly, as soon as the camera was turned on, I started to enjoy myself. When I'd finished, the crew were smiling. They thanked me, we shook hands then they disappeared. That night, to my amazement, the report on *Calendar* was introduced with my name. My face appeared briefly on the screen and I remember thinking, 'So what if the newspaper sack me for moonlighting. I've been on telly.'

I was offered a job by John Wilford on the strength of that report. I have no doubt that JB had something to do with it as well. And you know, I still enjoy myself whenever I'm performing for the camera. Thank Heaven I never had to go back to doing a proper job again!

[*Eventually, he did. After many years as a* Calendar *stalwart, Alan Hardwick became the first democratically elected Police and Crime Commissioner for Lincolnshire.*]

Robert Hall

Robert Hall, a Leeds University graduate and these days a top BBC reporter, remembers his start on Calendar:

Going to the YTV district office in Grimsby was quite a shock. We operated out of a shop near the Crest hotel in a newly redeveloped square. There were four of us: Margaret, who sat out front and to

Back row (L to R) Robert Hall, Roger Greenwood; Richard Madeley and Hugh Weekes.
Middle Row (L to R) Sita Guneratne and Marylyn Webb.
Front (L to R) Geoff Druett; Richard Whiteley and Alan Hardwick.

Here Robert Hall and his Grimsby-based crew are following up the aftermath of the disastrous Flixborough explosion near Scunthorpe in June 1974. It happened on a quiet Saturday afternoon, when only 72 people were on the site of the chemical plant; nevertheless, 28 people died and 36 were seriously injured. (L to R) Des Holmes (sound recordist), Paul Jackson (lighting), Ken Little (cameraman) and Robert.

most people was the local face of YTV; and behind a frosted glass screen, me; the cameraman, Ken Little, a short, almost spherical man who had originally worked the patch for Anglia TV; the sound man, Des Holmes, a Londoner who made it clear that he would rather be working in feature films; and Paul Jackson, the electrician, built like a rugby player and operating his own special employment rules.

It was explained to me early on that the custom was to shoot only in the mornings, since the film had to travel back to Leeds, and anyway it got dark in the afternoons; in addition, that Paul would not be with us on a Friday because that was the day he took a van to Leeds to sell fish, and anyway it was also 'exes' day (the day on which staff could collect expenses which they had incurred during the week), which also required his

presence in Leeds – this time at the cash office.

My memories of Ken are his undoubted skill behind the camera, his love of curries so hot that the sweat ran into his poppadoms, and his passion for vintage motorbikes.

Des, on the other hand, didn't seem to love much at all – he regarded me as a young whippersnapper and the rest of us as amateurs. He hated Grimsby, and rarely found the perfect conditions in which to record the sounds he needed. He used to vent his spleen to Trevor, the dubbing mixer in Leeds, whom he rarely met, by recording grumbling messages on the front of the day's sound tape:

'Morning Trev … Des here again, on another filthy wet day on the docks … rain running down my neck … just waiting for something to happen … it's been miserable all week.' I was out on Humberside for around two years, living in a bungalow in a village called Holton-Le-Clay, on the edge of a disused wartime airfield full of cars awaiting export. I drove what I thought was a very smart Ford Fiesta, equipped with the forerunner of today's mobile phones, call sign 'Brown 853'. It was operated by a company near Grimsby docks, and it enabled me to ask an operator to connect me with a phone number, which she would dial – a very useful gadget for someone commuting between Leeds, where I had a girlfriend, presenting duties, and far flung corners of Lincolnshire, because no one really knew where I was when I made the calls, and I could therefore be in two places at the same time.

On many mornings I would call David Garner, the news editor, who assumed I was well on the way to Grimsby, when in fact I was holding myself in readiness in the welcoming kitchen of Harold Caine, our Scunthorpe stringer cameraman, admiring his daughter and eating his sausages.

Bob Bairstow

John Fairley recalls:

When I took over as Director of Programmes, Paul Fox gave me two pieces of advice. The first was to sit next to Granada at Controllers' meetings. That was bad advice – it just made it easier for them to slip the knife between your ribs. The other was 'Listen to Bob'. That was advice without price. Bob taught me many of the dark arts of scheduling.

'That's not a Thursday programme,' he would decree. Or, 'I can squeeze that past

Bob Bairstow, long-time Controller of Presentation and arbiter of the YTV schedules, was never averse to reviving his early career skills as an assistant purser in charge of entertainment on cruise ships.

Thames, if you'll give me that new sitcom.' And so on.

And, at any YTV party, he would always give us a song.

Epilogue

In the autumn of 2009, I heard to my complete surprise that Archie Norman had been appointed Chairman of ITV. He was an old friend of my wife Kitty and me. And by an odd coincidence he lived in the same little house in Ribston Park, near Wetherby, that I had lived in when I was Director of Programmes at Yorkshire.

In fact, we were all due to have supper together in York a couple of days later. Archie had already been an MP, Chairman of the Conservative Party and, famously, the man who took a business called Asda from the modest Leeds factory I could see from my YTV office window to an international success story.

But I knew he knew nothing of television. So I decided he might as well start by seeing the rough side. I gave him a copy of Ray Fitzwalter's book about Granada, *The Dream That Died*.

'Our dream lived,' I said, somewhat pompously – and indeed, I think it did.

Watching Peter Kosminsky winning the 2016 BAFTA drama award for *Wolf Hall*, then seizing the opportunity to denounce government attempts to shackle the BBC, took me back to the days of *Shoot to Kill*. All that trouble had paid off.

The YTV studios have been completely rebooted by the new ITV regime and *Calendar* remains the dominant force in local programming. *Heartbeat* lived on for 20 years, and *Emmerdale* lives still. *Countdown*, sadly, did not survive long as a Leeds production after the death of Richard Whiteley. John Willis now runs the powerful documentary house of Mentorn. And when we all meet, as we do every spring at Rudding Park in Harrogate, it is to celebrate, not mourn, all those things we did, after we gathered in that trouser factory, now 50 years ago.

John Fairley

Afterthought

In 1968 *Calendar* relied on film as its only means of recording pictures. Most was shot by three or four staff crews, backed by a team of freelance 'stringers' using old fashioned 'wind-up' Bolex cameras – with no sound track. The film had to be transported to the processing labs, edited by hand, then loaded on to a set of Telecine machines for transmission. Frustratingly, it was slow and cumbersome and led to too many 'on-air' mistakes.

Today, every owner of a mobile phone is potentially a newsgatherer, and every reporter, most of whom shoot and edit their own material, can file 'live' from anywhere there is a signal. As a result of these astounding improvements in technology, *Calendar* is transformed; it's slick and stylish and skilfully presented by the estimable Margaret Emsley, the Head of News, and her team.

In the face of competition from a range of social media, its solid journalistic principles ensure that it remains as valuable to the viewing public today as it did 50 years ago.

Graham Ironside

Appendix

YORKSHIRE TELEVISION DRAMA PRODUCTIONS

Compiled by Nicky Storey

1968

The Best Pair of Legs in the Business
Written by Kevin Laffan. Featuring Reg Varney, Chris Chittell

Camille 68
Written by Alexandre Dumas fils. Featuring Genevieve Page, Georgina Hale

Funeral Games
Written by Joe Orton. Featuring Michael Denison, Ian McShane, Bill Fraser

Daddy Kiss It Better
Written by Peter Nichols. Featuring Michael Craig, Dilys Laye

Remember the Germans
Written by Leo Lehmann. Featuring Tony Britton, Anna Massey, Helen Lindsay, Alan MacNaughtan

A Bit of Discretion
Written by John Whitewood. Featuring Julia Foster, Gerald Sim, Noel Dyson

Where Did You Get That Hat?
Written by Carol Fisher. Featuring Desmond Llewelyn, Tenniel Evans, Zia Mohyeddin

Gazette
Created by Robert Barr. Various writers. Featuring Gillian Wray, Jon Laurimore, Gerald Harper

Tom Grattan's War
Various writers. Featuring Michael Howe, Richard Warner, Sally Adcock

The Bonus
Written by Ray Jenkins. Featuring John Stride, June Barry

The Right Attitude
Written by John Whitewood. Featuring Moray Watson, Dennis Waterman, Susan George

You Can Only Buy Once
Written by Kevin Laffan. Featuring Derek Benfield, Reginald Marsh, Joe Gladwin

West of Eden
Written by Anthony Skene. Featuring Horst Janson, Eleanor Summerfield

Money for Change
Written by Ronald Starke and Patrick Thursfield. Featuring Sylvia Syms, Ann Firbank

The Fireplace Firm
Written by Bill MacIlwraith. Featuring Roland Culver, Barbara Couper, Nora Nicholson

The Last of the Big Spenders
Written by Hugh Whitemore. Featuring Ian Carmichael, Faith Kent

Of Course We Trust You Arnold
Written by Robert Coole. Featuring George Cole, Richard Pearson

1969

Floating Man
Written by Leo Lehmann. Featuring Elizabeth MacLennan, Tony Britton, Ursula Howells

What's in it for Me?
Written by Anthony Skene. Featuring Frances Bennett, Jean Marsh, George Layton

The Long Sixpence
Written by Ray Jenkins. Featuring Billy Murray, Adrienne Posta, Terence Rigby

A Bit of a Holiday
Written by Charles Wood. Featuring George Cole, Gwen Watford, Edward Woodward

Bloxham's Concerto for Critic and Carpenter
Written by J. B Bodie. Featuring Barbara Murray, Clive Elliott

Park People
Written by Alun Lewis. Featuring Zena Walker, Julian Glover, Elizabeth Shepherd

Aren't We All?
Written by Frederick Lonsdale. Featuring Ann Bell, Judy Campbell, Corin Redgrave

Two Feet off the Ground
Written by Trevor Danby. Featuring Leslie Sands, Martin Shaw, Jennifer Hilary

Toys
Written by John Whitewood. Featuring Michele Dotrice, John Breslin

Steve
Written by Hugh Forbes. Featuring Jon Finch

Hazel and her New Gas Cooker
Written by Bill MacIlwraith. Featuring Patricia Routledge, Jack Hedley, June Brown

End of Story
Written by Leo Lehmann. Featuring Peter Barkworth, Roland Curram, Lally Bowers

Tiger Trap in the Street
Written by Michael Craig. Featuring Michael Craig, Rosemary Leach, Angela Douglas

Hester Lilly
Adapted by Elizabeth Taylor from her novel. Featuring Faith Brook, Michael Gwynn, Joan Hickson

Full Cheddar
Written by Hugh Whitemore. Featuring Daniel Massey, Vivien Merchant

The Reporters
Written by Leo Lehmann. Featuring Tony Britton, Anna Massey, Derek Francis, Alan MacNaughtan

Justice is a Woman
Written by Stanley Miller, adapted from the novel by Jack Roffey and Ronald Kinnoch. Featuring Margaret Lockwood, Iain Cuthbertson, John Laurie, Allan Cuthbertson

Castle Haven
Created by Kevin Laffan. Various writers. Featuring Sally James, Roy Barraclough, Gretchen Franklin, Kathy Staff

Parkin's Patch
Various writers. Featuring John Flanagan, Gareth Thomas

Hadleigh – Series I
Created by Robert Barr. Various writers. Featuring Gerald Harper

The Main Chance – Series I
Created by Edmund Ward and John Malcolm. Featuring John Stride

1970

Skyscrapers
Written by Thomas Strangmorn. Featuring Michael Bryant, Vivien Merchant

Dangerous Corner
Written by J. B. Priestley. Featuring Ian Hendry, Nicola Pagett

A Doll's House
Adapted by J. W. McFarlane from the play by Henrik Ibsen. Featuring Anna Massey, Julian Glover, Paul Daneman

A Man for Loving
Written by Jeremy Paul. Featuring Lorne Greene, Richard Greene

Unexpectedly Vacant
Written by Hugh Whitemore. Featuring Michael Denison, Dulcie Gray

Grady
Written by Edmund Ward. Featuring Anthony Bate, Diana Coupland

The Main Chance – Series II
Created by Edmund Ward and John Malcolm. Featuring John Stride. *TV Times* Best Actor Award to John Stride. Hollywood Festival of World Television Best Drama Series Award

Kate – Series I
Various writers. Featuring Phyllis Calvert, Penelope Keith, Jack Hedley

1971

Fly on the Wall
Written by Kevin Laffan. Featuring Julia Foster, Clive Francis, Christopher Timothy

The Chinese Prime Minister
Written by Enid Bagnold. Featuring Judy Campbell, Francesca Annis, Roland Culver, Judy Cornwell

Follyfoot
Created by Monica Dickens, inspired by her novel *Cobbler's Dream*. Various writers. Featuring Gillian Blake, Steve Hodson, Arthur English, Desmond Llewelyn. Special Prize for the Best Children's Entertainment Programme, Society of Film & Television Arts

The Ten Commandments
Various writers. Featuring Anthony Hopkins, Tom Bell, Judy Parfitt, Peter Sallis, Mary Ure, George Cole, Paul Eddington

Justice – Series I
Based on the novel by Jack Roffey and Ronald Kinnoch. Various writers. Featuring Margaret Lockwood, Philip Stone, Anthony Valentine. *TV Times* Best Actress Award to Margaret Lockwood.

The Organization – Series I
Written by Philip Mackie. Featuring Peter Egan, Donald Sinden, Anton Rodgers

1972

Emmerdale Farm
Created by Kevin Laffan. Various writers. Re-titled *Emmerdale* on 14 November 1989. Continuous transmission to present day.

A Summer Story
Written by Jack Ronder. Featuring Jack Hedley, Ian Hendry

A Bit of Vision
Written by Charles Wood. Featuring Roy Dotrice, Adrienne Corri, Annette Crosbie

When the Music Stops
Written by David Ambrose. Featuring Edward Fox, Mary Peach

When the Wheel Turns
Written by John Whitewood. Featuring Michael Bates, Rosemary Leach

Jo
Written by Ray Jenkins. Featuring Philip Baldwin, June Barry

The Piano Player
Written by Alun Owen. Featuring Angharad Rees, Clive Revill

Dear Octopus
Adapted by Dodie Smith from her play. Featuring Peter Barkworth, Hannah Gordon, Anna Massey

The Challengers
Written by Edmund Ward. Featuring Colin Blakely, Michael Gambon, William Gaunt, Joanna Van Gyseghem

Kate – Series II
Various writers. Featuring Phyllis Calvert, Penelope Keith, Jack Hedley. *TV Times* Most Compulsive Female Television Character Award to Phyllis Calvert.

The Main Chance – Series III
Created by Edmund Ward and John Malcolm. Featuring John Stride

The Organization – Series II
Written by Philip Mackie. Featuring Peter Egan, Donald Sinden, Anton Rodgers. The Writers' Guild Of Great Britain, Best British Television Drama Series Award

A Place in the Sun
Various writers. Featuring Moray Watson, Joyce Carey, Anton Diffring.

1973

Sarah
Written by Guy Cullingford. Featuring Pat Heywood, Ursula Howells, Mark Kingston. International Emmy Awards Citation for Outstanding Achievement in Entertainment Programming; Monte Carlo Television Festival Silver Nymph Award for the Best Television Script

The Ruffian on the Stair
Adapted by Joe Orton from his play. Featuring Michael Bryant, Judy Cornwell

Professional
Written by David Ambrose. Featuring Michael Bryant, Clare Kelly

An Afternoon at the Festival
Written by David Mercer. Featuring Leo McKern, Adrienne Corri

Reckoning Day
Written by David Ambrose. Featuring Norman Bird, Noel Dyson

Free as a Bird
Written by Roy Minton. Featuring June Brown

Young Guy Seeks Part Time Work
Written by John Bowen. Featuring Anna Massey, Anton Rodgers

Barrie with Love
Written by J.M. Barrie. Featuring Michael Denison, Judy Cornwell, Gwen Watford, Bernard Hepton, Cherie Lunghi, Edward Hammond, Ronald Culver, Joyce Carey.

Flight
Written by Alun Owen. Featuring Leslie Sands

The Brontes of Haworth
Written by Christopher Fry. Featuring Alfred Burke, Ann Penfold, Vickery Turner, Michael Kitchen

Beryl's Lot – Series I
Created by Kevin Laffan. Various writers. Featuring Carmel McSharry, Annie Leake, Tony Caunter

Conjugal Rights
Written by Philip Mackie. Featuring Ann Bell, Julian Glover, Ian Holm

Dolly Dialogues
Adapted by Philip Mackie from the novel by Anthony Hope. Featuring Felicity Kendal, Daniel Massey

Hadleigh – Series II
Created by Robert Barr. Various writers. Featuring Gerald Harper. *TV Times* Most Compulsive Male Television Character Award to Gerald Harper

Justice – Series II
Based on the novel by Jack Roffey and Ronald Kinnoch. Various writers. Featuring Margaret Lockwood, Philip Stone, Anthony Valentine. *Sun* newspaper, Best Actress Award to Margaret Lockwood

So it Goes
Written by Ray Jenkins. Featuring Anouska Hempel, Johnny Briggs, Peter McEnery, Faith Brook

1974

The Break
Written by William Fairchild. Featuring Robert Shaw, Mary Ure, Jack Hedley

Click
Written by Charlie Humphreys. Featuring George Baker, Ann Bell

What Would You Do?
Written by Charles Humphreys. Featuring Ian McShane

Who Killed Lamb?
Created by Anthony Skene and Michael Zagor. Written by Anthony Skene. Featuring Stanley Baker, Barbara Leigh-Hunt, Peter Sallis

Mr Axelford's Angel
Written by Peter Whitbread. Featuring Julia Foster, Michael Bryant. International Emmy for Best Fiction

A Kind of Bonus
Written by John Whitewood. Featuring Gerald Cross, Michele Dotrice, Michael Kitchen

A Bit of Adventure
Written by Charles Wood. Featuring George Cole, Gwen Watford

A Provincial Lady
Written by Ivan Turgenev. Featuring Gwen Watford, Michael Denison

The World of J. B. Priestley
Devised and written by Leslie Sands. Featuring J. B. Priestley, Michael Cashman, Noel Dyson, Robert Stephens

M/S or Jack and Jill
Written by John Osborne. Featuring Jill Bennett, Denis Lawson, Michael Byrne

The Arcata Promise
Written by David Mercer. Featuring Anthony Hopkins, John Fraser, Kate Nelligan

The Gift of Friendship
Written by John Osborne. Featuring Alec Guinness, Sarah Badel, Michael Gough

Silver Wedding
Written by N. F. Simpson. Featuring John le Mesurier, Noel Dyson, Bernard Hepton

Death or Glory Boy
Written by Charles Wood. Featuring Phil Davis

Good Girl
Written by Philip Mackie. Featuring Julia Foster, Peter Barkworth, Joan Hickson, Peter Bowles

Justice – Series III
Based on the novel by Jack Roffey and Ronald Kinnoch. Various writers. Featuring Margaret Lockwood, Philip Stone, Anthony Valentine

South Riding
Adapted by Stan Barstow from the novel by Winifred Holtby. Featuring Dorothy Tutin, Hermione Baddeley, Nigel Davenport, Judi Bowker, Clive Swift. The Society of Film and Television Arts Best Drama Series Award; The Broadcasting Press Guild of Great Britain Best Drama Series Award; The Writers' Guild of Great Britain Best Dramatisation Award; RTS Writers Award.

1975

Joby
Adapted by Stan Barstow from his novel.
Featuring Patrick Stewart

Love me to Death
Written by David Ambrose. Featuring
Anthony Valentine, Susan Penhaligon, Gwen
Watford, Robin Bailey

Left
Written by Alun Owen. Featuring Colin
Welland

Suzi's Plan
Written by Charles Humphreys. Featuring
Leslie Schofield

Raffles – Single
Adapted by Philip Mackie from the novel
by E. W. Hornung. Featuring Anthony
Valentine

Willow Cabins
Written by Alan Plater. Featuring Dorothy
Tutin, Clive Swift, Michael Bryant

The Boy Dave
Written by Guy Cullingford. Featuring Keith
Barron, Annette Crosby, Freddie Jones

Beryl's Lot – Series II
Created by Kevin Laffan. Various writers.
Featuring Carmel McSharry, Annie Leake,
Tony Caunter

The Hanged Man
Written by Edmund Ward. Featuring Colin
Blakely

The Loner
Written by Alan Plater. Featuring Les
Dawson, Cyril Luckham, Roy Kinnear

The Main Chance – Series IV
Created by Edmund Ward and John
Malcolm. Featuring John Stride

Luke's Kingdom
Various writers. Featuring Oliver Tobias

1976

Now is too Late
Written by Larry Wyce. Featuring Felicity
Kendal, Anton Rodgers, Michael Gambon

Huggy Bear
Adapted by David Mercer from his short
story. Featuring Maurice Denham, Joyce
Heron

The Power of Dawn
Written by Emlyn Williams. Featuring Alfred
Burke, Adrienne Byrne

Almost a Vision
Written by John Osborne. Featuring Jill
Bennett, Keith Barron

Beryl's Lot – Series III
Created by Kevin Laffan. Various writers.
Featuring Carmel McSharry, Annie Leake,
Tony Caunter

Dickens of London
Created by Wolf Mankowitz and Marc Miller.
Written by Wolf Mankowitz. Featuring Roy
Dotrice, Diana Coupland

Forget-me-not
Written by Alun Owen. Featuring Patricia Brake, Cyd Hayman

Hadleigh – Series III
Created by Robert Barr. Various writers. Featuring Gerald Harper

Murder: Hello Lola
Written by Gerald Vaughan-Hughes. Featuring Jill Bennett, Sebastian Shaw

Murder: Nobody's Conscience
Written by Edmund Ward. Featuring Anthony Bate, Mark Eden, Patricia Haines, Leslie Sands

Murder: A Variety of Passions
Written by David Ambrose. Featuring Felicity Kendal, Ralph Michael

1977

The Lover
Adapted by Harold Pinter from his play. Featuring Patrick Allen, Vivien Merchant

Spaghetti Two-Step
Written by Jack Rosenthal. Featuring Connie Booth

Short Back and Sides
Written by Alan Plater. Featuring Michael Bryant, Philip Stone

Love Lies Bleeding
Written by Charles Wood. Featuring Bridget Turner, Richard Pasco

The Best of Enemies
Written by Christopher Fry. Featuring Horst Janson

A Chink in the Wall
Written by John Bryden Rodgers. Featuring Maurice Denham, Joyce Carey

Ghosts
Written by Henrik Ibsen. Featuring Dorothy Tutin, Richard Pasco, Julia Foster

Treats
Written by Christopher Hampton. Featuring John Hurt, Tom Conti, Kate Nelligan

A Superstition
Adapted by David Mercer from his play. Featuring Anthony Andrews, Hugh Burden

The Cost of Loving
Written by Stan Barstow. Featuring Colin Welland, Patricia Routledge, Paula Wilcox, Philip Stone

Raffles – Series I
Adapted by Philip Mackie from the novels by E. W. Hornung. Featuring Anthony Valentine

Sister Dora
Written by Jo Manton. Featuring Dorothy Tutin

Beryl's Lot – Series IV
Created by Kevin Laffan. Various writers. Featuring Carmel McSharry, Annie Leake, Tony Caunter

1978

Home and Beauty
Written by Stanley Miller adapted from the novel by W. Somerset Maugham. Featuring Daniel Massey, Felicity Kendal, John Standing

A Question of Time
Written by Charles Humphreys. Featuring Barbara Ewing

Aren't We All
Adapted by Pat Sandys from a story by Frederick Lonsdale. Featuring Richard Vernon, Gwen Watford, Nicola Pagett

Mates
Written by Charles Humphreys. Featuring Lesley Dunlop, Maggie Wells

Across a Crowded Room
Written by Philip Mackie. Featuring Glynis Johns, Richard Johnson, Charles Gray, Peter Sallis

Games
Written by John Bowen. Featuring Geoffrey Palmer, Barbara Leigh-Hunt

The Marriage Counsellor
Written by Sheila Sibley. Featuring Felicity Kendal, James Grout, Gabrielle Drake

The Party of the First Part
Written by Alan Plater. Featuring Michael Gambon, Anne Stallybrass Jan Francis

Night School
Adapted by Harold Pinter from his play. Featuring Ian Holm, Brenda Bruce, Jean Kent

The Bonus
Written by Ray Jenkins. Featuring Judy Cornwell, Norman Bird

Park People
Written by Alun Owen. Featuring Sarah Badel, Roy Marsden, Ciaran Madden

The File on Harry Jordan
Adapted by Anthony Skene from the play by Jean Benedetti. Featuring Bernard Gallagher

The English Climate
Written by Paul Jones. Featuring Charles Keating

The Look
Written by Alun Owen. Featuring Donald Sumpter, Lisa Harrow

Just between Ourselves
Adapted by Alan Ayckbourn from his play. Featuring Richard Briers, Constance Chapman, Rosemary Leach, Rosemary McHale, Stephen Moore

Losing Her
Written by Hugh Whitemore. Featuring George Cole, Diana Fairfax, Nicholas Lyndhurst

Wilde Alliance
Various writers. Featuring John Stride, Julia Foster. *TV Times* Most Compulsive Female Character Award to Julia Foster

The Sandbaggers – Series I
Created by Ian Mackintosh. Various writers. Featuring Roy Marsden, Ray Lonnen, Jerome Willis

Charlie and Julie
Written by Charles Humphreys. Featuring Nicholas Clay, Derek Benfield, Gwen Nelson

1979

Flat Bust
Written by Peter Draper. Featuring Alyson Spiro, Roger Brierley, John Ringham

The Blacktoft Diaries: True or False?
Written by Alan Plater. Featuring James Cameron, Jo Kendall

A Village Wooing
Written by George Bernard Shaw. Featuring Judi Dench, Richard Briers

Casting the Runes
Adapted by Clive Exton from the original story by M. R. James. Featuring Edward Petherbridge, Bernard Gallagher, Jan Francis, David Calder

The Daughters of Albion
Written by Willy Russell. Featuring Anton Lesser

The Beast
Written by Hugh Jarmany. Featuring Zena Walker, Ray Smith

The Winter Ladies
Written by Guy Cullingford. Featuring Jessie Matthews, Rachel Kempson

Getting in on Concorde
Written by Rhys Adrian. Featuring George Cole, Sheila Allen

Going Back
Written by William Corlett. Featuring Brewster Mason, Patricia Lawrence

After Julius
Adapted by Elizabeth Jane Howard from her novel. Featuring Faith Brook, John Carson, Cyd Hayman

Thundercloud
Created by Ian Mackintosh. Various writers. Featuring John Fraser, Sarah Douglas, Derek Waring, James Cosmo

Flambards
Adapted from the novel by K. M. Peyton. Various writers. Featuring Steven Grives, Christine McKenna, Edward Judd

The Racing Game
Adapted from the novel by Dick Francis. Various writers. Featuring Mike Gwylim, Susan Woolridge, Mick Ford

1980

You're Not Watching Me, Mummy
Written by John Osborne. Featuring Anna Massey, Peter Sallis, Suzanne Bertish

The Pump
Written by James Cameron. Featuring Kenneth More, Ann Firbank

A Rod of Iron
Written by David Mercer. Featuring Alfred Burke, Nigel Hawthorne, Edward Woodward. International Emmy Award

Midnight at the Starlight
Written by Michael Hastings. Featuring Kevin Lloyd, Gerald Flood

Too Close to the Edge
Written by Michael Ferguson and Lawrence Shaw. Featuring Tim Preece, Joanne Whalley

The Specialist
Written by John Bowen. Featuring John Judd, Stephanie Turner

The Marquise
Adapted by Pat Sandys from the play by Noel Coward. Featuring Diana Rigg, Richard Johnson, James Villiers

The Schoolmistress
Adapted by Pat Sandys from the play by Arthur Wing Pinero. Featuring Eleanor Bron, Charles Gray, Nigel Hawthorne

The Sandbaggers – Series II
Created by Ian Mackintosh. Various writers. Featuring Roy Marsden, Ray Lonnen, Jerome Willis

The Good Companions
Adapted by Alan Plater from the novel by J. B. Priestley. Featuring Judy Cornwell, Brian Pringle, Jan Francis, Denis Lawson

Gate of Eden
Written by William Corlett. Featuring Maurice Denham, Pat Heywood, Gwen Nelson

1981

Hedda Gabler
Adapted by John Osborne from the play by Henrik Ibsen. Featuring Diana Rigg, Denis Lill, Alan Dobie

The Reason of Things
Written by Freda Kelsall. Featuring Alec McCowan, Margaret Tyzack, Tony Selby

Cupid's Darts
Written by David Nobbs. Featuring Robin Bailey, Leslie Ash

Storm in a Broken Teacup
Written by Larry Wyce. Featuring Patricia Hayes

A Little Rococo
Written by Anita Bronson. Featuring Judy Cornwell, Geoffrey Palmer, Paul Nicholas

The Concubine
Written by Pat Hooker. Featuring Clare Higgins, Judy Parfitt, Edward Palmer

Like I've Never Been Gone
Written by Lesley Davies. Featuring Ray Smith, June Barry

One in a Thousand
Written by Mike Stott. Featuring Alun Armstrong, Norman Bird

Singles
Written by John Bowen. Featuring Sherrie Hewson, Jeff Rawle

The Potting Shed
Adapted by Pat Sandys from the play by Graham Greene. Featuring Paul Scofield, Celia Johnson, Anna Massey

Eden End
Adapted by Donald McWhinnie from the play by J. B. Priestley. Featuring Eileen Atkins, Anthony Head

Pygmalion
Adapted by Pat Sandys from the play by
George Bernard Shaw. Featuring Twiggy,
Robert Powell, Arthur English

Brother to the Ox
Adapted by Stephen Wakeham from the
novel by Fred Kitchen. Featuring Sandra Voe

Stay With Me 'til Morning
Written by John Braine. Featuring Nanette
Newman, Keith Barron, Paul Daneman

Get Lost!
Written by Alan Plater. Featuring Bridget
Turner, Alun Armstrong

Second Chance
Written by Adele Rose. Featuring Susannah
York, Ralph Bates

Airline
Created by William Greatorex. Various
writers. Featuring Roy Marsden, Anthony
Valentine, Polly Hemingway

1982

The Houseboy
Written by Irving Wardle. Featuring Richard
Pasco, Geoffrey Palmer

The Reunion
Written by David Evans. Featuring Kate
Coleridge, Michael Culver, Diane Keen

The Breadwinner
Adapted by Pat Sandys from the play by W.
Somerset Maugham. Featuring Michael
Gambon, Jennie Linden, Judy Parfitt

Dogfood Dan and the Camarthen Cowboy
Written by David Nobbs. Featuring David
Daker, Gareth Thomas, Helen Cotterill

The Boxwallah
Written by David Blunt. Featuring Rachel
Kempson, Leo McKern

Grandad
Written by Mike Stott. Featuring Frank
Middlemass, Trevor Peacock

Harry's Game
Adapted by Gerald Seymour from his novel.
Featuring Ray Lonnen, Derek Thompson,
Linda Robson. TRIC Award for Best TV
Theme Music; Ivor Novello Award for
Best TV Theme Music; Pye Award for
Most Promising Writer New to Television;
Locarno Film Festival The Golden Leopards
Eye for Best TV Movie; Banff Television
Festival Best Television Movie; nominated for
an International Emmy

Horace
Written by Roy Minton. Featuring Barry
Jackson, Jean Heywood

1983

Salad Days
Written by Julian Slade and Dorothy
Reynolds. Featuring Ian Richardson, Ann
Beach, Gwen Cherrell

Kean
Written by Raymund Fitzsimmons.
Featuring Ben Kingsley

Not about Heroes
Written by Stephen MacDonald. Featuring
Stephen MacDonald, James Telfer

Gracie – The Pride of Our Alley
Written by Alan Plater. Featuring Polly
Hemingway, Barry Jackson

Bloomfield
Written by Roy Clarke. Featuring Michael
Elphick

Number 10
Written by Terence Feely. Featuring Alfred
Burke, Keith Barron, Dorothy Tutin, Dennis
Quilley, Celia Johnson

One Summer
Written by Willy Russell. Featuring David
Morrissey, Ian Hart, Spencer Leigh, James
Hazeldine

The Outsider
Written by Michael J. Bird. Featuring John
Duttine, Carol Royle, Joanna Dunham

1984

Thank You, Mrs Clinkscales
Written by Alan Plater. Featuring Anne
Stallybrass, Clive Duncan

Lucifer
Written by James Andrew Hall. Featuring
William Gaunt, Anne Reid

Dearly Beloved
Written by William Corlett. Featuring Lynn
Farleigh, Gareth Thomas

Sweet Echo
Written by Freda Kelsall. Featuring Renee
Asherton, Ralph Michael

Family Man
Written by Mervyn Watson. Featuring Julie
Walters, John Duttine

Home is the Sailor
Written by John Whitewood. Featuring
Evelyn Laye

A Matter of Will
Written by George Pensotti. Featuring
Brenda Bruce, Hugh Lloyd, Noel Dyson

Killer – Series
Various writers. Featuring John Thaw, Diane
Keen

Frankenstein
Adapted by Victor Gialanella from the novel
by Mary Shelley. Featuring John Gielgud,
Carrie Fisher, Robert Powell, David Warner

The Glory Boys
Adapted by Gerald Seymour from his novel.
Featuring Rod Steiger, Anthony Perkins,
Joanna Lumley

1985

On Your Way, Riley
Written by Alan Plater. Featuring Maureen
Lipman, Brian Murphy

Romance on the Orient Express
Written by Jan Worthington. Featuring John
Gielgud, Cheryl Ladd, Ruby Wax

Timeslip
Written by Jim Hawkins, based on a story by Robert Holmes. Featuring John Taylor

The Beiderbecke Affair
Written by Alan Plater. Featuring James Bolam, Barbara Flynn

The Winning Streak
Various writers. Featuring Dinah Sheridan, Leslie Sands

Sorrell and Son
Adapted by Jeremy Paul from the novel by Warwick Deeping. Featuring Richard Pasco

1986

Scab
Written by Geoff Case and Gordon Flemyng. Featuring Dicken Ashworth, Barrie Shore. Prix Futura Best Drama; RAI Special Prize Prix Italia

The Understanding
Written by Angela Huth. Featuring Constance Cummings, Rachel Kempson, Isobel Dean, Michael Aldridge, Samantha Bond

Demons
Written by T. R. Bowen. Featuring Robin Ellis, Glynis Barber, Lally Bowers, Gary Bond

Glorious Day
Written by Gwen Cherrell. Featuring Michael Cronin, Jo Rowbottom

The Clinger
Written by Martyn Wade. Featuring Richard Hope, Sallyanne Law

Let's Run away to Africa
Written by John Bryden Rodgers. Featuring Richard Pasco, Lynn Farleigh, Elizabeth Shepherd

West of Paradise
Written by Michael J. Bird. Featuring Art Malik, Alphonsia Emmanuel

Love with a Perfect Stranger
Written by Terence Brady and Charlotte Bingham. Featuring Daniel Massey, Marilu Henner

May we Borrow your Husband?
Adapted by Dirk Bogarde from the short story by Graham Greene. Featuring Dirk Bogarde, Charlotte Attenborough, Simon Shepherd, Francis Matthews

The Christmas Tree
Adapted by William Corlett from the novel by Jennifer Johnston. Featuring Anna Massey, Simon Callow, T. P. McKenna. The Golden Chest International Television Festival Special Prize, Best Actor's Performance to Anna Massey.

Flying Lady – Single
Written by Brian Finch. Featuring Anne Stallybrass, Frank Windsor

1987

Flying Lady – Series I
Written by Brian Finch. Featuring Anne Stallybrass, Frank Windsor

Dreams Lost, Dreams Found
Adapted by William Corlett from the novel by Pamela Wallace. Featuring David Robb, Kathleen Quinlan

Who's our Little Jenny Lind?
Written by Christine Parr. Featuring Dennis Waterman

Cloud Waltzer
Adapted by John Bryden Rodgers from the novel by Tory Cates. Featuring Kathleen Beller

1914 All Out
Written by Colin Shindler. Featuring Barry Jackson, Colette Stevenson. Rheims Festival of Television, Public Prize

The Beiderbecke Tapes
Written by Alan Plater. Featuring James Bolam, Barbara Flynn

The Lady's not for Burning
Adapted by Christopher Fry from his play. Featuring Kenneth Branagh, Cherie Lunghi, Angela Thorne

1988

The Contract
Adapted by Gerald Seymour from his novel. Featuring Kevin McNally, Bernard Hepton, James Faulkner

Home Movies
Written by Phil Clark, David Warburton, Owen Aaronovitch. Featuring Brian Glover, Owen Aaronovitch, David Warburton. Experimental Theatre Series, The Crucible Theatre, Sheffield

Climbing Out
Written by Kay Mellor. Featuring Brian Glover, Mark Drewry, Jill McCulloch. Experimental Theatre Series, Yorkshire Theatre Company, Leeds

Mohicans
Written by Garry Lyons. Featuring Brian Glover, Gina McKee, Ian Bleasdale, Jeremy Wall, Nick Ledgard, Lorraine Peters, Maggie Lane, Philip Wilde. Experimental Theatre Series, Major Road Theatre Company, Bradford

Safe as Houses
Written by Alan Dix. Featuring Richard Hewitt, Kay Purcell, Gillian Wright, Jenny Lingham, Chris Cornibert. Experimental Theatre Series, Major Road Theatre Company, Bradford

Hooligans
Written by Jon Gaunt. Featuring Brian Glover, Dave Findlay, Robert Wilkinson, Paul Nolan. Experimental Drama Theatre Series, Tic Toc Theatre Company, Coventry

Place of Safety
Written by Kay Mellor. Featuring Shaun Prendergast. International Film and TV Festival of New York Bronze Medal

Out of the Shadows
Adapted by Michael J. Bird from the novel by Andrea Davidson. Featuring Charles Dance, Alexandra Paul

The Attic – The Hiding Of Anne Frank
Written by William Hanley, based on the diary of Anne Frank and the books by Miep Gies and Alison Leslie Gold. Featuring

Mary Steenburgen, Paul Scofield. American Emmy Award for Outstanding Writing in a Mini-Series or a Special to William Hanley; American Peabody Award; American Christopher Award.

Tears in the Rain
Adapted by Freda Kelsall from the novel by Pamela Wallace. Featuring Sharon Stone, Christopher Cazenove, Anna Massey, Leigh Lawson

Sun Child
Written by Angela Huth. Featuring James Fox, Twiggy, Anna Massey, Duncan Preston

The Beiderbecke Connection
Written by Alan Plater. Featuring James Bolam, Barbara Flynn. BAFTA Original TV Music Award

1989

A Day in Summer
Adapted by Alan Plater from the novel by J. L. Carr. Featuring Jack Shepherd, Peter Egan, John Sessions, Ian Carmichael, Jill Bennett, Suzanne Bertish, Daragh O'Malley

Comeback
Adapted by David Ambrose from the novel Second Chance by John Mathers. Featuring Anton Rodgers, Kate Buffery. Golden Chest International TV Festival, Grand Prix

Flying Lady – Series II
Written by Brian Finch. Featuring Anne Stallybrass, Frank Windsor

Till We Meet Again
Adapted Andrew Peter Marin from the novel by Judith Krantz. Featuring Hugh Grant, Michael York, Courteney Cox, Juliet Mills

1990

Yellowthread Street
Adapted by various writers from the novels of William Marshall. Featuring Ray Lonnen, Mark McGann, Bruce Payne, Catherine Neilsen

Talking Takes Two
Written Paul Bond. Featuring Anton Rodgers, Gina McKee

Missing Persons
Adapted by David Cook from his novel. Featuring Patricia Routledge, Jean Heywood, Jimmy Jewel, Tony Melody

Shoot to Kill
Written by Michael Eaton. Featuring Jack Shepherd, T. P. McKenna, David Calder. The Broadcasting Press Guild Single Drama Award; The Royal Television Society Best Single Drama Award

The World of Eddie Weary
Written by Roy Clarke. Featuring Ray Brookes, Celia Imrie, Connie Booth, Anita Dobson, Brian Glover. Nominated for International Emmy

Magic Moments
Adapted by Charlotte Bingham and Terence Brady from the novel by Nora Roberts. Featuring Jenny Seagrove, John Shea

1992

Heartbeat – Series I
Adapted from the *Country Constable* novels by Nicholas Rhea. Devised by Johnny Byrne. Various writers. Featuring Nick Berry, Niamh Cusack, Bill Maynard, William Simons, Derek Fowlds, Frank Middlemass, Mark Jordon

Guests of the Emperor
Adapted by Vicki Patik and Walter Halsey Davis from the novel by Janice Young Brooks Featuring Gena Rowlands, Phyllis Logan, Judy Parfitt, Cherie Lunghi, Annabeth Gish

1993

Heartbeat – Series II
Adapted from the *Country Constable* novels by Nicholas Rhea. Devised by Johnny Byrne. Various writers. Featuring Nick Berry, Niamh Cusack, Bill Maynard, William Simons, Derek Fowlds, Frank Middlemass, Mark Jordon, Tricia Penrose

Heartbeat – Series III
Adapted from the *Country Constable* novels by Nicholas Rhea. Devised by Johnny Byrne. Various writers. Featuring Nick Berry, Niamh Cusack, Bill Maynard, William Simons, Derek Fowlds, Frank Middlemass, Mark Jordon, Tricia Penrose, David Lonsdale.

15: The Life And Death Of Philip Knight
Written by Jeremy Brock. Featuring Philip Newman, Holly Aird, Suzanne Bertish. The Howard League Media Award; Prix Europa Special Prize; Golden Chest International Television Festival Grand Prix

1994

Heartbeat – Series IV
Adapted from of the *Country Constable* novels by Nicholas Rhea. Devised by Johnny Byrne. Various writers. Featuring Nick Berry, Niamh Cusack, Bill Maynard, William Simons, Derek Fowlds, David Lonsdale, Tricia Penrose, Mark Jordon

A Pinch of Snuff
Adapted by Robin Chapman from the novel by Reginald Hill. Featuring Gareth Hale, Norman Pace, John Woodvine, Freddie Jones

Mission Top Secret – The Polish Pony Puzzle
Various writers. Featuring Jean Anderson, Ian Bleasdale

Ellington – Single
Written by Don Webb based on an idea by Derek Lister. Featuring Christopher Ellison, Anna Chancellor, Sean Chapman, Perry Fenwick

The Wanderer
Written by Roy Clarke. Featuring Bryan Brown, Kim Thomson, Tony Haygarth

1995

Heartbeat – Series V
Adapted from the *Country Constable* novels by Nicholas Rhea. Devised by Johnny Byrne. Various writers. Featuring Nick Berry, Niamh Cusack, Bill Maynard, William Simons, Derek Fowlds, Mark Jordon, Tricia Penrose, David Lonsdale, Peter Benson, Kazia Pelka. Winner of TRIC Award ITV/ C4 Programme of the Year

Paparazzo
Written by Guy Andrews. Featuring Nick Berry, Fay Masterson

Strike Force
Written by Nick McCarty. Featuring Tim Bentinck, James Faulkner, Fiona Dolman

1996

Heartbeat – Series VI
Adapted from the *Country Constable* novels by Nicholas Rhea. Devised by Johnny Byrne. Various writers. Featuring Nick Berry, Jason Durr, Derek Fowlds, William Simons, Bill Maynard, Tricia Penrose, Mark Jordon, David Lonsdale, Peter Benson, Kazia Pelka

Ellington – Series
Various writers. Featuring Christopher Ellison, Perry Fenwick, Beth Goddard, Sean Chapman

Respect
Written by Richard La Plante. Featuring Nick Berry, Jayne Ashbourne, Mark Addy

1997

Heartbeat – Series VII
Adapted from the *Country Constable* novels by Nicholas Rhea. Various writers. Devised by Johnny Byrne. Featuring Jason Durr, William Simons, Bill Maynard, Derek Fowlds, Mark Jordon, Tricia Penrose, David Lonsdale, Peter Benson, Kazia Pelka

Black Velvet Band
Created by Chris McHallem. Written by Jonathan Critchley. Featuring Nick Berry, Todd Carty

1998

Heartbeat – Series VIII
Adapted from the *Country Constable* novels by Nicholas Rhea. Devised by Johnny Byrne. Various writers. Featuring Jason Durr, William Simons, Bill Maynard, Derek Fowlds, Mark Jordon, Tricia Penrose, David Lonsdale, Peter Benson, Kazia Pelka, Fiona Dolman

The Inspector Pitt Mysteries: The Cater Street Hangman
Adapted by T. R. Bowen from the novel by Anne Perry. Featuring Eoin McCarthy, Keeley Hawes, Peter Egan

Verdict
Various writers. Featuring Sue Johnston, Emilia Fox, Michelle Collins, Keith Barron, June Brown, Sarah Lancashire

1999

Heartbeat – Series IX
Adapted from the *Country Constable* novels by Nicholas Rhea. Devised by Johnny Byrne. Various writers. Featuring Jason Durr, William Simons, Derek Fowlds, Bill Maynard, Mark Jordon, Tricia Penrose, David Lonsdale, Fiona Dolman, Kazia Pelka, Philip Franks, Peter Benson

Lost for Words
Adapted by Deric Longden from his novel. Featuring Thora Hird, Pete Postlethwaite. International Emmy Outstanding Drama Programme; American Peabody Award

2000

Heartbeat – Series X

Adapted from the *Country Constable* novels by Nicholas Rhea. Devised by Johnny Byrne. Various writers. Featuring Jason Durr, Derek Fowlds, William Simons, Bill Maynard, Mark Jordon, Tricia Penrose, Philip Franks, David Lonsdale, Peter Benson, Fiona Dolman, Geoffrey Hughes

At Home with the Braithwaites – Series I

Created and written by Sally Wainwright. Featuring Amanda Redman, Peter Davison, Sarah Smart, Sylvia Syms, Julie Graham

Blind Ambition

Written by Eric Deacon. Featuring Robson Green, Imogen Stubbs

2001

Heartbeat – Series XI

Adapted from the *Country Constable* novels by Nicholas Rhea. Devised by Johnny Byrne. Various writers. Featuring Jason Durr, Derek Fowlds, William Simons, Geoffrey Hughes, Mark Jordon, Tricia Penrose, Philip Franks, David Lonsdale, Peter Benson, Duncan Bell

At Home with the Braithwaites – Series II

Created and written by Sally Wainwright. Featuring Amanda Redman, Peter Davison, Sarah Smart, Sylvia Syms, Julie Graham

The Innocent

Written by Jan McVerry and Stephen Mallatratt. Featuring Caroline Quentin, Paul Rhys, Clare Holman

2002

Heartbeat – Series XII

Adapted from the *Country Constable* novels by Nicholas Rhea. Devised by Johnny Byrne. Various writers. Featuring James Carlton, Jason Durr, Derek Fowlds, William Simons, Geoffrey Hughes, Mark Jordon, Tricia Penrose, Duncan Bell, David Lonsdale, Peter Benson.

Shipman

Written by Michael Eaton. Featuring James Bolam, James Hazeldine

At Home with the Braithwaites – Series III

Created and written by Sally Wainwright. Featuring Amanda Redman, Peter Davison, Sarah Smart, Sylvia Syms, Julie Graham

Birthday Girl

Written by Jonathan Harvey. Featuring Sarah Lancashire

2003

Heartbeat – Series XIII

Adapted from the *Country Constable* novels by Nicholas Rhea. Devised by Johnny Byrne. Various writers. Featuring James Carlton, Derek Fowlds, William Simons, Mark Jordon, Tricia Penrose, Peter Benson, Geoffrey Hughes, Duncan Bell, David Lonsdale

The Royal – Series I

Various writers. Featuring Wendy Craig, Ian Carmichael, Julian Ovenden, Michael Starke, Robert Daws, Denis Lill, Amy Robbins, Michelle Hardwick, Andy Wear, Linda Armstrong

The Royal – Series II
Various writers. Featuring Wendy Craig, Ian Carmichael, Michael Starke, Robert Daws, Amy Robbins, Denis Lill, Michelle Hardwick, Andy Wear, Linda Armstrong

The Royal – Series III
Various writers. Featuring Wendy Craig, Ian Carmichael, Michael Starke, Robert Daws, Amy Robbins, Denis Lill, Michelle Hardwick, Andy Wear, Linda Armstrong, Paul Fox, Anna Madeley

At Home with the Braithwaites – Series IV
Created by Sally Wainwright. Various writers. Featuring Amanda Redman, Peter Davison, Sarah Smart, Sylvia Syms, Julie Graham

2004

Heartbeat – Series XIV
Adapted from the *Country Constable* novels by Nicholas Rhea. Devised by Johnny Byrne. Various writers. Featuring Jonathan Kerrigan, Derek Fowlds, William Simons, Mark Jordon, Tricia Penrose, Peter Benson, David Lonsdale, Sophie Ward, Steven Blakeley, John Duttine, Gwen Taylor

The Royal – Series IV
Various writers. Featuring Robert Daws, Amy Robbins, Wendy Craig, Ian Carmichael, Michael Starke, Andy Wear, Linda Armstrong, Denis Lill, Michelle Hardwick, Paul Fox

Steel River Blues
Created by Patrick Harbinson and Jonathan Critchley. Various writers. Featuring Daniel Casey, Stuart Graham, Daniel Ryan

2005

Heartbeat – Series XV
Adapted from the *Country Constable* novels by Nicholas Rhea. Devised by Johnny Byrne. Various writers. Featuring Jonathan Kerrigan, Derek Fowlds, William Simons, Mark Jordon, Tricia Penrose, Peter Benson, David Lonsdale, Gwen Taylor, John Duttine, Sophie Ward, Stephen Blakeley

Falling
Adapted by Andrew Davies from the novel by Elizabeth Jane Howard. Featuring Michael Kitchen, Penelope Wilton. RTS Yorkshire Best Drama of the Year

2006

Heartbeat – Series XVI
Adapted from the *Country Constable* novels by Nicholas Rhea. Devised by Johnny Byrne. Various writers. Featuring Jonathan Kerrigan, Derek Fowlds, William Simons, Mark Jordon, Tricia Penrose, Peter Benson, David Lonsdale, Gwen Taylor, John Duttine, Steven Blakeley

The Royal – Series V
Various writers. Featuring Robert Daws, Amy Robbins, Wendy Craig, Ian Carmichael, Michael Starke, Andy Wear, Linda Armstrong, Michelle Hardwick, Denis Lill, Paul Fox

2007

Heartbeat – Series XVII
Adapted from the *Country Constable* novels by Nicholas Rhea. Devised by Johnny Byrne.

Various writers. Featuring Joe McFadden, Derek Fowlds, William Simons, Tricia Penrose, Peter Benson, David Lonsdale, Gwen Taylor, John Duttine, Steven Blakeley

The Royal – Series VI
Various writers. Featuring Robert Daws, Amy Robbins, Wendy Craig, Ian Carmichael, Paul Fox, Denis Lill, Michael Starke, Linda Armstrong, Michelle Hardwick, Andy Wear

2008

Heartbeat – Series XVIII
Adapted from the *Country Constable* novels by Nicholas Rhea. Devised by Johnny Byrne. Various writers. Featuring Joe McFadden, Derek Fowlds, William Simons, David Lonsdale, Peter Benson, Gwen Taylor, John Duttine, Tricia Penrose, Stephen Blakeley. RTS Yorkshire Best Single Drama, Series or Serial of the Year

The Royal – Series VII
Various writers. Featuring Wendy Craig, Robert Daws, Amy Robbins, Ian Carmichael, Michael Starke, Denis Lill, Andy Wear, Paul Fox, Linda Armstrong, Gareth Hale, Michelle Hardwick

The Royal Today
Various writers. Featuring Paul Nicholas, Leah Bracknell

2009

The Royal – Series VIII
Various writers. Featuring Wendy Craig, Amy Robbins, Robert Daws, Denis Lill, Andy Wear, Gareth Hale, Glynis Barber, Michelle Hardwick, Linda Armstrong

FEATURE FILMS

Stiff Upper Lips
Written by Paul Simpkin and Gary Sinyor. Featuring Peter Ustinov, Prunella Scales, Samuel West, Brian Glover, Frank Finlay, Sean Pertwee, Georgina Cates

Death Train
Written by David S. Jackson from a storyline by Alistair McLean. Featuring Pierce Brosnan, Patrick Stewart, Alexandra Paul, Christopher Lee

THEATRE

Heartbeat: The Musical
Written by Keith Richardson and Sarah Bagshaw. Featuring Andy Pelos, Reuven Gershon

VIDEO

Changing Places
Written by Jonathan Critchley. Based on the *Heartbeat* novels by Nicholas Rhea. Devised by Johnny Byrne. Featuring Nick Berry, Juliette Gruber

Don't Look Now! The Dingles Do Venice
Written by Tim Dynevor. Featuring Lisa Riley, Steve Halliwell, Paul Loughran, Mark Charnock, Ken Morley

The Dingles Down Under
Written by Lou Wakefield. Featuring Lisa Riley, Paul Loughran, Steve Halliwell, Billy Hartman, Alun Lewis, Jane Cox

Emmerdale: Revenge
Written by Mark Illis from a storyline by Rebecca Levene. Featuring Chris Chittell, Mark Charnock, Malandra Burrows

Acknowledgements

We would like to thank the many people who have contributed photographs from their personal collections and delved into their memories to provide us with background information and details of programmes, people and events which are slowly but surely slipping out of living memory. Their names appear by their photographs, or in the index.

In particular, we would like to thank the following:

ITV, for allowing us to reproduce many photographs from the old Yorkshire Television files, and the picture agency, Shutterstock, which holds the archives, for allowing us access to their files and guiding us in our many searches.

Valerie Kleeman, for permission to reproduce photographs from Alan Whicker's collection; and Catherine Kirby, the archivist who enabled us to find them.

Amanda-Jane Read and Tim Fee, for advice and facilitating access to photographs from the history of *Emmerdale*.

David Gregory, of the Wharfedale Inn, Arthington, for the cover photographs.

Darren C. Miller, for personal photographs from several YTV film 'shoots'.

Hanna Richardson of the Goathland Hotel (aka the Aidensfield Arms), for finding and providing photographs from the heyday of *Heartbeat* filming.

Dave Berhens of the *Yorkshire Post*, for researching and providing photographs of *Calendar* from the early days.

Shirley Rubenstein, Alan Plater's widow, for permission to quote from his memoir.

Dan Waddell, for permission to quote from his book *We Had Some Laughs* about his father, Sid's, career in Darts.

Christine Edmondson, Angie Lavelle and Danuta Skarszewska, three long-serving PAs (production assistants), now known as Script Supervisors, for patiently disinterring people and pictures from the dim and distant past.

Terry Ricketts, Don Atkinson and Gus Lupton, formerly of the Props department, for essential background details of past programme personnel and productions.

Gillian Ironside, for collating and cataloguing a large and random collection of pictures into an accessible library

Sheena Ironside, for her eagle eye in spotting errors and omissions, and for creating a logical relationship between text and photographs.

And, lastly, George Chamier, a creative and supportive editor.

Index